I0105341

And others, Andrew Seth

Essays in Philosophical Criticism

And others, Andrew Seth

Essays in Philosophical Criticism

ISBN/EAN: 9783337086213

Printed in Europe, USA, Canada, Australia, Japan

Cover: Foto ©Thomas Meinert / pixelio.de

More available books at **www.hansebooks.com**

ESSAYS

IN

PHILOSOPHICAL CRITICISM

EDITED BY

ANDREW SETH AND R. B. HALDANE

WITH A PREFACE BY

EDWARD CAIRD

LONDON

LONGMANS, GREEN, AND CO.

1883

All rights reserved

DEDICATED TO THE MEMORY

OF

THOMAS HILL GREEN

WHYTE'S PROFESSOR OF MORAL PHILOSOPHY

IN THE UNIVERSITY OF OXFORD

CONTENTS.

ESSAYS

IN

PHILOSOPHICAL CRITICISM.

PREFACE.

THE various contributors to a volume of Essays such as the present may naturally be supposed to be animated by some common purpose or tendency; and I have been requested to say a few words to indicate how far such a common purpose or tendency exists.

In the first place, then, I have to state that the Essays have been written quite independently by their several authors, and that any agreement which exists among them is due, not to an intention to advocate any special philosophical theory, but rather to a certain community of opinion in relation to the general principle and method of philosophy. In other words, it may be described as an agreement as to the direction in which inquiry may most fruitfully be prosecuted, rather than a concurrence in any definite results that have as yet been attained by it. Such an agreement is consistent with great and even vital differences. For any idea that has a principle of growth in it, any idea that takes hold of man's spiritual life on many sides, is certain, as it developes, to produce wide divergencies, and even to call forth much antagonism and conflict between its supporters. A doctrine that passes unchanged from hand to hand, is by that very fact shown to have exhausted its inherent force; and those ideas have been the most fruitful both in religion and philosophy, which, accepted as a common starting-point, have given rise to the most far-reaching controversy. Nevertheless, so long as in such controversy it remains possible to appeal to one principle, so long as the differences are due to the various development of one way of thinking in different minds, the division and opposition is a sign of life, and may be expected ultimately to be overcome by the same spiritual energy which has produced it.

The writers of this volume agree in believing that the line of investigation which philosophy must follow, or in which it may be expected to make most important contributions to the intellectual life of man, is that which was opened up by Kant, and for the successful prosecution of which no one has done so much as Hegel. Such a statement of their philosophical creed, however, would be misleading, if it were not further explained and limited. For a reference to definite names is in philosophy often taken to imply a kind of discipleship which cannot be acknowledged by those who believe that the history of philosophy is a living development, and who, therefore, are adherents of a school only in the sense that they trace the last steps of that development in a particular way. The work of Kant and Hegel, like the work of earlier philosophers, can have no speculative value except for those who are able critically to reproduce it, and so to assist in the sifting process by which its permanent meaning is separated from the accidents of its first expression. And such reproduction, again, is not possible except for those who are impelled by the very teaching they have received to give it a fresh expression and a new application. Valuable as may be the history of thought, the literal importation of Kant and Hegel into another country and time would not be possible if it were desirable, or desirable if it were possible. The mere change of time and place, if there were nothing more, implies new questions and a new attitude of mind in those whom the writer addresses, which would make a bare reproduction unmeaning. Moreover, this change of the mental atmosphere and environment is itself part of a development which must affect the doctrine also, if it is no mere dead tradition, but a seed of new intellectual life. Anyone who writes about philosophy must have his work judged, not by its relation to the intellectual wants of a past generation, but by its power to meet the wants of the present time—wants which arise out of the advance of science, and the new currents of influence which are transforming man's social and religious life. What he owes to previous writers is, so to speak, a concern of his own, with which his readers have directly nothing to do, and for which they need not care. For them the only question of interest is, whether in the writer they have immediately to deal with, there is a living source of light which is original in the sense that, whatever may be its history, it carries its evidence in itself. And this evidence must lie in its power to meet the questions of the day, and in the form in which they arise in that day. A volume of Essays such as the present, touching on so many important topics, can be only a small contribution to that critical reconstruction of knowledge which every time has to accomplish for itself. But it will, I believe, serve the purpose of its writers, if it shows in some degree how the principles of an idealistic philosophy may be brought to bear on the various problems of science, of ethics, and of religion, which are now pressing upon us.

A better indication of the spirit and aims with which the writers of this volume have written, than can be given in any such general statement as the above, may be found in their wish to dedicate it to the memory of Professor Green; an author who, more perhaps than any recent writer on philosophy, has shown that it is possible to combine a thorough appropriation of the results of past speculation with the freshness and spontaneity of an original mind. To Professor Green philosophy was not a study of the words of men that are gone, but a life transmitted from them to him—a life expressing itself with that power and authority which belongs to one who speaks from his own experience, and never to 'the scribes' who speak from tradition. It may be permitted to one who had the privilege of a long and unbroken friendship with him to take this opportunity of saying a few words on his general character, as well as on the special loss which philosophy has sustained in his death.

Those friends who can look back on Professor Green's life with the intimate knowledge of contemporaries cannot fail to be struck with the evidence of consistency and unswerving truth to himself, which it presents. His fellow-students at the University were specially impressed by two features of his character, which then stood out with the greater clearness from their contrast with the usual tendencies of youth. The first was the distinctness with which he lived by conviction and not by impulse. No man could be less pedantic; he had, indeed, a kind of humorous grasp of character and situation which made pedantry always impossible to him. But it seemed to be for him a moral impossibility to act at all, unless he had thought out his course and come to clearness of decision regarding it. Hence at times his manner might quench or repel the ready fire of immediate youthful sympathy in those around him, and might seem to keep even those who were most intimate with him at a distance from his life. Really, however, no one was more capable of friendship, and he was one with whom every tie which he had once formed only grew stronger with time, and was unaffected even by absence and want of intercourse.

The other characteristic was the intensity of his political and intellectual interests. In this respect his character seemed to invert the usual order of development. What is called the ' enthusiasm of humanity,' or at least a sympathy with great intellectual and political movements, was with him a primary, and one might almost say an instinctive, passion; and it was rather out of this and, as it were, under its shadow, that for the most part his personal feelings and affections grew up. Hence he was, in some sense, intellectually old in his youth, and he seemed to become younger at heart—less restrained and self-centred, and more open to individual interests—as he grew older.

He was, in the best sense, a democrat of the democrats. I use this word for want of a better, but what I mean is, that from a somewhat exclusive interest in the essentials of humanity—in the spiritual experiences in which all men are alike—and from a natural disregard for the outward differences of rank and position and even of culture, by which these essentials are invested and concealed, his sympathies were always with the many rather than with the few. He was strongly inclined to the idea that there is an ' instinct of reason ' in the movement of popular sentiment, which is often wiser than the opinion of the so-called educated classes. The belief in the essential equality of men might, indeed, be said to be one of the things most deeply rooted in his character, though it showed itself not in any readiness to echo the commonplaces of Radicalism, but rather in an habitual direction of thought and interest to practical schemes for 'levelling up' the inequalities of human lot, and giving to the many the opportunities of the few. This characteristic ' note ' of his mind is expressed by his last published writing —an Address to the Wesleyan Literary Society of Oxford, ' On the work to be done by the new Oxford High School,' which ends with the following words:—'Our High School then may fairly claim to be helping forward the time when every Oxford citizen will have open to him at least the precious companionship of the best books in his own language, and the knowledge necessary to make him really independent; when all who have a special taste for learning will have open to them what has hitherto been unpleasantly called " the education of gentlemen." I confess to hoping for a time when that phrase will have lost its meaning, because the sort of education which alone makes the gentleman in any true sense will be within reach of all. As it was the aspiration of Moses that all the Lord's people should be prophets, so with all seriousness and reverence we may hope and pray for a condition of English society in which all honest citizens will recognise themselves, and be recognised by each other, as gentlemen. If for Oxford our High School contributes in its measure, as I believe it will, to win this blessed result, some sacrifice of labour and money—even that most difficult sacrifice, the sacrifice of party spirit—may fairly be asked for its support.'

In philosophy Professor Green's whole work was devoted to the development of the results of the Kantian criticism of knowledge and morals. To Hegel he latterly stood in a somewhat doubtful relation; for while, in the main, he accepted Hegel's criticism of Kant, and held also that something *like* Hegel's idealism must be the result of the development of Kantian principles rightly understood, he yet regarded the actual Hegelian system with a certain suspicion as something too ambitious, or, at least, premature. ' It must all be done over again,' he once said, meaning that the first development of idealistic thought in Germany had in some degree anticipated what can be the *secure* result only of wider knowledge and more complete reflexion. This attitude of mind was, indeed, characteristic of one who scarcely felt that he had a scientific right to any principle which he had not submitted to a testing process of years, and who never satisfied himself—as men of idealistic tendencies are too apt to satisfy themselves—with an intuitive grasp of any comprehensive idea, until he had vindicated every element of it by the hard toil of an exhaustive reflexion. Hence he was almost painful in the constancy of his recurrence to certain fundamental thoughts, which he never seemed to have sufficiently verified and explained, and which he was ever ready to reconsider in the light of new objections, even those that might seem to be comparatively unimportant to others. In this he showed how a deep faith in certain principles may be united with the questioning temper of science, and even with a scrupulous scepticism which is ever ready to go back to the beginning, that it may exhaust everything that can be said against them. For such a mind there must always be a wide division between faith and reason, or (what in philosophy comes to the same thing) between a principle and its development into a system. Its appropriate activity must be rather to lay and to try the foundations than to build the superstructure. But it is the result of such work, and of such work alone, to secure that the foundations are immovably fixed on the rock.

Professor Green's great influence on the life of the University and the City of Oxford, to which so many testimonies have been given since his death, was not due to any of the usual sources of popularity. Wanting in superficial readiness of sympathy, wanting also in the sanguine flow of animal spirits, and by constitutional reserve often prevented from expressing what he felt and wished to express, he yet gradually created in those around him a sense of security in trusting him which was due to the transparent purity of his aims and to the entire absence of personal assumption and petty ambition. It was due, it may be added, to the secret fire of ethical enthusiasm, which gradually made itself felt through the unpretending simplicity and business-like directness of his manner. His very reticence and unwillingness to speak, except upon knowledge and from necessity, gave an additional, and sometimes an almost overpowering, weight to his words when he did speak. And in later years the consciousness of the success of his work, both speculative and practical, (however he might underestimate it), and also the consciousness of the sympathy, which he found in his home and in a widening circle of friends who understood him, seemed to soften the strength of his character and give him greater freedom in the use of his powers. There are not a few among the Oxford men of the last fifteen years to whom, as was once said of another teacher, ' his existence was one of the things that gave reality to the distinction between good and evil.' The loss of such an educative influence cannot be easily replaced; but, so far as his literary work is concerned, there is reason to believe that his forthcoming volume upon Ethics, though not quite completed, will prove a better representation of his thought and aims to those who were not immediately brought in contact with him than anything from his pen that has as yet been given to the world.

EDWARD CAIRD.

I.

PHILOSOPHY AS CRITICISM OF CATEGORIES.

A HUNDRED years have passed since Kant, in a note to the Preface of the first 'Critique,' declared his age to be pre-eminently the age of an all-embracing criticism, and proceeded therewith to sketch the outlines of what he called the critical philosophy. The latter has grown to be a great fact even in that dim general consciousness in which humanity keeps record of the deeds of its past. But a hundred years have apparently not been long enough for commentators and critics to make clear to a perplexed public the exact import of what Kant came to teach. And if Kant had survived to dip into the literature of the centennial and see the different doctrines with which he is credited, one can fancy the indignant disclaimers that would have filled the literary journals. The agreement is general that Kant's contribution to philosophy forms a bridge between one period of thought and another; but opinion is sadly divided as to the true philosophic succession. Hence it is probably better, in any treatment which aims at philo-sophical persuasion, to regard Kant not so much with reference to the systems of which his own has been the germ as with reference to the whole period which he closed. If we get in this way to see what notions it was that he destroyed, then we may possibly reach a certain unanimity about the principles and outlines of the new philosophy. When we know on what ground we stand, and what things are definitely left behind, we are in a position to work for the needs of our own time, taking help where it is to be found, but without entangling ourselves in the details of any particular post-Kantian development.

An unexceptionable clue to the way in which Kant was accustomed to regard his own philosophic work is furnished by the use he makes of the term criticism. Criticism, as everyone knows, is generally mentioned by Kant in connection with dogmatism and scepticism, as a third and more excellent way, capable of leading us out of contradiction and doubt into a reasoned certainty. The term thus contains, it may be said, Kant's own account of his relation to his predecessors. That account—often repeated in the Kantian writings—bears a striking similarity at first sight to Locke's description of his discovery that most of the questions that perplex mankind have their source in the want of 'a survey of our own understandings.' 'Were the capacities of our understandings well considered, the extent of our knowledge once discovered, and the horizon found which sets the bounds between the enlightened and dark parts of things—between what is and what is not comprehensible by us—men would perhaps with less scruple acquiesce in the avowed ignorance of the one, and employ their thoughts and discourse with more advantage and satisfaction in the other' ('Essay,' Book I. chap. i. § 7). But Locke's aim was practical, not professionally philosophical; and, being an Englishman, he had not been much troubled by the metaphysical system-builders. Kant, on the other hand, has the latter continually before his mind; 'the celebrated Wolff' in particular had made a deep impression upon him. But he perceived that not one of the metaphysicians was able to establish his system as against the equally plausible constructions of others, or in the face of the sceptical objections brought against such systems in general. The disputes of the Schools seemed best likened to the bloodless and unceasing combats of the heroes in Walhalla. A scepticism like David Hume's appeared the natural end of these ineffectual efforts to extend our knowledge. Profoundly convinced, however, that scepticism is not a permanent state for human reason, Kant tried to formulate to himself the necessary causes of the failure of the best meant of these attempts to construct a philosophy. This is how he differentiates his own work from Hume's. Hume, he says, was satisfied with establishing the fact of an actual failure on the part of metaphysics, but he did not show conclusively how this must be so. Hence in the general discredit which he threw upon the human faculties he involved much of the knowledge of the natural world which no one disputes, but which it is impossible to vindicate on the principles of Humian scepticism. Besides, though an effectual solvent of preceding systems, Hume's method offers no guarantee that other philosophers will not arise, more subtle and persuasive, winning many to accept their constructions, and calling for a second Hume to repeat the work of demolition. What is essential is to set the bounds between our necessary knowledge and our equally necessary ignorance. We must submit to critical evaluation, not *facta* of reason, but reason itself. Proof must be had not merely of limitation or finitude in general, but of a determinate boundary line that shuts off knowledge from the field of the unknown and unknowable. That is, we demonstrate on ground of principle not only our ignorance in respect to this or that subject, but in respect to all possible questions of a certain class. There is no room for conjecture. In this region of complete certitude alone can reason take up its abode; and to mark out the firm 'island' of truth is the task of *criticism*.[1]

All the conclusions of the system-builders are vitiated, Kant explains, by the fact that they have not submitted the conceptions and principles which they employ to a preliminary criticism in order to discover the range of their validity. Conceptions which are familiar to us from daily use we assume to be of universal applicability, without considering what are the conditions of our present experience, and whether these conditions may not be of essential import in determining for conceptions the range of their application. Conceptions quite unimpeachable under these conditions may be quite unmeaning when these conditions are removed. Metaphysic which is oblivious to such considerations Kant calls dogmatic. Thus, when philosophers conclude that the soul is immortal because it is a substantial unit and therefore indiscerptible, their argument is altogether in the air, for they have omitted to consider whether such a conception as substance can have any meaning except as applied to a composite object in space. Similarly, when Locke attempts to prove the existence of God by the 'evident demonstration that from eternity there has been something,' he is importing the conceptions of time and causality into the relations between God and the

---

[1] Cf. Kant's 'Methodenlehre' at the end of the *Critique of Pure Reason*. The special reference is to the second section of the first chapter.

universe, without reflecting whether time and causality are available ideas when we venture beyond the context of our sense-experience.

Nothing could well be more satisfactory than this. But in such an undertaking everything depends upon the thoroughness with which the idea of criticism is applied; and Kant unfortunately left the most fundamental conception of all uncriticised. He dogmatically assumed the conception of the mind as acted upon by something external to it. In other words, the mechanical category of reciprocity, which psychology and ordinary thought may justifiably employ for their own purposes, was taken by him as an adequate or philosophic representation of the relation of the knowing mind to the objective world. The distinction between mind and the world, which is valid only from a certain point of view, he took as an absolute separation. He took it, to use a current phrase, abstractly—that is to say, as a mere fact, a fact standing by itself and true in any reference. And of course when two things are completely separate, they can only be brought together by a bond which is mechanical, external, and accidental to the real nature of both.

Hence it comes (in spite of the inferior position to which Kant explicitly relegates empirical psychology) that the 'Critique of Pure Reason' sets out from a psychological standpoint and never fairly gets beyond it. 'In what other fashion is it to be supposed that the knowing faculty could be roused to exercise, if not by objects which affect our senses?' Kant hardly waits to hear the answer, so much does it seem to him a matter of course. Such a self-revelation is too naïve to be got rid of by saying that this sentence in the first paragraph of the Introduction expresses no more than a provisional adoption of the standpoint of ordinary thought, in order to negate it and rise above it by the progressive criticism of the remainder of the book. That this point of view is negated and surmounted in the 'Critique,' I do not in the least doubt; but it is just as certain that Kant did not mean to express here a merely provisional standpoint from which he could intelligibly launch his own universe upon the reader. The passage may be matched by many others taken from any stage of Kant's speculations. They recur too often to be explained otherwise than by the admission that, while his new method is the conclusive refutation of the claims of psychology to function as philosophy, Kant himself never consciously called in question the fundamental presupposition of psychological philosophy, much less subjected it to the criticism which his principles demanded.

Many untenable Kantian distinctions to which students—and especially students trained in English philosophy—take exception at the outset, are connected in principle with this initial psychological dualism. Such are, for example, the sheer distinction drawn between the form and the matter of experience, between *à priori* and *à posteriori*, and the equally abstract way in which Kant uses universality and necessity as the criteria of formal or perfectly pure cognition. Since the whole of Kant's scheme of thought appears to rest upon these distinctions, it is not to be wondered at if many conclude that the rest of the system must be entirely in the air. It is not the less true, however, that this is a case in which the pyramid does not stand upon its apparent base.

Such disjunctions in Kant are due to the effort of reflection to escape from the unlimited contingency of the Humian position, while retaining the ultimate presupposition of the unrelatedness of mind and things, from which the scepticism of the earlier thinker resulted. What the mind learns from things must necessarily, on this hypothesis, be so many bare facts or atoms of impression cohering simply as they have been accidentally massed in the piecemeal process of acquisition. Kant is forward to endorse Hume's conclusion on this point; that 'experience' cannot yield universality and necessity, is the ground common to both Kant and Hume which furnishes the starting-point of the 'Critique.' On the one hand, Kant found himself faced by this assumption, on the other, by the existence of judgments continually made, and whole sciences constructed, whose universal and necessary application it would be mere affectation to deny. The lines of his own theory were virtually settled by these two admissions. If the necessity which we find in experience is confessedly not derivable from the atomic data furnished to the mind by things, then it must be infused into these data by the action of the mind itself. We have thus the spectacle of experience as the product of an interaction taking place between 'the mind' and things. The element contributed by the action of things Kant calls the matter of experience; the contribution of the mind he calls the form. On his own principles the 'matter' ought to be pure matter or unlimited contingency, containing in itself no germ of methodical arrangement, while the 'forms' of the mind should compel this mass into order and system. But it is of course impossible for Kant to maintain himself at the point of view of a distinction which in this shape simply does not exist. He is forced to admit that, for the particular applications of the general forms or laws imposed on experience by the mind, we remain dependent upon things. But, in such cases, if the particular application is given in the matter, then à fortiori the law or principle in its general form must be so given. It must be possible, by an ordinary process of generalisation and abstraction, to formulate in its generality the principle which the specific instances exemplify. In other words, Kant admits that what is 'given' to the mind is not pure matter, not mere particulars, but matter already formed, particulars already universalised, that is to say, related to one another, and characterised by these relations. The task of the knower is simply to read off, or at most laboriously to bring to light, what is there complete before him in his material. There is not the slightest doubt that, when we remain at the point of view of the abstract distinction between mind and the world which we have signalised in Kant, empiricists are correct in insisting that not the matter of his experience only, but the form as well, is derived by the individual from the world with which he is set in relation. The mind is not the seat of universals and the world a jumble of particulars, the former being superimposed upon the latter for the production of knowledge. Neither mind nor the world has any existence as so conceived. How, for example, can the unfilled mind of the child be regarded as creatively producing order in a chaos of pelting impressions, or what do we mean by postulating a mind at all in such a case? If they prove nothing else, such considerations prove the complete impossibility of treating knowledge from a psychological standpoint. We conclude, therefore, that matter and form are shifting distinctions, relative to the point of view from which they are contemplated; and the same is true of the world and the mind, of which opposition, indeed, the other is only another form. From the standpoint of a theory of knowledge it will be found that the mind and the world are in a sense convertible terms. We may talk

indifferently of the one or of the other; the content of our
notion remains in both cases the same.

A similar criticism applies to the criteria of universality
and necessity as employed by Kant. No sooner are the
words uttered than people begin to ransack their minds in
order to discover whether, as a matter of fact, they ever
make such judgments as are here attributed to them. The
absolute necessariness which Kant affirms of certain judgments becomes a species of mystic quality. Some thinkers
persuade themselves that they recognise this quality in the
judgments in question; others, more cautious, maintain that
whatever stringency the judgments possess may be sufficiently accounted for without resorting to what they brand
as an 'intuition.' Thus, when a conscientious associationist
like Mill comes forward and denies that he finds any absolute
universality and necessity whatever in his experience, Kant's
argument is brought to a complete standstill. The question
of fact on which he builds being denied, there is no common
ground between him and his opponent. Few things can be
imagined more unfortunate than this reduction of the controversy between Kant and empiricism to a discussion about
the existence or non-existence of some mystical necessity in
the propositions of geometry. Yet this actually happened in
the earlier stages of Kantian study in England. Wherever
'intuitions' come into play, the point in dispute is referred
to a merely subjective test, and controversy necessarily
fritters itself away into a bandying of 'yes' and 'no' from the
opposite sides. No one who has learned Kant's lesson so as
to profit by it, should have any hesitation in finding Mill's
hypothetical theory of demonstration to be truer in conception than any theory which insists on a difference of kind
between the necessity of geometrical and that of any other
propositions. All necessity is hypothetical or relative, and
simply expresses the dependence of one thing upon another.
No truth is necessary except in relation to certain conditions,
which being fulfilled, the truth always holds good. The more
general or simple the conditions on which any truth depends,
the wider is the range of its validity; and truths which, like
those of geometry, depend only on the most rudimentary
elements or conditions of experience, will of course be universally and necessarily valid *for all experience depending on these
conditions.* This, as every student ought to know, is the only

necessity which Kant's theory eventually leads him to attribute to the propositions of geometry. It is the more unfortunate that he should seem to base his argumentation upon the assertion of an abstract or absolute necessity. But this is only one of many instances in which the true sense of Kantian terms must be defined by the completed theory. Necessity of the latter type is not so much doubtful in fact as it is contradictory in notion. 'Necessity' invariably raises the question 'why?', and the answer must consist in showing the conditions. Something may be necessary in relation to conditions which are themselves of limited application; in that case we never speak of it as necessary unless when these conditions are themselves under consideration. When we speak of anything as being necessary in a pre-eminent sense, we mean that our assertion depends for its validity on nothing more than the system of conditions on which experience is founded. There is no abstract opposition, therefore, between the necessary and the contingent, such as Kant presents us with; the difference is not one of kind but of degree.

This interpretation of necessity is particularly worth keeping in mind in connection with the Kantian categories or conceptions of the understanding; for Kant's treatment of these so-called à priori elements as the contribution of the mind has again led him into false issues—or at least it has led many of his followers and opponents. It is supposed, for example, that the whole question turns upon the mental origin of certain conceptions, and this, as has been seen, is a fact which may very properly be denied. It appears to be forgotten amid the pros and cons of such an argument, that mental origin is in itself no clue to the function of a conception or the range of its validity, unless we connect our assertion with a whole theory as to the nature of experience in general. This, it must be allowed, Kant has not neglected to do; and his ultimate proof of the necessity of conceptions like substance and cause is simply that without them experience would be impossible. They are the most general principles on which we find a concatenated universe to depend. Their mental origin falls in such a deduction completely into the background; and Kant is only obliged to assert it because of the absolute opposition which he set up between the necessary and the contingent, and the presupposition with which he started that experience can give us nothing but contingency. The conceptions derive their necessity from their relation to experience as a whole. Kant proceeds, indeed, to describe the conceptions in this relation as modes of mental combination, according to which the Ego lays out the variety poured in upon it from without. As nothing can come within experience except so far as it fits itself into the structure of the mental mould, the necessary validity for experience of these combining multiples is evident. But nothing is gained by isolating these conditions, principles, or categories from the experience in which they are disclosed to us, and hypostatising them as faculties or modes of faculties—methods of action inherent in the mind. On the contrary, this is essentially a mischievous step; for when we talk thus, we are inevitably held to refer to the individual mind, and the difficulties, or rather absurdities, of such a position have already come under our notice. It is to be regretted, therefore, that Kant frequently described his un-- dertaking as a criticism of faculties, instead of keeping by the more comprehensive and less misleading title (which, as we have seen, he also employs) of a criticism of conceptions. Unfortunately this is not merely a verbal inconsistency; it represents two widely different views of the critical philosophy.

Kant's general scheme is sufficiently well known to render any minute account of it superfluous in this connection. It was framed, as has been seen, to account for the fact of universal and necessary judgments, and its form was conditioned by the previous acceptance of Hume's fundamental assumptions. Kant's way out of the difficulty was contained in what he called his Copernican change of standpoint. If there is no necessity to. be got by waiting on the world of things, let us try what success attends us if objects are made to wait upon us for their most general determinations. The form or 'ground-plan' of experience which Kant discovers in following out this idea, consists of twelve categories, conceptions, or methods of combination, according to which the matter of sense is arranged in the perceptive or imaginative spectra of space and time, the process of arrangement being ultimately guided by three ideals of intellectual completeness, and being referable at every point to the unity of the transcendental Ego. Or, in Kant's psychological language, the mind is furnished, first, with the *à priori* forms of space and time in which all its impressions must be received; and secondly, with twelve principles of intellectual synthesis, by submission to which the impressions of sense first become objects in a world of related things. The relations of space and of objects in space,[1] as dependent upon the nature of the mind-form and of the mind-imposed laws of combination, may thus evidently be known with complete certainty. We are in a position, so far as these points are concerned, to anticipate experience; universality and necessity are saved. But the counter-stroke is obvious. We anticipate experience—and to that extent, as Kant paradoxically puts it, legislate for nature—simply because it is our own necessity, and not the necessity of things, which is reflected back to us from the face of this mind-shaped world. We purchase the sense of certainty in our knowledge at the cost of being told that our knowledge is not in a strict sense real knowledge at all. The world of real objects (improperly so called, inasmuch as they never *are* objects) on which Kant represents us as waiting for the matter of our experience, is necessarily cut off from us by the constitution of our powers of knowing. Here Kant draws the line which he said Hume neglected to draw—the line dividing the region of complete certitude from that of necessary and eternal ignorance. The first region is the field of phenomena, related to one another in space and time—the context of possible experience, consisting of the mind-manipulated data of sense. The second, from which our faculties debar us, is the world of things-in-themselves, considered not merely as the unknown region where our sense-experience takes its rise, but as a world in which room may possibly be found for such non-spatial entities as God and the soul, and the aspects of human life which seem to depend on these ideas.

The nature of these results determines the special sense which the term criticism assumes in Kant's hands. The term originally describes merely the method of procedure, but it naturally becomes descriptive also of the definite view of the universe to which his method leads him. The critical

---

[1] Time, Kant proves in the 'Refutation of Idealism,' is knowable only in relation to space. He says elsewhere that inner sense receives its whole filling from outer sense. The correlation of time and space being necessary, the limitation of knowledge is correctly described in the text as limitation to the contents of space.

philosopher, accordingly, is one who clearly apprehends what is implied in calling the deduction of the categories *transcendental*. A transcendental deduction is one undertaken solely with reference to experience—one which leaves us, therefore, completely without justification for employing the deduced conceptions in any other reference. And if it be considered that experience in this connection implies for Kant the relation of the mind to an unknown object—means, in fact, the application of the categories to the matter derived from that object—it is evident that when the latter element falls away, the conceptions must become so many empty words. Experience so conceived is called sense-experience, in order to describe our partially receptive attitude and the compound character of our knowledge. It yields us a knowledge only of material things and their changes, and the attempt to gain any other species of knowledge by means of the categories Kant compares to the flapping of wings in the unsupporting void. Criticism means, then, the recognition of this limitation, and it pronounces experience so limited to be merely phenomenal in character. Experience actual and possible represents, in other words, not things as they are in themselves, but only a certain relation of the human mind towards the world of reality. Our ignorance in this respect is inevitable and final; and if there are other avenues by which—in the case of the Self and God—we may penetrate to noumenal existence, yet the conviction we reach is not such that we can rightly speak of it as knowledge. All knowledge remains in the Kantian scheme phenomenal— phenomenal in the sense that there is a reality behind, which we do not know.

If now it be asked, by what right Kant draws the line exactly where he does, and cuts off from knowledge everything but a spatial world of interacting substances, the answer must be that his conclusion depends ultimately on his uncritical acceptance of the dualistic assumption of preceding philosophy. We express the same thing in another form, when we say that the result is due to the attempt to construct a theory of knowledge from the standpoint of psychology. This standpoint brings with it the distinction between 'sense,' as the source of knowledge, and 'understanding,' as a faculty of 'comparing, connecting, and separating,' the material supplied by sense. This is Locke's distinction, and it is Kant's too.[1] Kant minimises the contribution of sense; he speaks of it on occasion as a mere blur, and in itself no better than nothing at all. But the *amount* referred to sense does not affect the principle of the distinction; so far as it is made in this form at all, its consequences will be essentially the same—either with Hume, the denial that (so far as we know) any real world exists, or with Kant, the denial that such a world can ever be revealed to us by knowledge. Hence the importance of observing that the distinction is not a deduction from the theory of knowledge, but a presupposition drawn from another sphere. The division of the mind into receptivity and spontaneity is the mere correlate of that view of the universe from which the Kantian criticism was ultimately destined to set us free—the view which represents the relation of the world to consciousness as a case of interaction between two substances. The effect of the distinction on the form of the Kantian theory appears in the separation of the Æsthetic from the Analytic, and the hard and fast line drawn in consequence between space and time as forms of sensibility and the categories as functions of the understanding. Kant gets the perceptive forms in the Æsthetic by an independent set of arguments, while in the first part of the Analytic his categories seem to drop at his feet as pure intellectual conceptions. Hence the categories do not appear to him as limited or inadequate *in their own nature*, but because of their subsequent association with sense and its forms. It would be nearer the truth to say that the Kantian categories are themselves the reason why the world appears to us in space; space is merely the abstraction or the ghost of the world of interacting substances which these categories present us with. If the Kantian categories can give us nothing beyond a world of material things, the defect is in their own intellectual quality and not in any limitation extraneously attached to them. They are bonds of connection, yet they may be said to leave the elements

[1] As it happens, Kant's phraseology in the opening paragraph of the Introduction corresponds exactly with Locke's account of knowledge given in Book II. chap. xii. of the *Essay*. 'The materials being such as he has no power over, either to create or destroy, all that a man can do is either to unite them together, or to set them one by another, or wholly separate them.' Kant's language looks like a reminiscence of this passage, when he speaks of impressions producing ideas, and rousing 'the faculty of the understanding *to compare, connect, and separate* these, and so to work up the raw material of sensuous impressions into a knowledge of objects.' Of course Kant's 'raw material' turns out afterwards not to mean so much as Locke's 'simple ideas.'

they connect still independent of one another. The categories of quantity, while in one sense they express a connection between all things, express even more emphatically the
complete indifference of every individual point to its neighbours; and though the categories of relation—summed up,
as they are, in reciprocity—undoubtedly express a system of
elements in which this mutual indifference is overcome, yet
the individuals brought into connection are not seen to have
any necessary relation to one another in the sense of being
members together of one whole. The individuals appear
endlessly determined by their relations to one another, but
there is involved in this very endlessness an unavoidable
sense of contingency. If we are to have a real whole and
real parts—parts, that is, whose existence can be understood
only through the whole that determines them—we must have
recourse to other categories than these. But the imperfect
relatedness just referred to is the essential mark of what we
call the world of sense; and for a theory of knowledge, if it
retain the term sensible world, that world is definable simply
by this characteristic, and not by an imaginary reference of
its contents to an impressing cause. It is defined, in other
words, by the categories that constitute it, and by the relation of these categories to the other modes in which the
mind endeavours to harmonise the world. With reference
to Kant, then, the point to be insisted on is, that the categories which he offers as the only categories are *inherently*
inadequate to express a synthesis more intimate than the
mutual relatedness + mutual externality of things in space.
The world, therefore, necessarily presents this aspect when
viewed solely by their light. They are not got independently
of sense (we might reply to Kant) and afterwards immersed
in it; they are the categories *of* sense. Their true deduction is not from the table of logical judgments; it is given in
the 'system of principles' in the second part of the Analytic,
where they are proved to be the ultimate conditions on which
a coherent sense-experience depends. In Kant's technical
language, the categories do not require to be schematised,
because apart from schematisation they do not exist even
as conceptions. The conception of substance, for example,
means just that relation of a permanent to shifting (or con-
ceivably shifting) attributes which is familiar to us in the
sensible world. The logical relation of subject and predicate,

which Kant seems to say is the pure category before it is soiled by sense, is merely the image of this real relation expressed in language.[1]

There is thus no justification for a separation of space from the categories, space being simply the ultimate appearance of a world constructed on these categories alone. When this is admitted, the mere fact that we perceive things *in space* is no imputation upon the reality of our knowledge. In itself space is no limitation; it is an intellectual bond, it is one point of view from which we may represent the world as one. This mode of knowledge becomes limited and unreal only when it claims to be the ultimate aspect from which the universe is to be regarded. The nature of space affords no grounds then for a division of knowledge into absolutely phenomenal and absolutely noumenal, such as we find in Kant. The so-called phenomenal world of sense is as real as the so-called noumenal world of ethics, that is to say, its account of the universe is as legitimate so far as it goes; but to claim for either an absolute truth is the essential mark of dogmatism, whether the claim be advanced by the man of science or by the metaphysician. Both are accounts which the mind gives to itself of the world, relatively justified points of view from which experience may be rationalised. It is the province of a theory of knowledge to point out the relation of the one point of view to the other, and, in general, while showing the partial and abstract nature of any particular point of view, to show at the same time how it is related to the ultimate or concrete conception of the universe which alone admits of being thought out without self-contradiction. The opposition between phenomenal and noumenal worlds is thus replaced by one between more abstract and more concrete points of view. That is to say, the opposition itself is no longer of the rigid or absolute nature which it was before. The truth of the one point of view does not interfere with the truth of the other; the higher may rather be regarded as the completion or fulfilment of the lower.

Let us now see how far Kant helps us towards such a philosophic conception. Reasons have been given for disallowing his absolute limitation of knowledge by erecting

---

[1] The relation of the table of logical judgments to the Kantian categories (where it actually exists and is not a matter of forced interpretation) is thus seen to be reversed.

behind it a realm of unknowables. These unknowables are simply the impressing things of preceding philosophy, uncritically assumed, and removed into a somewhat deeper obscurity. But the theory which derives knowledge from impressions is essentially a physiological theory which we, as spectators, form of the rise of knowledge in an organised individual placed in relation to a world which we already describe under all the categories of knowledge. What we observe is, strictly, an interaction between two things which are themselves objects in a known world. And if we afterwards extend inferentially to our own case the conclusions which our observations suggest, we are still simply repeating the picture of a known environment acting on a known organism. The relation is between phenomenal things and a phenomenal organism in which they set up affections, not between a transcendent or metempirical somewhat and intelligence as such. In other words, when we have framed our notion of the world, and of our own position as individuals in it, we can give even to such a misleading metaphor as impression a certain intelligible meaning; but to step outside of the world of knowledge altogether and characterise it by reference to something beyond itself—this is the type of all impossibility. Yet it is no less than this that Kant and the neo-Kantians undertake to do when they pronounce our knowledge phenomenal, implying by that term the existence of something hidden from us in its own transcendency. While adhering, therefore, in the fullest manner to Kant's position that the categories are only of immanent use for the organisation of experience, we deny altogether that the existence of transcendent entities may be justly inferred from such a statement. Only to those who are haunted by the ghosts of the old metaphysic can the proposition appear in the light of a limitation of human reason; to others adhesion to Kant's position, so far as it asserts immanence, becomes a matter of course. What they combat in Kant's scheme is the assumption that his twelve categories are the only categories implied in our experience, and the belief, corresponding to this assumption, that they give a completely coherent and exhaustive account of that experience.

Kant himself, however, is prone to confess that experience is not exhausted by these categories, if by experience is understood the whole life of man. The world of ethical action (to take his own crucial instance) remains completely unintelligible when viewed from the standpoint of mechanism. Determination by ends is the characteristic feature of this world ; and action so determined cannot be understood, Kant says, except under the idea of freedom.   That is to say, the attempt to explain it by the categories of natural causality is equivalent to a denial of the existence of the facts in question.   Such a procedure means that in our levelling zeal we obliterate the specific difference of two sets of facts ; whereas in reality the difference is the fundamental feature of the case which calls upon us for a rationale of its possibility.   Now it is matter of common knowledge that for Kant himself moral experience was *the* reality.   In the Preface to the ' Critique of Practical Reason ' he speaks of the idea of freedom as the ' topstone of the whole edifice of a system of pure reason, *speculative as well as practical*; and no attentive reader of the first Critique can fail to notice the vista ever and anon opened up of a world of supersensible reality into which we are eventually to be carried by the march of the argument.   The whole critical scheme of sense-experience is thereby invested with a palpably preparatory character.   Kant fully recognises, and indeed enforces, this aspect of his work when he comes to review its scope and method in the Preface to the second edition.   The whole investigation is there represented as merely ' making room ' for the extension of our knowledge on the basis of practical data ; criticism simply fulfils the function of ' a police force ' in keeping the unregulated activity of the speculative reason within bounds.   It might well seem, then, as if, in going on to treat the presuppositions of morality, we were merely passing from one sphere of rational experience to another. Kant's method, too, is essentially the same in all the three Critiques.   It is an analysis of certain experiences with a view to determine the conditions of their possibility.   One would expect, therefore, that the different sets of conceptions to which his analysis leads him, would be treated impartially, and on their own merits, or looked at merely in their relation to one another as parts of one rational explanation of experience.   If there is no flaw in our deduction of the conceptions, it seems very like stultifying the transcendental method to talk of differences between them in respect of objective truth or validity.   Kant, however, as is well known, draws a variety of such distinctions. Thus, in the 'Critique of Judgment' he finds the idea of organisation to be as essential to a complete account of nature as he had previously found the conception of substance to be for a narrower range of experience. Yet he arbitrarily holds the former to be of merely regulative utility—a fiction or contrivance of the mind to aid it in investigation—while the latter is allowed to be constitutive of nature as such. And so again Kant restricts the terms experience and knowledge to the sense-phenomena of the first Critique, while the presuppositions of ethical experience are made at most matters of rational belief or moral certainty. It is impossible to decorate the one with pre-eminent titles without a corresponding disparagement of the others. The term experience is in these circumstances a question-begging epithet. When such distinctions are drawn, it inevitably tends to make men regard the 'Critique of Pure Reason' as alone embodying Kant's substantive theory of the world. The categories of life, of beauty, and of morality come to be looked on as appendices of a more or less uncertain character, the acceptance or rejection of which does not interfere with the finality of the categories of sense. This is unquestionably the form in which Kantian results are most widely current at present. It is a form for which Kant himself is chiefly responsible, through his habit of 'isolating' different spheres of experience for the purposes of his analysis, and neglecting afterwards to exhibit their organic relation to one another. None the less is it a form which ignores explicit intimations like those quoted above from the two Prefaces, and one which is based on that very notion of the relation of mind to reality which Kant came to destroy. After all, too much stress has probably been laid upon the difference of nomenclature which Kant adopts, and it ought to be remembered that though he refuses to call his moral faith knowledge, he yet holds that it, and it alone, brings him into contact with reality.

If we now return to Kant's account of the phenomenal nature of our knowledge, and abstract altogether from the illegitimate reference of our sense-objects to the transcendental thing-in-itself, another meaning of the phenomenality of sense-experience begins to emerge. The opposition is no longer between the world of sense and its unknown correlate (or cause), but between the world of sense as nature or the realm of causal necessity, and the 'intelligible world,' as Kant calls it, or the realm of ends, in which the will determines itself by its own law. Noumenal personality and freedom are reached in the notion of the self-legislative and self-obedient will. The condemnation of phenomenality comes upon the world of sense because of the contrast which its externality of connected part and part offers to the self-centred finality of a conception like the self-determining will. If this is not the meaning of phenomenality which is most prominent in the 'Critique of Pure Reason,' still it is continually appearing there also; and in proportion as it comes into the foreground, the other reference of objects to their transcendental correlates tends to lose its importance and almost to disappear. Anyone may convince himself of this by turning to Kant's official chapter 'On the ground of the division of all objects into phenomena and noumena.' He will find that the conception of noumena or non-sensuous objects is there defined as a 'Grenzbegriff,' a limitative conception, or, more exactly, as a conception which sets bounds to the sphere of sense (ein die Sinnlichkeit in Schranken setzender Begriff). The conception is problematical, Kant says, inasmuch as it does not give us a knowledge of intelligible or non-sensuous objects as actually existing, but merely affirms their possibility. Its utility lies in the fact that by it we prevent sense-knowledge from laying claim to the whole of reality. Evidently it would be unfair to interpret the term problematical here as if Kant meant by using it to throw doubt on the actual existence of what he sometimes calls 'the non-sensuous cause' of our ideas. 'In what other fashion is it to be supposed that the knowing faculty should be roused to exercise,' he might repeat, 'if not by objects which affect our senses?' The question of the origin of the matter of sense remains for Kant just where it was, but he is speaking here in quite another connection, and that problem has fallen out of view for the time. He is engaged in limiting sense so as to 'make room' for the *mundus intelligibilis* which he is afterwards to produce as guaranteed by the practical reason. It is the existence of freedom and its implicates that is declared to be, in the meantime, merely problematical. The phrase intelligible world is never used by Kant, so far as I know, except of the world of ethically determined

agents—an additional proof that we are right in attributing
to him here a point of view which judges the inadequacy of
sense not by reference to a somewhat beyond the confines
of intelligible experience altogether, but by reference to a
higher phase of experience itself. The lower point of view
is not, strictly speaking, abolished by the higher, but it is
perceived that to try to take the sensible world absolutely or
by itself would be to render it unintelligible. Isolated in this
way, the world of interacting substances would have all the
irrationality of a series that cannot be summed, of multiplicity without unity, of externality without internality. It
is impossible, in Kant's language, to treat nature as an end
in itself, as something there on its own account; yet reason
demands this notion of the self-sufficing and self-justifying,
as that in which alone it can rest. Kant recognises that it
is only intelligence, and especially intelligence in its moral
aspect, that supplies the lacking notion; nature itself, he .
says, assumes a unity which does not otherwise belong to it,
and becomes a ' realm ' or system, when viewed in relation
to rational beings as its ends.[1]

It is thus on account of its incomplete and self-less
character that the *mundus sensibilis* appears phenomenal,
when regarded from the standpoint of the intelligible world.
And reason is compelled, Kant says, to pass beyond the
phenomenal and occupy such a standpoint, ' if we are not to
deny to man the consciousness of himself as intelligence, *i.e.*,
as rational and through reason active, which is to say, a
free cause.' [2] The importance of the change in the ·point
of view can hardly be over-estimated. Self-consciousness is
here put forward explicitly as the one noumenon to which all
phenomena are referred, and by which they are, as it were,
judged and declared to be phenomenal. This is the real Copernican change of standpoint which Kant effected, or at
least which he puts us in the way of effecting; and it must
be pronounced fundamental, seeing that it reverses the whole
notion of reality on which the old metaphysic was built. The
dominating categories of philosophy in the present day are
still, it is to be feared, those of inner and outer, substance and
quality, or in their latest and most imposing garb, noumenon

---

[1] Cf. *Grundlegung zur Metaphysik
der Sitten. Werke*, IV. 286 (ed. Harten-
stein). ·

[2] *Werke*, IV. 306. The expression
' Standpunkt ' is used by Kant himself.

and phenomenon.   And these are so interpreted as to represent the intellect clinging round the outside of things, getting to know only the surface of the world, and pining and wailing for the revelation of that intense reality, the ' support of accidents,' which yet is unrevealable, and mocks our cries. A true metaphysic teaches that if we so conduct ourselves, we do in very truth ' pine for what is not.' This unapproachable reality is entirely a fiction of the mind; there is nothing transcendent, no unknowable, if we once see that a phenomenal world is a permissible phrase only when taken to mean something in which reason cannot rest, and that the ultimate noumenon is to be found in self-consciousness, or in the notion of knowledge and its corollaries. The centre of the world lies then in our own nature as self-conscious beings, and in that life with our fellows which, in different aspects, constitutes alike the secular and the divine community. The spirit fostered by physical science, and the mood familiar to all of us—the mood which weighs man's paltry life and its concerns against the ' pomp of worlds' and the measureless fields of space—is in reality less philosophical than that of the poet and humanist to whom this pomp is barren save as the background of the human drama. Ordinary people get most of their metaphysics through religion or through poetry, and they probably often come nearer the truth in that way than if they went to the professed philosophers.

Kant's ethics are part therefore of the strength and not of the weakness of their author. They are not to be regarded as a calling in of faith to repair the breaches of knowledge ; on the contrary, they are founded on Kant's deepest philosophical conceptions. But for all that, the superstructure contains much questionable material ; and as we are not engaged in a process of hermeneutics, it is essential to arrive for ourselves at a general notion of how the ethical point of view stands related to the mechanical. This will serve as an illustration of the main thesis of the essay, the distinction of categories or points of view. It is at the same time the more necessary in the present case as Kant has expressed the relation chiefly by negations, and has left the sensible and intelligible systems separated by an apparently impassable gulf. The positive predicate of freedom which he applies to the ethical world is, on the other hand, so ambiguous, and to men of scientific training so ominous, that it has been more productive of misconception than of enlightenment. It may be said at once, then, that if Kant's account of freedom contains anything which seems to lift man, as it were, out of all the influences and surroundings that make him what he is, and from this height makes him hurl a decisive and solely self-originated fiat into the strife of motives beneath—then, undoubtedly, this idea is not only at variance with the teaching of physical and social science, but is fatal to all rational connection in the universe. But the self in such a conception is a bare unit, an abstraction which has no existence in fact. So long as we take up with such notions of the self, we must inevitably seem to be battered about by the shocks of circumstance. The man whose self could be emptied of all its contents and reduced to this atomic condition would be, in a strict sense, no more than the moving point which exemplifies the composition of forces. In reducing the abstract self to this position, and so abolishing it, determinism is entirely within its rights; it is in vain that the upholders of 'free-will' try to save for this self even a power of directing attention on one motive rather than another. But happily the real self is not this ghost of argumentative fancy. A man cannot be separated from the world which lies about him from his infancy—and long before it—moulding him after its own image, and supplying him with all sorts of permanent motives in the shape of creeds and laws, customs and prejudices, creating, in a word, the concrete personality we are held to refer to when, in ordinary speech, we name this or the other individual. The self-conscious individual is not something identical with himself alone, and different from everything else; he is not even exclusive as one thing in nature is exclusive of other things. The whole past and the whole present are transformed, as it were, by self-consciousness into its own nature. A man's motives do not seem to him, therefore, to come to him from without; they are the suggestions of his good or evil self. And if he reviews his past experience, when his self, as others might say, was in the making, he cannot himself take this external view. It is impossible to him because it abolishes the one presupposition from which he cannot depart; it abolishes himself. Much rather he will say that he has made himself what he is; he identifies himself necessarily with all his past, and of every deed he can say 'Alone I did it.' In short, though the external view with its tabulation of motives may be useful for statistical purposes, and may yield scientific results that are not to be despised, it is absolutely valueless in ethics or the explanation of moral experience as such. The presupposition of ethical action, as of intelligence generally, is the Ego. It is true that, as explained above, we do not suppose the Ego in action to bring an inexplicable force into play any more than we suppose it, as intellect, to add any determinations to things which were not there already. But just as any metaphysic which does not base itself on self-consciousness, as the fundamental presupposition and the supreme category of thought, is forced openly or tacitly to deny the conscious life, so a science of ethics which does not assume as its basis the self-determination of the rational being, remains outside of moral experience altogether. Moral experience consists entirely in this self-reference; if this be destroyed the whole ethical point of view vanishes. Let us contrast with this the point of view of physical science from which we started. From this standpoint every moral action is simply an event, and as an event forms a term in a series of mechanical transformations. This is certainly one way of regarding the actions in question; they are such events, and for science that is the legitimate and true method of treating them. All that we contend is that the scientific explanation does not exhaust their significance; so far as they are actions, that is, related to the moral consciousness, it gives no account of them at all. The world of ethics is superimposed therefore upon that of science, not as contradicting it, but as introducing a totally new order of conceptions, by which actions which are for science mere factual units in a series, become elements in a life guided by the notion of end or ought. Their sole ethical meaning is in relation to this ideally judging consciousness, and to that extent they cease to be facts conditioned by other facts. The ethical consciousness identifies itself with each of its actions, and each therefore is immediately referred to the standard of duty. Ethically, that is to say, the action is not referred backward in time to the circumstances and predispositions of which, as motives, it is the legitimate outcome; but the man brings his action face to face with a 'Thou shalt,' which he finds within him,[1] and according to

---

[1] The 'matter' which the law commands, depends of course upon his social

its conformity or want of conformity with this law he approves or condemns his conduct. The former method of looking at his actions is appropriate to a spectator—a psychologist, a statistician, a scientific educator, &c.—but not to the man himself. As soon as an individual begins to seek excuses for his fault by showing how 'natural' it was in the circumstances, he has fallen from the ethical point of view. He is assuming the position of a spectator or scientific observer, and however justifiable this standpoint may be for others, it certainly means the destruction of the ethical consciousness in him who deliberately adopts it in his own regard. The proper category of ethics is not cause and effect, but end, with its correlative obligation.

The world of ethical ends, however, is only one of the conceptions or points of view by which reason makes the world intelligible to itself ; and by treating it as the sole antithesis of the world of sense, Kant ran the risk, as was hinted above, of falling into a fresh dualism. It is not even well to speak of the one as 'intelligible' by pre-eminence, lest the sensible world lose its reference to consciousness altogether. We might do worse than recall in this connection Kant's demonstration of the intellectual elements in sense-experience. We do not get 'facts' given to us in the mechanical scheme of science, and in ethics a point of view from which to regard this factual world. Bare facts in this sense have no existence save for an abstract thought which conceives them as the pegs on which relations may be hung. The process of knowledge does not consist in the discovery of such *individua*, but in the progressive overthrowal of such ideas of the nature of the actual. In this process the scientific account of things forms one of the ways in which the mind seeks to present the world as an intelligible whole ; it is a *theorising* of the world, and, as it turns out, the theorising is incomplete and ultimately contradicts itself. Such considerations prepare us to expect a progress by more gradual stages from the less to the more complete conception of the universe than is found in Kant's great leap from mechanism to morality. Here again Kant helps us on the way. The 'Critique of Judgment,' according to his own account of it,

environment and his past ; but the 'form' of law exists wherever consciousness exists, since rights and duties are involved in the most rudimentary notion of society.

is intended to bridge over the gulf between the world of the understanding, outlined in the first Critique, and the world of reason or of free determination, outlined in the second. There is as usual much that is artificial in the scheme of faculties with which Kant connects his investigation. So far as we are concerned here, the best method of approaching the 'Critique of Judgment' is simply by reference to the aspects of nature which it endeavours to explain. Its importance lies in its recognition of certain points of view which are continually recurring in our contemplation of the world, but which find no place in the critical idea of nature. These are the æsthetic and the teleological judgment of things, or, in less technical language, the phenomena of beauty and of organisation.[1]

The weakness of the book lies in the presupposition on which it proceeds, that the record of objectivity has been definitively closed in the first Critique. In other words, Kant believes knowledge to be limited by the imagination ; nothing is real (in the domain of knowledge) unless what can be constructed in relations of space. Now the 'Critique of Judgment' consists virtually in the production of two sets of negative instances ; a living body and an object considered as beautiful are not exhausted in the space-relations which constitute them. Imagination knows only parts that are external to one another, and to that extent independent of one another; but in the organism this externality and independence disappear. The parts are only parts through the whole of which they are parts. Part and whole acquire, in fact, a meaning in which their necessary correlation is for the first time apparent—a correlation or union so intimate as to be inadequately expressed by terms which contain, like part and whole, a quantitative suggestion. Similarly the category of cause breaks down when applied to the organism, for all the parts are mutually cause and effect; and the organism as a whole is at once its own cause and its own effect (*causa sui*). It organises itself. In all this Kant's description of organic phenomena is unexceptionable ; he pleads the case well against himself. But unfortunately the negative instances he produces did not lead to a recasting of his theory. They

---

[1] To avoid confusion, the significance of the æsthetic judgment, or of the categories of art, for our ultimate notion of the world, is not touched upon in the present essay.

only led to a fresh distinction. The new aspects of nature
could not be recognised as constitutive or objectively valid,
but they might be accepted as regulative points of view for
the investigation of phenomena. But as there is no ground
for this distinction except in presuppositions which have
been shown to be irrelevant, we shall make no scruple of
ignoring it, and treating the relation of organism to mechanism not as subjectivity to objectivity but as a more adequate
to a less adequate interpretation of the same facts.

It must be observed that the notion of organism given
above constitutes no assertion of the existence of a vital force
as a separate cause of the phenomena of life. This is the
kind of deduction which metaphysicians of the kind that
have brought the name into disrepute were quick to draw.
But it is easy to see that by explanations of this sort we are
just setting up a duplicate of the thing to be explained, or
in other words, hypostatising it as its own cause. Besides,
when the physiologist comes to close quarters with a
living body, he finds everywhere a mechanism of parts
connected with one another and communicating with the
surrounding world. Motion is handed on from one member
of this system to another without the intervention of any
other than mechanical contrivances; and so far from a
necessity arising for a transcendent cause, there is nowhere
a gap to be found in the circle of mechanical motions where
its introduction could be effected. The physiologist, in short,
in describing the action of the different parts of the organism,
is in precisely the same position as the psychologist in giving
an account of mental states and processes. The empirical
psychologist analyses the most complex states into their
elements, and builds up ethical and religious sentiment out
of simple desires and aversions, and all by a process essentially mechanical, without any reference to the unity of the
conscious life for which these states exist. Just as the
psychologist has neither occasion nor right to consider any
special power which he calls the Ego, so the physiologist in
the case of the organism. He works within the conditions of
organic existence, as the psychologist within those of consciousness, but neither requires for the purposes of his
special science to make any explicit reference to these conditions. Hence it comes that physiology, so far as it treats
the living body as a whole, represents it as merely a mecha-

nical conjunction of parts in space. The abstraction is not only defensible but necessary; none the less, however, is it a complete abstraction from the significance of the same parts viewed as members of a living system. Viewed organically, or in their relation to the whole, they are seen to be mutually implicative, and, within certain limits, mutually creative. The presuppositions of mechanism are so far overthrown that at the organic standpoint the mutual exclusiveness of the parts disappears; the organism, *quâ* organism, is not in space at all. If we persist, therefore, in looking at the parts abstractly or in their separateness, and if we tender this as the complete account of them, we are leaving out of sight the very fact which constitutes the phenomenon to be explained.[1]

So far from mechanism being objective and the notion of organism only subjective, we should be compelled, if we were in the way of talking in this strain, to reverse the relation. For even as applied to so-called mechanical things, if the category of causality be thought out into reciprocity, and if reciprocity be conceived as complete, the result is that we arrive at a closed circle of perfect mutual conditionedness, in which all play of actual causality is brought to a standstill. The universe becomes like the sleeping palace of Dornröschen: there is no point where movement might be introduced into this dead picture. We sublate in this way the conceptions with which we started, and only find the contradiction solved for us (at least temporarily) in the notion of the organism.

If the categories of reciprocity and abstract individuality fail us in speaking of the living body, still less will they serve us when we come to treat of conscious individuals and what is called the social organism. Step by step we have combated the intellectual vice of abstraction, but it is when we reach self-consciousness that the nature of this fault becomes fully apparent. When we examine the conceptions of ordinary and scientific thought in the light thrown upon them by that supreme category of which they are all the imperfect reflections, the whole series of stages from which the individual knower views the world appears as a gradual deliverance from an abstract individualism, or, as Spinoza said, from the imaginative thought that insists on taking the individual as a thing by itself. When we reach the only true individual,

[1] Cf. the working out of this point in the second essay of this volume, pp. 52-60.

the self-conscious being, we find that individuality is not the exclusive thing we had imagined it to be. The self is individual only to the extent that it is at the same time universal. It knows itself, *i.e.*, it *is* itself, just because it includes within its knowledge not only one particular self, as an object in space and time, but also a whole intelligible world embracing many such selves. A mere individual, supposed for a moment possible, would be a self-less point; and it was the assumption of the reality of such self-less points that led us into contradiction at a lower stage. In the notion of the self we find that what is outside of, or different from, a man in the narrow sense, yet enters into and constitutes his self in such a way that, without it, he would cease to be anything more than the imaginary point just referred to. The individual is individualised only by his relations to the totality of the intelligible world. In a more restricted sense, his individuality is constituted by the social organism of which he is a member; he cannot be an individual except so far as he is a member of society. If this is the relation of society to the individual, it is at once apparent how false any theory must be which tries to take the individual as a mere individual, and regards society as an aggregate of such beings combined together for mutual advantage. The doctrine of *laissez-faire* and the theory of the police-state are immediate deductions from the individualistic premises. It is natural from such a point of view that the State should be treated as a mechanism external to the individuals, and constructed by them merely that they may live at ease and enjoy their goods. But the logic of practice refutes both these principles. The economic doctrine has been largely modified even by those who promulgated it, little as their professed philosophical principles give them a right to do so; and the external view of the State is refuted not only by its practical action in numberless spheres of life, but by every patriotic emotion that passes over individuals or peoples. If the State is the artificial aggregate it is represented as being, how shall we explain Shakespeare's impassioned apostrophe to .

> This happy breed of men, this little world,
> This precious stone set in the silver sea . . .
> This blessed plot, this earth, this realm, this England . . .
> This land of such dear souls, this dear dear land.

This little world— a more felicitous phrase could hardly be desired to describe what the true State must always be to its citizens.   The State is not Leviathan, as Hobbes supposed, swallowing up the individual, but the ethical cosmos into which he is born, and by which his relation to the wider cosmos of universal experience is mediated.   These, however, are considerations which are insisted upon elsewhere in the present volume, and which are being recognised, one is glad to see, in other quarters, even though it be as yet without a consciousness of their ultimate philosophical bearing.   Still we are not entitled to depart from individualistic metaphysics in one point unless we recognise the fallaciousness of its method everywhere.   We need not fear by so doing to sacrifice what are called the rights of individuality.   Socialism, for example, is the recoil from individualism, not the refutation of it.   Individualism and socialism are alike refuted by the true notion of self-consciousness, which combines all-inclusiveness with intensest concentration in a way which might have seemed impossible, had we been engaged in an abstract argument and not simply in an analysis of concrete reality. While this notion is held fast, the members in whom the social organism is realised will not cease to know themselves as personalities, and to demand that the free play of their lives be not sacrificed to imaginary needs of the body politic.

Our whole criticism of categories thus leads us up to the notion of self-consciousness or knowledge.   Here we may connect ourselves for the last time with Kant.   The shortcomings of his theory of knowledge have been somewhat severely criticised in the earlier part of the essay.   It has been seen that he vitiated his analysis to a great extent by confusing a psychological or a spectator's account of the growth of knowledge with a transcendental analysis of its conditions.   It has also been shown how the presuppositions that sprang from this confusion prevented him from seeing the mutual relations of the categories in their true light as simply stages or phases of explanation (of greater or less abstractness) which necessarily supersede one another in the development of knowledge.   But in spite of the absolute line which Kant drew at reciprocity, he explicitly announced the emancipation of the category of categories—the unity of apperception—from the dominion of the conceptions which were its own creatures.   It can be compassed, he says, by none of them; it can be known only through itself.   Know-

ledge is related as such to an universally synthetic principle
which calls itself ' I,' and which is described by Kant as the
transcendental Ego to distinguish it from the empirical con-
sciousnesses which constitute, as it were, the matter of this
formal unity.   Kant's view of this unity as merely logical
and merely human prevented him from recognising that he
had found the true noumenon here as well as in the ethical
sphere.   Nevertheless his assertion of the unity of the subject as the ultimate principle of thought leads directly to the
conception of knowledge as necessarily organic to a subject,
and as constituting in this form the complete Fact from which
all so-called facts are only abstractions.   Here the line
between dogmatism and criticism may be drawn without
prejudice to Kant's essential meaning.   Dogmatism, or the
use of uncriticised conceptions, means practically the un-
questioning application of the categories of mechanism to the
relation between consciousness and things.   Mind and matter
are hypostatised, and the category of reciprocity is employed
to describe their union in knowledge.   How far Kant was himself a dogmatist in this sense has been already considered ; at
all events the whole of modern philosophy before Kant is based
upon this conception.   ' In order to make his theory work,'
says Professor Fraser in his recent notice of Locke in the
' Encyclopædia Britannica,' 'he (Locke) begins by assuming
a hypothetical duality beneath phenomena—some phenomena
referable to external things, others referable to the conscious self—and in fact confesses that this dual experience is
the ultimate fact, the denial of which would make it impossible to speak about the growth and constitution of our
thoughts.'   It is to be noted that what is spoken of is not a
duality with reference to knowledge—in which case knowledge itself would be the ultimate fact ; there is an assumption of two facts or things out of whose (contingent) relation
to one another a third fact arises as something additional.
The derivative fact acts as a kind of mirror in which actuality,
consisting of the first two facts, is reflected.   Now if we start
with the notion of a self-existent self (an entity which, whatever it is, cannot by any chance be a *self*) and a self-existent
world, it is easy to make a watershed of experience in the
fashion indicated, and so to appear to establish the hypothetical duality with which we started.   This, as Professor
Fraser says, is what Locke did ; and all psychological

philosophy does so still.   As it becomes more acute, speculation is necessarily led, as idealism or materialism, to dissolve
one of these substances into a series of changes in the other,
while scepticism calmly points out to both disputants that
the arguments which apply in the one case apply in the
other also.   But idealism, materialism, and Humism have
meaning only with reference to the assumption of a duality
of self-existing substances to which experience is referred as
to its causes.   They exist as the denial of one of the factors,
or as the assertion of the impossibility of proving either, but
they do not attack the abstraction on which this hypothesis
of dual existence was originally founded.   Hume is a sceptic
because he cannot prove either mind or matter to be real in
the sense in which Cartesian and Lockian metaphysics understood reality.   But if such realities are no more than fictions
of abstract thought, then a sceptical disproof of our knowledge
of them is so far from being a final disproof of the possibility
of any real knowledge that it is rather to be taken as indis-
pensably preliminary to the attainment of a true notion of
what reality is.

Such a notion is attainable only through a transcendental
analysis of knowledge — an analysis, that is, which shall
regard knowledge simply as it is in itself, without any presuppositions of existences which give rise to it.   An analysis
of this sort, so far as it remains true to its transcendental
standpoint, will not be tempted to substantiate the conditions
of knowledge apart from the synthesis in which it finds
them.   It will simply relate them to one another as different
elements in, or better perhaps, as different aspects of, the
one concrete reality.   This is why Kant's treatment of the
'I think' is so different from Descartes' procedure with his
'Cogito.'   Kant, like Descartes, finds the presupposition of
knowledge and of intelligible existence in an 'I think'; but
he never forgets that it is only in relation to the world, or
as the synthesis of intelligible elements, that the self exists
or can have a meaning.   A world without this unifying
principle would fall asunder into unrelated particulars; the
synthetic principle itself, apart from the world which it unifies,
would be no more than the barren identity, $I = I$.   Even this
consciousness of self-identity is reached only through the
synthesis of objects to which it stands in relation.   This
necessity of correlation may be treated without injustice as

the fundamental feature of the transcendental method. So
far is it from being a figure of speech that the self exists
only *through* the world and *vice versâ*, that we might say with
equal truth the self *is* the world and the world is the self.
The relation between them is that of a subject to its predicate
when the predication is supposed to be exhaustive. The subject
is identical with its completed predicate without remainder.
So the self and the world are only two sides of the same
reality; they are the same intelligible world looked at from
two opposite points of view. But, finally, it must not be forgotten that it is only from the point of view of the self or
subject that the identity can be grasped; this, therefore, is
the ultimate point of view which unifies the whole.

It will easily be understood that, in speaking thus of the
self of knowledge, abstraction is made from any particular
self in experience. No one who has mastered Kant's distinction between the transcendental and the empirical Ego
is likely to have any difficulty here. At the same time, the
theory of knowledge makes no assertion of the existence of
the transcendental self otherwise than as the form of these
empirical individuals. To raise the question of existence in
this shape is to fall back once more into mechanical or spatial
categories, and to treat the ultimate synthesis of thought as
if it were a thing that could exist here or there. Separate
facts, however, are the type of reality only to that abstract
thought which has faced us in every sphere. The transcendental self, as the implicate of all experience, is, for a
theory of knowledge, simply the necessary point of view
from which the universe can be unified, that is, from which
it becomes an universe.

Thus the Kantian criticism with its claim to map out
knowledge and ignorance has assumed under our hands the
less pretentious form of a criticism of categories. The attempt is no longer made to determine the validity of reason
as such; the trustworthiness of knowledge is and must be
an assumption. But this does not mean that every reasoned
conclusion is true. Knowledge is not a collection of facts
known as such once for all, and to which we afterwards add
other facts, extending our knowledge as we might extend an
estate by adding acre to acre. This is not a true picture
of the march of knowledge. On the contrary, every advance
of science is a partial refutation of what we supposed we

knew; we undertake in every new scientific theory a criticism and rectification of the conceptions on which the old was constructed. On the largest scale the advance of knowledge is neither more nor less than a progressive criticism of its own conceptions. And, as we have seen, this is not all. Besides the continual self-criticism carried on by the individual sciences, there is the criticism which one science or department of inquiry passes upon another. The science of life cannot move hand or foot without the category of development, which in its biological acceptation is foreign to the inorganic world; and the science of conduct is founded upon the notion of duty, of which the whole world of nature knows nothing. But so long as this mutual criticism is left in the hands of the separate sciences themselves, it tends to degenerate into a strife in which there is no umpire. Philosophy, as theory of knowledge, can alone arbitrate between the combatants, by showing the relation of the different points of view to one another, and allowing to each a sphere of relative justification. When physical science, for example, begins to formulate its own results and to put them forward as an adequate theory of the universe, it is for philosophy to step in and show how these results depend entirely upon preconceptions drawn from a certain stage of knowledge and found to be refuted in the further progress of thought. Philosophy in the capacity of a science of thought should possess a complete survey of its categories and of their dialectical connection; but this 'Wissenschaft der Logik' will probably never be completely written. In the meantime it is perhaps better if philosophy, as critic of the sciences, is content to derive its matter from them and to prophesy in part. Examples of this progress and connection among conceptions or points of view have been given in the preceding pages, and whether we apply to them the name dialectic or not is of little matter. This critical office in which philosophy acts, as it were, as the watch-dog of knowledge is important enough not to compromise the dignity even of the queen of the sciences. She is critic not only of the special sciences, but especially of all metaphysics and systems of philosophy.

Most men of science believe that metaphysics consists in the elaboration of transcendent entities like an extraneous Deity, or Mr. Spencer's Unknowable, or the Comtian noumena.

But the theory of knowledge teaches us that all such constructions in the void have their genesis in a belief that the substance is something different from all its qualities, or that the cause is not identical with the sum of its effects. We learn, on the contrary, that cause and effect, substance and quality, and all similar conceptions are not names for two different things, but necessary aspects of the same object, and that therefore, when we are dealing, not with limited objects, but with the universe as the synthesis of all objects, it is a mere repetition to invent a cause of this synthesis. To be delivered from bad metaphysics is the first step and the most important one towards the true conception of the science. True metaphysic lies, as we have tried to show, in that criticism of experience which aims at developing out of the material of science and of life the completed notion of experience itself.

ANDREW SETH.

II.

THE RELATION OF PHILOSOPHY TO SCIENCE.

WHILE the Berkeleian reduction of *esse* to *percipi* has become matter of common knowledge among educated men, students of philosophy have of late years grown familiar with a line of criticism of an order more penetrative if more pretentious. The point of this criticism may be defined in its own somewhat uncouth language, as a claim to have exhibited even the simplest phases of sensation as possible only through the operation of an intelligible synthesis which cannot itself be made an object of experience, because only through it is experience possible. And just as the Berkeleian principle has come to be regarded as amounting to little more than a rather barren truism, so the criticism of experience is often treated with a considerable decrease of respect arising from its vagueness. But while both principles suffer from the too great generality of their terms, they may claim, each in its own way, to have effected in speculative thinking revolutions of a sufficiently definite character. The influence of Berkeleian empiricism without and within the field of philosophy is currently and adequately recognised. It is the object of these pages briefly to sketch out one branch of the case on behalf of the theory of knowledge.

Kant gave a new significance to the old question whether knowledge was limited by imagination, that is, actual or possible presentation under the forms of space or time. Experience for him implied two elements equally radical and logically independent of each other, but of which it was a gross misunderstanding to speak as separable in any other sense. In the constitution of experience it was implied that transcendental thought (thought which itself could never as such become the object of experience) should operate as a synthetic activity in the pure forms of space and time. Only through such a logical combination was the real constituted, and except in space and time there could be no real. It followed from this that knowledge was for Kant limited by imagination, or in other words, that what could not be represented as constituted by relations of space or time was not real. But the real, or experience, was only an element in Kant's system. There was at the other extreme the moral universe of which it was the characteristic that it ought to be but was not— that it must remain an unrealizable creature of reason. Obviously the universe, that is, every possible object of knowledge in the wider meaning of the word, was not exhausted by these two conceptions. Between them came the subject matter of what Kant called the criticism of judgment—those æsthetic and (in the Aristotelian sense) teleological relations of which it was the characteristic that while they could not be expressed in terms of space or time, they were yet real in the sense that the real universe of perception necessarily suggested them to thought, and never was, as a matter of fact, conceived wholly apart from them.

Kant's meaning may perhaps best be illustrated by a reference to another part of his system. Experience is, for him, constituted in twelve fundamental modes of the synthesis of thought. But there is no object in experience which can be conceived as constituted in one or more of these modes to the exclusion of the rest. They are only logically separable. When we say of something that it is a cause or a substance, we are simply abstracting, for the purpose of clearness of individual knowledge, from its other relations. That which in one reference presents itself as cause or substance, in others presents itself as quantity or quality. But just because finite mind (*i.e.* for Kant, mind which has by making itself its own object, or becoming self-conscious, limited itself in space and time after the fashion of objects in general) is incapable of attending to any other than a limited aspect of its object at one time, we *speak* as though the object were *only* a cause or a substance, a quantity or a quality. Attention is in short concentrated on one relation in actual or possible perception, to the exclusion of others. So it is with the æsthetic and teleological aspects of things. It is true that they exist only for thought or judgment in the meaning in which it is distinguished from actual or possible perception, and cannot be realised in space and time, but they are just as inseparable from the object of perception as are those other categories which are abstracted from when we concentrate attention upon an object in a particular relation in perception.   For Kant, then, the relation of reciprocity, as the most concrete of the categories, is the highest relation of reality.   Teleological and æsthetic significance belong to objects only in so far as they have been invested with these features by the subjective operation of thought.   In the world of real experience there is nothing higher than mechanism, and the mechanical aspects of organised bodies are the highest aspects which experimental science can recognise.   Yet such is the constitution of knowledge, that we cannot but regard the world as though it were also constituted by such relations as those of beauty and organisation, relations not less real than its mechanical aspects.

So far as it goes, it is difficult to impeach this reasoning. Apart from their æsthetic and teleological aspects, objects are not objects at all, but mere abstractions.   It is impossible to conceive a universe which should be constituted out of relations of a nature exclusively mechanical.   On the possibility, for example, of our conceiving what we call an organism as that in which the whole, while indistinguishable from its parts, yet determines them, depends, as we shall find later on, the possibility of our knowledge of some of the most common features of nature, the features which embrace what we call life.   Therefore we may take it that the question whether there are or are not relations higher than those of mechanical arrangement in space and time is identical with the question whether the world as we know it does or does not exist.   But when it passes beyond this general proposition, Kant's doctrine becomes eminently unsatisfactory.   It is not easy to see why the higher relations should be treated by him as merely subjective, while those of mathematics and physics are regarded as in reality constitutive of objects.   For, as we have seen, objects are no more to be conceived as constituted exclusively by the one sort than by the other.   Nor is it intelligible to speak of their æsthetic and teleological aspects as existing merely in the percipient mind.   For mind as percipient, for Kant, creates the objective universe which it perceives, and is not itself an object of perception.   No doubt mind, when it makes itself its own object, does become an object of perception, limited, like all individual objects, by time and space relations, but in this aspect mind is conceived in quite a different reference from that in which it is taken to be the creative synthesis of transcendental thought.   Accordingly, to speak of certain relations of things as existent only for the subject is to use language which, upon Kantian principles, is either meaningless or contradictory.   That mind as the object of experience cannot be the subject of knowledge, Hume and the physiologists have shown, by disproving upon this hypothesis, the reality of the objective universe.   On the other hand, Kant has proved that if even the illusion of an objective universe is real, the subject in knowledge can never be an object disclosed in experience, or, what is the same thing, be a finite individual.   It is therefore impossible for the consistent Kantian to distinguish the characteristics of the object into such as really belong to it, and such as really exist only in the mind.

The truth is that the terms in which Kant put to himself the problem of knowledge were never divested of a psychological reference.   For him the process of knowing, notwithstanding the new departure in his conception of its position, was always more or less conceived as a process taking place between two objects of experience.   It was not until after his time that the principle which he had laid down as against Hume and the physiologists was worked out to its full development.   The fully developed theory need here be only briefly characterised.   The fundamental fact beyond which we cannot get is the fact of self-consciousness.   This fact contains within itself elements which, while inseparable in existence, are yet distinguishable in thought.   We find a self limited by an objective universe. But the one cannot be separated from the other, and we come to find that, although it is only as apparently external to and independent of one another that these two elements can be made objects of knowledge, they must yet be assigned to a common position as moments in a higher synthesis of thought.   But this synthesis can never become an object, i.e. conscious of itself, save under this form of limitation.

Such a theory is not a theory of creation, much less of origin in time, but simply an analysis of the fundamental unity of knowledge.   In becoming conscious of itself thought finds itself limited by itself in space and time as one of many individuals, and as such the process of knowledge so far as known, *i.e.* as real, is a finite subjective process. But even finite self-conscious knowledge is potentially infinite, *i.e.* is, in ultimate analysis, thought, not as presented to itself in self-consciousness, but as identical with the creative synthesis. For such a doctrine there can be no real distinction, as with Kant, between the forms of space and time and the categories of thought; space and time can be nothing else than the fundamental forms of the limitation which the self finds confronting it in consciousness. And the other categories, themselves in a like sense the objective relations of intelligence, must be looked upon as phases differing from the fundamental characteristics of externality not in kind but in degree.

From such a point of view we should expect to find that the process of conscious knowledge exhibited certain characteristics—characteristics of a kind of which Kant was in some measure actually aware. We should expect, from the nature of its limitation, to find knowledge to be a process in which certain relations or aspects of its objects are *actually* under known conditions present to consciousness, while others, which are *potentially* present, and in that sense equally real, are abstracted from. An illustration of this is the distinction drawn in mathematical physics between kinetics and kinematics. The latter science looks at objects from the point of view (in the language of the theory of knowledge under the categories) of change of position. Kinetics, on the other hand, brings in the conception of force as producing such change of position. It brings in an entirely new series of relations or categories, without which its subject matter would be as unintelligible to the physicist as is colour to the blind. But no physicist really supposes that he is dealing with anything else than a metaphysical abstraction as distinguished from a real object in a purely kinematical investigation. His abstraction no more exhausts the reality which it represents symbolically, than does the abstraction of the pure mathematician when he speaks of a straight line or of the numerator of a differential coefficient. In the same way we shall find—what apparently is not so clearly understood by materialists or spiritualists—that the categories of mechanism do not exhaust reality in its aspect of life. But it is time to turn to another side of this subject.

As we have seen, the term mind has a double significance. It may mean that which is in analysis found to be the ultimate reality to which all existence is referable. This was the view of mind which was known to the Greeks, and which Kant found to be the true way out of the dilemma put by Hume. In this sense, mind is not a substance or individual object of experience, but the creative synthesis of thought which, just because it is that which constitutes experience, cannot as such be made an object of experience. We infer it as the only possible explanation of the fact of experience, and we conclude further that it manifests itself in fundamental modes, which definitely differ from one another, but which mutually imply each other and are related in a dialectical development. Such a development is, of course, no affair of space and time, for space and time are themselves, as has already been stated, but two of its stages. In the other meaning of the term, mind is conceived as it appears, as its own object—having transformed its nature and become a definite part of experience. In this aspect it is the subject matter of empirical psychology, and falls under that distinction between subject and object, which, as a relation created by thought, really falls within it. It is in this way that mind is at the same time creator and created, at once infinite and yet a finite self. Our subjective knowledge is ever attended with that consciousness of limitation which points to its infinite nature. To treat mind as an ordinary object of investigation is to abstract from the very fact that only for mind do objects exist at all. The more definitely intelligence is brought like other matters into consciousness by abstraction, the further is the result from the reality, however much we may have gained for ordinary purposes.

These remarks may, for the present, in some degree serve to explain what is meant when it is said that the process of finite or conscious knowledge is essentially a process of abstraction, and that whether its method be looked at on its inductive or its deductive side. It necessitates the isolation of definite relations presented by its object through the application to that object of a general conception. In the case of certain branches of natural science, these general conceptions are chiefly those which make possible the apprehension of mechanical arrangement in space and time of parts external to and exclusive of one another, and the principal aim of these departments of natural science is to regard nature simply from this point of view. But it is one thing to take such a course for the purpose of advancing knowledge, and quite another to say that because, for a certain point of view, the object can only be regarded as if it existed in a certain way, therefore it exists in the world of fact only in that way. No doubt we can bring to reflection upon the object a particular category only because through that category the object is created in perception or (to pass beyond Kant) exists. But this does not mean that the object is constituted through that category alone. As we shall find later on, the failure to appreciate this distinction has been a fertile source of difficulty in science. The blunder amounts to the confusion of a difference which exists only for individual knowledge, with a supposed difference in reality or objective knowledge. A familiar example of this mistake is the notion that causation, or the unvarying sequence of two independent facts, is a distinct process in time, taking place as a fact complete in itself. Causation is in truth but an abstract way of looking at a phenomenon, which is what it is quite as much through the relation of identity or of substance and accident. There is no such fact in nature as an unvarying succession of two unconnected events as cause and effect. If we examine such a supposed relationship we find that it resolves itself into a case of identity, in which the effect is simply the sum of its conditions. On the other hand, if we try to present the occurrence to ourselves merely as a case of identity, we find that we have excluded an essential element, that of change in time. Causation and substantiality are abstract categories or limited ways of thinking of things in knowledge, rather than independent ways of existence in nature. A like criticism applies to the famous distinction between the discrete and the continuous aspects of quantity, the distinction which gave rise to the familiar puzzle, first solved by Aristotle, of Achilles and the Tortoise. All such distinctions are not only legitimate, but the absolutely necessary outcome of reflection. But, although they are only possible because reality or objective knowledge presents phases of which these are abstractions, such phases are necessarily related to and imply one another, and are incapable of any such separation or independence as appears in the abstractions of self-conscious reflection. The task of these pages is to try to exhibit some of the consequences to scientific conceptions which have resulted from a failure to appreciate this deduction from the theory of knowledge.

The boundlessly varying expanse of nature presents for reflection a sort of scale of modes of existence. Here we have the inorganic world, of which the distinguishing feature is the chemical arrangements and processes among parts that seem generally to determine each other as at once causes and effects in a relation of reciprocity. Again, there is present to consciousness a world of organisation in which what is characteristic is apparently the determination of parts by a whole which is not a cause distinct from them, but some principle or tendency which will not allow itself to be exhibited as any relation of these parts in space and time. Under another phase there are disclosed to us as facts of experience phenomena of conscious life. Now it is not to be supposed that such distinct phases are so many absolutely independent and distinct ways of existence lying side by side. The extreme antithesis to this view is that which follows from the theory of knowledge as expounded by Kant. As we have already seen, objective nature consisted, for Kant, only in those aspects of bodies which embraced the mathematical and physical relations of things, and stopped short with the categories of substance, cause, and reciprocity. All those other aspects of nature which relate to its æsthetic and teleological characteristics, were for him merely subjective creations of the percipient mind. From such a point of view, the aspects under which bodies appear as external to one another in space, as connected with one another, or as consisting of parts connected as substances, causes, or mutual determinants, constitute one kind of knowledge. The other aspects are not qualities separable as objects in space and time from the first kind, but different sorts of knowledge, the categories of which cannot be applied to the aspects which nature presents in its more immediate reference. Thus we can no more express the properties of a body *quâ* organised in terms of the categories of mechanism, than we can express the properties of a stone in terms of the categories of moral judgment.

The practical significance of Kant's teaching may be illustrated very clearly in its bearing on the phenomena of consciousness. When we perceive around us other organisations akin to those which we associate with ourselves, we attribute to them those psychical accompaniments of which we are conscious as somehow making up in association with our bodies our existence as human beings. These psychical phenomena we do not *perceive* as external qualities, but naturally *attribute* in a way which does not present to us any obscurity until we come to reflect upon it. What then are these phenomena, and how are they bound up with the physical phenomena which precede them? The pure 'Naturforscher' who strives to attain to the astronomical knowledge of nature of Laplace's ideal spirit, and who, limiting his categories to those of mechanism, strives to explain and express nature simply in terms of these categories, says that the two sets of phenomena are causally related in that the one set invariably accompanies the other. It is no matter that he denies any attempt to find a *nexus*, and confines himself to a simple assertion of the sequence of two sets of events; he none the less employs the category of causality and interprets his facts as a common case of cause and effect. Just because he makes the unproved assumption of the applicability of this category, an assumption which can only be weighed in the proper balance from the standpoint of a theory of knowledge, Kant calls him a dogmatist. Now the special view taken by Kant himself of this relation, following as it does from his principles, is very different. For him the phenomena of consciousness are perceived in time only, and by inner sense, a sense which is conceived by him as distinct from the outer sense by which external nature is perceived. Therefore it is for Kant a gross fallacy to speak of the phenomena of the one sense as causally connected with the phenomena of the other sense. The category of causality only applies to the determination of phenomena belonging to the same sense. It is only phenomena of the same sense which are determined by creative synthesis in the relations of sequence and co-existence, and consequently finite intelligence cannot attribute these categories of sequence and co-existence to the phenomena of different kinds of knowledge, however closely they may appear to be related. It is what Kant would call

E

a mistaken assumption of the dogmatist (*i.e.* the person who applies categories without having duly examined into their applicability), to speak of consciousness as the effect, sequent, or concomitant of physiological phenomena, or as the other side or manifestation of an unknowable substance or thing in itself.[1] But, it may be asked, must not the phenomena of conscious life, those of sensation for example, if they exist at all, be forms, or modifications of forms, of energy? Certainly so, if these so-called phenomena are brought under the categories of mechanism, that is to say, regarded as, like energy, something actually or possibly perceived as existing in space and time. But in reality there can arise no question in regard to the conservation of energy or any other physical law. For we are at once relieved from the dilemma that there must either be an exception to the uniformity of such a principle or not, so soon as we understand that such a dilemma arises from our assumption that we are dealing with the case of phenomena related in the same way as the phenomena which come under, because they are constituted through, the categories of substance, causality and reciprocity. No doubt we perceive other conscious beings. But in the case of mind and body, when we talk of these as distinct, we do not perceive two independent existences of a physiological structure and of psychical phenomena. The phenomena of self-consciousness are presented in knowledge in a different way, not as external phenomena, and not as existing with parts, and in relation to other phenomena in the multiplicity of space and time. In our perception of conscious beings outside us, we rather *interpret* the physical facts which we perceive by higher categories than their own, and as so interpreted their existence in externality is abstracted from. No doubt we can, and for the advancement of knowledge must, at times regard other persons and even our bodies simply as physical or mechanical arrangements. But in so doing we have abstracted from a point of view from which they appear to us as something more, and so appear in a way not less real than the way of their physical or mechanical aspects. For unreflecting perception, psychical and physical phenomena are naturally associated. But the distinction between them is implicitly present in the simplest cases, and becoming in reflection at

---

[1] Cf. note on page 61.

once explicit, demands an abstract judgment as to its nature.[1]

The phenomena of self-consciousness are thus not facts of external nature coming under the categories of mechanism. Kant arrives at a similar result with regard to the phenomena of teleology. We do, as a matter of fact, find nature presenting the aspect of organisation as life and growth. How is this aspect to be explained? The dogmatist propounds the dilemma that it must be regarded either as the manifestation of a special vital principle, a possible object of external perception, or as a complicated case of mechanical arrangement. And the scientific dogmatist properly rejects the first hypothesis in favour of the second. But for Kant there is no such difficulty. The categories of teleology belong, as we have seen, to a kind of knowledge quite distinct from external perception, that which he terms the faculty of judgment. While we must think of objects as if they existed under teleological relations, we do not find them so existing in external perception. The general knowledge of nature or experience is no doubt made up of both kinds of knowledge. But the relations which are the objects of the one kind do not exist as external facts alongside of the relations which are presented in the other. Life and growth are not processes taking place in space in the same sense as the interaction of molecules. In our general knowledge of nature there are two distinct classes of relations which are not reducible to each other. Therefore, to try to explain organisation as a mechanical arrangement is to hypostatise an abstraction—the mechanical aspect of what appears for the unreflecting consciousness as an organised body.

We shall return to this subject presently, but at this point it is necessary slightly to correct the general form of the statement. We have been applying not the detailed principles of what we have seen to be the more developed theory of knowledge, but those of the Kantian criticism. But the fallacies in question have the same explanation for Kant and for his more modern successors. For Kant they arise from the applications of the categories of one kind of knowledge to the subject matter of another. For the more fully

[1] Cf. the late Professor Clifford's theory of ejects. It is perhaps not too much to say that recent philosophical thought in this country suffered an irreparable loss in the absence of an acquaintance with Kant's *real* teaching about the nature of knowledge on the part of this brilliantly original thinker.

developed theory the same misapplication is the explanation, the difference lying in this, that the distinction between the sorts of knowledge is not even for finite thought the insuperable distinction between kinds which we find in Kant, but a distinction of degree. The fundamental relations or categories in knowledge being conceived as *dialectically* implied by each other, we see more readily how it is that in nature organisation and growth exhibit for reflection mechanical aspects, and how consciousness comes to be so naturally associated with organisation. From the relations of pure mathematics up to those of self-consciousness we have a chain of aspects of nature not one of which is reducible to another, but which are yet inseparably united together in thought. If the Kantian analysis with its distinctions between inner and outer sense and spheres of knowledge is from its accommodation to psychological tendencies more readily intelligible, it is a less adequate explanation of the continuity of the phases of nature. But whether or not we can arrange these phases systematically or exhibit the categories as a system, is for the purposes of practical criticism of categories irrelevant. If we can affirm that upon the principles which are the foundation of the point of view of these pages, the nature of thought must be generally such as necessitates the deductions we have indicated, it does not concern us to go further.

We are now in a position to illustrate the argument of the preceding pages by a critical examination of such crucial scientific conceptions as that of organisation and the cognate idea of development. These ideas are derived from the phenomena of what is called life. Now life, like beauty, is one of those ultimate facts in experience which we may try to explain but cannot get rid of. And it follows from what has been said that it is a mistake to regard it as realised in certain objects to the exclusion of others. The distinction between what lives and what is mechanical substance is a distinction of point of view and not of objects in space. No doubt we speak of such a distinction as if it existed between objects; but this is due not to perception but to reflection. When we see a house and a man we may certainly distinguish them as inanimate and animate. But this only means that the man is naturally considered in a way in which the house is not. Looked at merely as objects in space there is really no distinction between them. Both are regarded as mechanical arrangements, and in the case of neither is the reality exhausted. On the other hand, looked at exclusively as a living being, the man in a sense has ceased to be an object in space. In perception there are involved many points of view which only reflection distinguishes. As we have seen, it is not only a legitimate but a necessary procedure to consider things in an abstract reference. And this is just what physiology, as conceived by the majority of scientific men, does in regard to organisation. It abstracts from the point of view of life, and treats the organism as merely an exceedingly complicated mechanical arrangement, employing the category of causality to the exclusion of higher categories. No doubt physiology through this abstraction succeeds in advancing knowledge as it could not otherwise be advanced, for it in this way becomes an exact science, i.e. a science proceeding by measurement. But at the same time it gets into difficulties by the inadequacy of its category to its object, and it is forced either to admit that there is a limit to the extent of its explanations or to deny the reality of the supposed facts. An illustration of the strength and weakness of the physiological method may be found in the following description. An electrical stimulus is applied to the tongue by means of the electrodes of an induction machine. A flow of saliva into the mouth is observed to follow the stimulation. This circumstance is capable of a lucid mechanical explanation. An impulse is conveyed from the part stimulated along an afferent nerve to a group of nerve-cells in the medulla oblongata. The effect of this is suddenly to release nerve-energy stored up in these cells and cause it to be discharged along efferent nerves leading to the salivary glands. The stimulus thus applied to the gland-cells causes them to do work in secreting the saliva observed to flow into the mouth. The physiologist thus finds here a delicate mechanism consisting of nerves, nerve-cells, and gland-cells, and he traces a causal series commencing with the stimulation of the afferent nerve and ending with the secretion of saliva by the gland. He has a purely mechanical problem before him apparently indistinguishable from any other mechanical problem, starting as he does with the conception of a series of parts existing outside of and independent of one another.

Each of these independent things is successively considered first as effect and then as cause, or, in another mechanical aspect, it is considered that energy is passed on from the initial stimulus through several internal processes back again to the outside world. It is true that the organism is of such a nature that this energy in its passage liberates a great deal of additional energy, but this does not affect the explanation. Perfectly satisfactory as is what we have got here so far as it goes, it is yet, when the facts are examined more closely, seen to fall short of them. The category employed is adequate to the investigation of the case of a simple mechanical arrangement, but not to the case of that arrangement considered as a normal function of the organism to which it belongs. A purely physiological account of the action of the organism simply traces energy from the surroundings through the organism and out to the surroundings again. If this is to be taken to be a full account of the process it is inadequate, for it ignores the fact, characteristic of life, that the energy spent by the organism on its surroundings is not dissipated at random on these surroundings, but is so directed as to cause them to give back again to the organism, sooner or later, just as much energy as the organism has previously expended. In other words, the distinguishing feature of vital activity is self-preservation, or the conservation of the organism in a state of functional activity; and this is just as true of the most complicated actions of the human body as of the movement of the amœba towards a source of nourishment.

But besides this characteristic a living structure has a capacity of adapting itself to an infinite number of changing circumstances, which is wholly unintelligible upon any conceivable mechanical ' scheme.' How, for instance, is the process to be explained by which in the case of a newt there grows a new hand in the place of one which has been amputated? By the amputation the vital activity of the animal is hindered. Accordingly, in order that its functional arrangements may be kept in action, it is necessary that the hindrance arising from the mutilation should be overcome by provision being made for the carrying out of the function of the lost limb. What happens is that the cells of all sorts of tissue in the stump of the limb soon begin to divide, and gradually group themselves so as to form a bud of embryonic tissue. This bud, as a matter of fact, gradually grows into the form of the lost hand, the cells gradually so modifying themselves as to form, all in their proper places, bone, connective tissue, epithelium, nerve and muscle, until at last a proper hand occupies the place of the old one. Every cell performs its appropriate duty until the whole business is accurately finished without fail. Is it conceivable that each of the thousands of separately existing cells concerned in the process should have a mechanism within it, which would cause it in spite of all obstacles to take up the position, and undergo the modification requisite for the proper performance of its work in the newly developed hand? Or is it conceivable that mechanical pressure of any kind should cause the bud to grow into a perfect hand? The alternative hypothesis is that each cell is directly determined in its action simply by what it has to do in order that the vital activity of the newt may be restored to its normal condition.

The fact is that every part of the organism must be conceived as actually or potentially acting on and being acted on by the other parts and by the environment, so as to form with them a self-conserving system. There is nothing short of this implied in saying that the parts of the organism can adapt themselves to one another and to the surroundings. And in this light we must correct the description which went no further than the assertion of a relation of cause and effect.

The action of a muscle upon a joint seems at first impression a simple case of a merely causal relation. But in the living body the action of the muscle is controlled by nervous impulses proceeding from ganglion cells in a nervous centre, and these ganglion cells act upon the surroundings through the muscle as part of a self-conserving system. The action of the muscle has a purpose in relation to the life of the individual of which it is a part, and is not thrown away at random upon the surroundings. In reality the muscle is determined by, just as much as it determines the surroundings. But this feature of the facts is abstracted from when joint and muscle are considered separately from their surroundings. Such an abstraction is at times necessary for the purposes of science, but we must not suppose that it is adequate to the reality.

The first matter which is of consequence here is that

whether or not the point of view is necessarily other than mechanical, it has at least changed. The conception of the nerve, muscle, and joint as separate and independent parts, respectively related merely as cause and effect, has given place to a conception which takes them as in conjunction with their environment making up a process of reciprocal determination, and recognises that no explanation can be sufficient which fails to do this. In short there has been a transition from the category of causality to the less abstract, though still mechanical, category of reciprocity. But is it possible to stop here? In every true case of reciprocal action the interacting bodies are considered as still external to and independent of one another. In the case of a planetary system, for which the appropriate conception is reciprocity, any planet can be detached from the system, and yet remain for the most part what it was before. It has an existence independent of its relation to other planets and the centre of the system, a relation which is after all unessential to it. But it is different in the case of the system of life. If a sea-anemone is cut in two, the parts do not simply heal up and form two halves. They either die, or else each half buds out and changes into a new and perfect whole. A single cell of some of the lowest compound organisms will, if detached, instead of living an independent life, reproduce the whole organism. In the higher animals this power appears only in the reproductive cells, but there are everywhere traces of a tendency in each living cell when isolated to reproduce the whole organism of which it formed a part. It would thus appear that the parts of an organism cannot be considered simply as so many independent units, which happen to be aggregated in a system in which each determines the other. It is on the contrary the essential feature of each part that it is a member of an ideal whole, which can only be defined by saying that it realises itself in its parts, and that the parts are only what they are in so far as they realise it. In fine the relations of life are not capable of reduction to the relations of mechanism.

The difficulty is one which has long been familiar to men of science, and attempts have frequently been made to minimise it. So long as science is regarded as made up properly only of the results of observation and experiment, and abstract conceptions are admitted only for the purpose of facilitating the acquisition of these results, the inadequacy of the mechanical standpoint is not practically important. But it always happens that after a time observers begin to generalise and seek to obtain a systematic view of their work as an entirety. And then it is that trouble arises. If, for example, we seek to conceive biological relations as cases of the interaction of atoms or molecules, we find it necessary to resort to some such hypothesis as that these atoms or molecules are endowed with consciousness, and we come face to face with the contradictions which, as we have seen, perplex those who try to bring consciousness within the categories of things in space. If, on the other hand, we turn to the old conception of external design or supernatural intervention, we not only commit a like error, but find ourselves wholly unable to reconcile this new notion with the context of experience. Now on the theory of knowledge such difficulties arise simply from a misapplication of categories. Whether we treat life as a case of the interaction of molecules, or as the manifestation of a special vital force, we are alike dogmatically applying mechanical categories to phenomena to which they are not adequate. The phenomena of life exist for consciousness in a point of view distinct from that of the phenomena of mechanism, in the same sense as is the point of view under which the world is perceived as beautiful or as morally good. This is a result of the nature of knowledge, and it follows from it that life can never be reduced to mechanism. In a way the classes of facts which are constituted through each special kind of relation may be looked upon as exhibiting a sort of endless series the limits of which are the relations of the next higher and the next lower order. And these limits are asymptotic in a sense more profound than that of the mathematician. For there can be absolutely no evolution in time of one of such relations out of another. We can, for example, conceive the vital relation as less and less apparent until we do not seem to distinguish it from a mechanical arrangement. But we can never hope to find a case of *abiogenesis* as a matter of fact, any more than we can really construct the moral consciousness upon physical principles. Only the suppression of a point of view which is yet implicitly there enables us to imagine that we do so. It is quite legitimate to suppose that the universe has become what it is from a state of existence as a mass of incandescent vapour. But in such a conception we have already got implicitly present all the categories which we afterwards find prominent. The idea of a mass of vapour as an object existing in merely mechanical relations, and without reference to a percipient consciousness, would be a meaningless abstraction. At least such an object is only an object for knowledge, and with knowledge is present, whether in clear consciousness or not, the whole series of the categories of knowledge.

In the conception of the environment of the organism there is implied the higher class of relations. In a sense the surroundings of the organism just as much as its own structure are implicated in its life. What is really implied in such words as 'function,' 'purpose,' 'means,' and 'end' is that we are looking at the organism, not as acted on by things outside it, but as in teleological connection with that which is different from, but not existent independently of it. We have in fact discarded those categories of mechanism which were found so useful in a different kind of enquiry in reference to the phenomena of life. When we have reached a standpoint from which we refuse to separate the individual organism from its surroundings and from its relation to other individuals, we see how the species may itself be looked upon as a compound organism, or as a member of which each individual attains its true significance. And we begin to comprehend the meaning of the death of the individual, an event which otherwise appears arbitrary and unintelligible.

These considerations may serve to throw some light on an idea which is wider than that of organisation, the idea of development. Now the first point which falls to be made in connection with this idea, is that it cannot be expressed as a simple result of action from without. As we have seen, it is not correct to separate the surroundings in thought from the organism, and treat them as independent things, for the organism only realises itself in its surroundings. It is not the case that the 'fittest' survive after the fashion in which the roundest shot only reach the bottom of the sloping board used by shotmakers to eliminate those that are imperfect. Development is in all cases the realisation of what was not there at the beginning of the process. Yet the resulting difference is not conceived as impressed from without, but as freely produced from within itself by that which developes. A little consideration shows that such branches of biological science as embryology and morphology become possible only through the conception of development. For the uneducated observer the examination of the sections of an embryo in different stages of progress brings no light. For him the points of difference are as striking as the points of similarity, and there is no indication of continuity. But in the case of a trained embryologist this is not so. Such an observer at once recognises the sections as exhibiting the stages of a progress in which there becomes only more fully realised in change something which remains identical, notwithstanding the alteration of all that from a merely mechanical point of view constitutes its existence.

Again, when the botanist says that leaves, petals, stamens, carpels, &c., are organs which are morphologically identical, he means something more than a mere similarity in appearance. Were nothing more than this signified, then assuredly Cuvier would have been right in maintaining that the idea of morphological identity was trivial and gave no new light. The differences were in that case just as real as the identity, and there would be no justification for emphasizing the one more than the other. But for the modern comparative morphologist stamen and leaf are none the less identical because of a difference which is felt to present no real hindrance. For he brings with him to his problem the conception of development.

If there were no point of view higher than that of mechanism, such conceptions as those which have now been briefly examined would be meaningless. But it is just because there is such a point of view, possible by reason of the fact that the phenomena which it embraces are constituted through higher categories than those of spatial and temporal arrangement, that as science advances men are driven back to the use of these higher conceptions in spite of their attempts to dispense with them. For such attempts lose their meaning as soon as it is recognised that to abandon them in no sense implies the admission of an exception to the uniformity of nature. The man who insists on regarding organisation and development as mechanical, and the man who insists on the existence of supra-mechanical

substances and causes, are alike dogmatists, whose principles are really untrue to those facts of common sense with
which science and philosophy alike must start. If, then, a
critical examination of categories can reconcile the truth
which lies at the bottom of each point of view, and without
for a moment seeking to intrude into the domain of observation and experiment, yet throw light on conceptions which
are necessarily used in obtaining and arranging the results
so reached, surely such a criticism becomes a matter of the
last importance. We shall show later that the method of such
an investigation, so far from being that of à *priori* reasoning, is not distinguishable in principle from the method of
science. Meanwhile it is desirable to say that it is in no
reference such an attempt to rationalise nature as would
sometimes seem to have been the real purpose of that somewhat unintelligible treatise the ' Naturphilosophie ' of Hegel.
The theory of knowledge does not seek, as Hegel seems to
have thought (whether or not he really meant it), to deduce
nature from intelligence. Nor does the critical point of
view find in nature a fossilisation of intelligence in which
the categories of thought are strewn about, severally realised
in things external to one another. It does not concern us
even to consider the possibility of an attempt which lies far
away from our purpose, or even to put the question whether
it does not itself imply first such a misapplication of categories as on Hegelian principles is inadmissible. What we
have to do is merely to show from the nature of intelligence
how certain different points of view are actually or potentially present in the simplest state of consciousness, and to
correct scientific conceptions when they confound one of
these points of view with another.

So far as the scope of this essay permitted, its method
has been exemplified by the examination, in the light of a
certain view of knowledge, of the scientific conceptions of
organisation and development. It is obvious that the same
principle of criticism applies to the conceptions of many
other departments of inquiry which do not lie within the
scope of these pages. But it may not be amiss at least to
mention one or two of these. It is a mistaken application
of categories which, for example, gives rise to the controversy
about free will and necessity. So soon as it is recognised
that volition is really not to be looked upon as a process

taking place in space,[1] the dilemma that it must either be caused or uncaused disappears. Will and motive are not independent external existences related as cause and effect. They are phenomena of a higher point of view whose relation is rather that of reason and consequent. A like criticism applies to the idea of the state as a mere aggregate of isolated individuals. A less abstract category would prove more adequate to the facts in embracing, in the conception of the individual, his determination by the social organism of which he is a member. And in the light of such a conception the shortcomings of the abstractedly individualistic doctrines of the Manchester school in political economy become apparent. But it is not merely in its application to aspects of the universe higher than those of mechanism that this process of correction is important. It is no doubt quite correct to lay stress upon the mathematico-physical relations of matter, and to reason from them in an abstract

---

[1] The question of the relation of will and motive is not strictly relevant, but it is so important as illustrative of the necessity of examining the facts of experience in the light of a criticism of categories, that it is desirable to amplify the reference in the text. It may be objected that the relation, though not one of externality in space, may yet well be one of succession in time. This objection will hardly, however, be raised by anyone who has acceded to the earlier stages of the argument. Space and time are not things separable from, or independent of, one another. Viewed in such a light they are merely abstract figments. The relations of externality and succession, of outside-one-another-ness and after-one-another-ness, imply each other in the same way as identity implies difference or substantiality implies causation. They exist only in co-ordination as contributing to the constitution of a highly concrete reality which they do not exhaust, however essential to it in certain aspects. This is the strength of the contention of Czolbe and Ueberweg, that the phenomena of consciousness (which we prefer, from the standpoint of this essay, to speak of as psychological rather than as psychical) must be regarded as extended in space. It follows that there is no such thing as a succession in time which is not the succession of events in space. It may be convenient for the purpose of explanation to abstract from the spatial aspects of such a concrete succession (cf. the procedure at pp. 49, 50), but for no other purpose is it legitimate. Kant made the mistake of taking such an abstraction for an independent existence in his separation from outer sense of inner sense as apprehension under the form of time only. The differences in the different points of view or aspects which are co-ordinated in the consciousness of nature and of self are, as has been shown, differences not of kind but of degree, and each degree is to that below it, as τέλος or form to matter (cf. Aristotle's doctrine in the *De Anima*). To separate, as Kant does, inner and outer sense, *i.e.*, mind and matter, or to regard, as Hegel apparently does, the different categories as existing in isolation or externality to one another in nature, is to apply the category of reciprocity, where, in fact, the highest categories are rather requisite to the state of the case. Thus it is that the point of view of succession can never be adequate to the investigation of motive and volition. The general point of view in which the phenomena of consciousness are presented to us is higher than, just because it is the relative completion of, that in which we conceive ourselves as organisms in nature.

reference. But even such appropriate abstractions when hypostatised in thought into real existences, share the general fate of all other abstractions, and give rise to contradictory conclusions. We can no more consistently represent to ourselves matter as constituted by the reciprocal determination of points of attraction and repulsion in space, than we can conceive matter and energy as independent existences. Such abstract conceptions, however great their value as regulative, *i.e.* for the purpose of advance in knowledge, are not adequate as descriptions of a reality which is essentially concrete and inexhaustible in its properties.

That the principle which has now been dwelt on at some length has not received more attention in the past is no doubt due in great measure to the faulty manner in which it was presented by Kant. Kant's great mistake was, as has already more than once been pointed out, the assumption that the sphere of imagination was co-extensive with that of knowledge up to and including the relations of mechanism, and that all beyond this, that which was for him the subject of judgment as distinguished from perception, was unreal. Such a doctrine was the necessary result of the distinction of the categories as modes of potential synthesis from space and time as the forms in which they created the real. But for a more advanced theory of knowledge, space and time become themselves indistinguishable in kind from other relations in experience, and consequently the different aspects of experience are regarded as differing not in kind but in degree. All that is is seen to exist in necessary relationship and implication, and such lines of demarcation in things as language indicates are seen to be fictions of finite knowledge, properly created only for the purposes of its own advancement. One result of such a point of view is the impossibility of attempting a philosophical classification of the sciences. No doubt a classification is conceivable which should arrange the subject matter of knowledge according as the relations of which it consisted approximated to or rose above the relations of simple externality and succession. But such a classification could never coincide with those distinctions between the sciences which actually exist. As has already incidentally appeared, the sciences are defined quite as much by convenience as by the categories which they employ, and it constantly happens that one science employs several distinct sorts of categories and overlaps the sphere of another. If the sciences are to be classified at all, it must be simply with reference to their positions in advancing finite reflection and without any hope of throwing light on the nature of things. This must remain the case so long as self-consciousness remains finite; in other words, it is a necessary result of the constitution of knowledge.

It remains to be asked what the position of the theory of knowledge is in relation to what is generally meant by science. Its object is the fact of self-consciousness, and this fact it must assume as something ultimate given to it, just as all sciences assume their own objects. Now self-consciousness presents the peculiarity that while ordinary objects of knowledge fall wholly within the field of the object as distinguished from the act of knowing, this one only partially does so, inasmuch as it is at once knowledge as presented to itself and the act of presentation. As the act of thought can never as such be presented to thought as an object, it follows that if the nature of thought is to be investigated at all, it must be so by means of some method which does not presuppose a distinction between knowledge and its object. Such a method was attempted by Hegel, with what degree of failure or success it is no part of the business of these pages to inquire. It is enough to point out that for the purposes of a theory of knowledge such a process of investigation as the Hegelian dialectic is not necessary. What is essential is at the very most such a method as what is understood in a general and not a philological reference as the Kantian, which from the nature of experience sought to determine a conception of the nature of knowledge that would explain it. It is no true objection to say that such procedure is the procedure not of science but of metaphysics. For the method of Kant was just the method which is common to all branches of investigation, the devising of a conception, and the acceptance or rejection of that conception according as it does or does not upon application explain the facts. This is the method of the exact as well as of the non-exact sciences, and the point of difference between the two classes is simply that in the one the adequacy of the conception is determined by measurement—that is, the comparison by intuition of spatial

magnitudes, in the others it is not. Any objection which
prevails against the method of the theory of knowledge
must likewise prevail not only against such branches of
inquiry as political economy, but also against a vast deal in
what are called the exact sciences that is not reducible to
measurement. The most prominent fallacy of the exploded
à *priori* reasoning of the old-fashioned metaphysics was
that it was applied to a class of objects in regard to which
the test of the adequacy of the conception ought to have
been an exact test. In the case of philosophy in its modern
acceptation, as in that of political economy and the kindred
sciences, the objection becomes irrelevant.

It is clear that if there be any truth in the reasoning of
the preceding pages, the theory of knowledge must have a
place assigned to it in relation to the whole body of
scientific inquiry. If science did nothing more than observe
and record the facts of nature, such a discipline might be
dispensed with. But science is concerned not merely with
facts but with reasoning about conceptions abstracted from
these facts, reasoning as to which, just because it deals with
abstractions symbolical of only one phase of the many-
phased reality, there can be no talk of verification. That
there is a tendency in all reasoning to hypostatise these
abstractions, to regard them not in their proper light as
simply fragments of thought, but as representing real
existences, is as obvious as it is natural. That this tendency
has led to all sorts of difficulties, as science has proceeded
out of the region of actual sense-perception, is matter of
historical knowledge. If, then, it is correct to say that
science is forced to go beyond what is immediate, it is
difficult to avoid the conclusion of the necessity of a department of inquiry which shall deal critically with the abstractions of the inquirer, shall assign to them their true
position and value, and shall make clear the real nature of
scientific method. Such an inquiry can from its very
nature assume no other form than that of a theory of
knowledge. The question is not between philosophy and
no philosophy, but between philosophy and bad philosophy.

It is claimed on behalf of Kant and Hegel that they have
jointly elaborated the principles of knowledge. But this
does not mean either that to Kant and Hegel are we to look
for the whole truth, or that the inquiry is to be further de-

veloped through the study of German philosophy.   No doubt
the pages both of the ' Kritiken ' and the ' Encyclopaedie ' contain almost the only exposition of what we are in search of.
It may without much presumption be said that those who have
not mastered the lesson of Kant and Hegel, whether to accept
or to reject it, are not in a position to discuss the questions
they raise, any more than one who knows nothing of biology
would be entitled to discuss the theory of evolution.   But
the days of philosophical systems are for the present at all
events gone by, and with them the days of devotion to mere
abstract thinking.   The work of philosophy must now be the
application of what thought has won for itself to questions
of the kind which it has been here sought to indicate, and to
the cognate questions of other departments of knowledge.
No doubt there must often be great difficulty in determining
at what point a problem ceases to be properly one of science
and becomes one of knowledge.   The history of the past
relations of science and philosophy has shown that so long as
the two spheres of inquiry remain in different hands—in the
hands of persons who are more or less ignorant of each others'
subjects—so long will science have cause to reject many of
the inferences of philosophy as the intrusion into her domain
of something akin to à *priori* reasoning.   But it is no less
true that under these conditions the philosopher must have
equal cause to complain of the man of science, in that he
perpetually raises difficulties insoluble for himself in his own
department by the dogmatic application of mistaken categories.   Such considerations point towards what seems to
be becoming the conclusion of the present time, that science
and philosophy can no longer be kept wholly apart from one
another.   The inquirer who is to do anything more than
simply observe and record, who desires to systematise his
results and to generalise from them, must have assimilated
the philosophical theory of experience.   The philosopher, on
the other hand, must, to progress in the direction which the
time requires, have the problems which arise within experience before him as they can only come before the scientific
observer.   But science is a wide subject, and philosophy if,
the most abstruse because the least immediate of studies,
is a narrow one.   It would therefore seem that the work
of philosophy in the near future must pass into the hands of
specialists in science who are at the same time masters of

philosophical criticism. There is no finality in thought. Progress is always relative, and this form of philosophical advance can hardly be a permanent form. But for a time, at least, the work would seem as though it must remain in the hands of a new class of men. For such a class the mastery of the critical investigations of Kant and Hegel, or at least of conceptions which have been profoundly influenced by these writers, will be absolutely essential. But such a discipline can form simply a part, though not the least part, of preparatory culture.

R. B. HALDANE.
J. S. HALDANE.

III.

LOGIC AS THE SCIENCE OF KNOWLEDGE.

' THE Science of Knowledge ' is a title which everyone concedes to logic. But when we ask what it is that in virtue of this title logic ought to be or to do, we gather the most various answers both from the conception and from the execution of logical treatises.

The purpose of this essay is to illustrate the treatment of logic as a systematic science, in contrast with the spirit of compromise which prevails in modern philosophy, and is in matters of science little better than a spirit of confusion. The writer has selected a title which indicates, as he believes, the nature of that science which Plato imagined and which Aristotle formulated, when knowledge began to be distinguished from common sense and from instinct.

The philosophical idea of knowledge which these great men created has been justified a thousandfold by the history of science; and that the justification has not in the main been owing to the labours of their interpreters, but to the direct constructive efforts of countless minds, ignorant or contemptuous of the forms which claimed the place of that idea, is irrefragable proof that the nature of knowledge can be known. The exhibition of this nature in a system of stages or types, embodying the essential phases and the ideals of knowledge, is the process which these pages are intended rather to advocate than to realise.[1] The purpose

---

[1] Among recent works the writer is especially indebted to the logical treatises of the late Professor Lotze, and of Prof. Sigwart, and he has adopted the doctrine of hypothesis in induction from *Principles of Science*, by the late Professor Jevons, whose unfortunate death is a great loss to independent thought in England. Older works it is unnecessary to mention, excepting that those who, like the writer, believe Mr. Mill's position to have been fundamentally untenable, are the more bound to acknowledge his services to logic, on which he probably had a more healthy influence than any other logician since Hegel.

of this sketch is only to indicate the combined unity and comprehensiveness which such a point of view may confer on the treatment of logic, and to protest, by the way, against certain compromises which really compromise the simplicity and truth of logical science.

The present paper will conveniently fall into three sections. The first will be an attempt to determine the nature and conditions of a science of knowledge, while the two others will be devoted to explaining the relation of logic when thus conceived to metaphysics and the real world, and to the traditional types of formal logic with their modern offshoots.

1. A science of knowledge is not quite the same thing with a science of thought, nor even with a science of thought *as* thought. In order that the two should coincide, it would be necessary to restrict the province of thought to the mediate and immediate judgment, when *bonâ fide* put forward as knowledge, excluding all mental acts which do not, like the judgment, claim to be the assertion of fact or truth. Such restriction of thought as thought would not be warranted by common language ; hardly, perhaps, by psychology. The mental act which corresponds to an imperative sentence is a thought, but does not claim to be knowledge ; so, too, is a conscious exertion of the abstract fancy, which judges, but claims for its judgments no positive connection with the whole of experience, *i.e.* does not put them forward as true.

Our science then takes for its province only such thought as claims to be knowledge, and that is, we may say at once, in every case, some form of the judgment, excluding the acts of conscious fancy, and the lie or wilful error. Logic has to do not with the moral lie, but only with the 'lie in the mind' which presents itself under the disguise of knowledge.

When does thought claim to be knowledge? We say, when it claims to correspond to fact; and it is knowledge, we believe, in as far, and only in as far, as it does correspond to fact. Now 'fact,' whatever it may be, is beyond the control of the individual mind, and is discovered or constructed by the process, primarily related to the individual mind, which we call 'experience.'

Experience is then the criterion of knowledge. But experience practically presents itself to us, not as a fixed standard, but in a number of growing systems which we call the special sciences; and in each the correspondence of thought to fact can only be judged by the relation of the system to its material.   This means, as the material is not available for judgment till it is organised into knowledge, that knowledge in each growing system is always in process of passing judgment on itself, and nothing else can judge it.

So far, we are only saying what is admitted, we suppose, ever since Kant; that no general criterion can apply to the material of knowledge, and that the reality of knowledge depends on its material.

But these considerations bring us face to face with a grave difficulty in the conception of a science of knowledge. *Primâ facie,* the relations which give thought its character of certainty can only be investigated by the direct march of experience, the direct inquiry whether this or that thought is indeed true.

Few would now put forward the traditional 'laws of thought' as a test of knowledge which will meet this embarrassment.   It will be admitted that they are not false only in as far as they are unmeaning.   It will also be generally admitted that the attempt to treat logic as an organ of discovery is for similar reasons inevitably self-contradictory. But we must observe upon a compromise which commended itself to Mill, and is, in fact, a sort of parody of a true treatment of logic.

We grant, it may be said, that logic can never tell us whether the composition of cellulose is $C_6H_{10}O_5$; no doubt we must obtain particular facts from those who know them; but of an inference at least logic is sovereign judge.   If we are supplied with premises we can tell whether a conclusion is rightly drawn from them, or what other conclusion would be so.

But the distinction is untenable.   An inference is a judgment, though a judgment whose ground or reason is explicitly set forth.   Whether such a judgment is true as it stands, *i.e.* for the reason which it sets out, or true only in part, *i.c.* as a true conclusion from false premises, is no less a question of fact than is the truth of an immediate judgment.   The conditions required by formal logic for the technical validity of a syllogism amount to demanding that the mediate judgment in which it consists shall be taken as true.   Unless it is true in fact it cannot be true as an inference. It is said that a true conclusion may follow from false premisses. But of course this is not the case if we regard the conclusion as an inference, as a mediate judgment. The assertion is that a certain rule connects this predicate with this subject. The mere logician cannot say 'this is true;' and if he cannot say 'this is true,' he cannot say 'this inference is valid.' He can only say 'it is stated in a form which is appropriate to the exhibition of an adequate rule for determining a subject by a predicate,' *i.e.* 'it is stated as if it were valid.'

Who then is to answer the question whether, *e.g.*, a principle will bear the new application proposed to be put upon it? Clearly the question can only be answered by the consequences of each new application to the entirety of the science in question, *i.e.* by the limits which experience dictates.

No doubt it may seem that an inference is bound by its form, and that its form is accessible to the logician's criticism. If thrown into another form, it may be said, the inference becomes other, but it must stand by the defects of the form which, as given, it presents. But this objection rests on something like an equivocation. The true form, that which has a real grasp of the matter and consists in systematic thought-relations, is not in particular cases accessible to the logician as such. All that he can reach is the grammatical expression, and all the fallacies that he can detect are those which occur, however rarely, from a confusion of the import of sentences.

Truth and validity then cannot be separated; validity is only the truth of an explicitly conditioned judgment. Both depend on the movement of experience.

How then can we save the conception of a science of knowledge? For the essence of knowledge is truth, and it seems that the relation which constitutes truth cannot enter into our science.

This issue, on which the whole possibility of logic rests, is familiar to us in several forms. How is it possible that we should know more than we have actually felt and seen? How can any judgment be more than descriptive; which amounts to asking, in other words, How synthetic judgments are possible which are at once universal and necessary? All these issues are summed up in the question to which we must now turn—' What is the distinction between the matter and the form of thought ? '

The truth, it has been said, is the whole. No isolated judgment, in its isolation, is necessary, or indeed has any import. We may gather this from the admission that, in order to see the necessity of any judgment, we must understand the terms. This means no less than that we must master a certain system in which the judgment which we are to apprehend is bound up, and then we shall perceive how unintelligible that part of our world, or it may be our entire world, would become if we denied that judgment. This is excellently illustrated by Whewell's account of coming to feel that the contradictory of certain judgments is inconceivable. Thus it is not to be demanded of a science of knowledge that it should conjure certainty out of nothing, or, on the other hand, embrace in itself the whole range of special science. Logic does not arise till men are convinced that knowledge is real; it has no power or authority over minds that should *bonâ fide* deny this reality. (Not that we admit such denial to be possible.) It is only when the difference between truth and error, between proof and guesswork, has become the basis of civilisation, of the practice of law courts and the predictions of science, that attention is turned, as in the time of Plato, to the distinction between knowledge, common sense, and ignorance.

It was said above that truth lay in the correspondence of thought to fact. It is now said that truth lies in the entirety of experience. The two expressions are equivalent ; a fact is that which experience as a whole compels us to believe. If this were not so ; if facts were isolated as neither a grain of sand nor anything else is isolated, then, as we may partly fancy by the help of a violent abstraction, truth, granting that there was to be truth, would consist in the correspondence of each several thought to some archetype, and there could be no inference,[1] nor any but descriptive judgments, nor any science of knowledge. There would be none of those degrees of relation between each judgment and the whole of what is known which constitute the more and less of truth and certainty. There would be,

---

[1] There might be generalisation about the isolated facts, if we suppose them to have enough community to generalise about. But no fact could be criticised, doubted, or inferred.

that is, no distinction between the matter and the form of thought.

But this is not so. Beginning with the sentence, the linguistic equivalent of all living thought, men are led to observe a certain structure which repeats itself, though not without differences, in all mental operations that embody knowledge. As this structure is freed from the accidents of particular languages it is seen to be identical with that systematic unity the more and less of which constitutes the more and less of knowledge. This unity in its rudimentary form is the judgment. A synthetic judgment *à priori* would be a judgment, not tautologous, but yet so determining the whole arrangement and cohesion of our experience that if it were untrue we should have to give up the pretension to connected intelligence. Whether any judgment can be known as having this character is doubtful; but it is the logical ideal to which every proved fact must approximate, and is fairly realised in such judgments as those of which Whewell naïvely maintained that we learn to find their contradictory inconceivable. We cannot, *e.g.*, refuse to admit that a straight line is the shortest way between two points. And why not? Because in attempting to deny it we make nonsense of our idea of space. It is proved, like every first principle, by being necessary to the conclusions drawn from it. Such systematic unity in its various shapes and types, known to us not so much by what we call them as by what they do for our knowledge, is the form of thought. To understand this unity in its different but kindred manifestations, to appreciate the demands which in its various phases it makes upon its material, and to formulate these demands as the logical ideal of knowledge, is what we understand by the function of logic as a science. The relation of logic to science then is reflective and illustrative: it proposes not so much to criticise as to interpret. We would not, however, lay it down that no logician can be of service to science. Lookers on see most of the game; and it might well be that the wider studies of Mill, Lotze, or Jevons might lead them to fruitful considerations, not to speak of Lotze's eminence in certain branches of science. But whatever is so done for discovery by logic is done *per accidens*; it is not as a logician that the philosopher is of service, but as a scientist or amateur.

In this purely narrative paper we may be permitted further to give the bearings of this position by discussing the relation of such a logic to metaphysic and to the formal logic of tradition.

2. How is logic distinguished from metaphysic? Logic has been defined to be the science of thought as knowledge; metaphysic will be allowed to consist in the science of reality as such.

I. The distinction cannot be that logic deals with the intellect and metaphysic with something beyond or external to the intellect. There are only two grounds on which such a distinction can be proposed :—*a.* The restriction of logic to a consideration of the shapes and figures of thinking without reference to their connection with reality. But beside such a logic as this there is room for a further science, about which the question whether it dealt with the work of intellect or not would arise over again; *i.e.* metaphysic is not treating of something external to the intellect because it goes beyond the range of ' formal ' logic.

β. But there is also the well-known ground of a thoroughgoing distinction between thought and existence. Metaphysics may then be held to busy itself with ascertaining what elements of experience are due to each of these factors, and may state its guesses either about the world outside the mind, or about the world as given in the nature of the mind, as the outcome of its search for what is really real. In the second of these cases it may be identified with logic, and in the first distinguished from logic, and both with equally little ground.

II. It is idle, if not impossible, to separate logic from metaphysics as the exhibition of a process from the exhibition of its results; that is, as a critical investigation of knowledge from a summary of its outcome to be taken as reality. In science there is no such thing as a net result. Even in dealing with *data* of number and extension, it is essential to bear in mind the processes by which they have been obtained; otherwise we cannot know what they really represent. To base processes on results is unavoidable; it is a makeshift which is needful for lengthened operations. But to exhibit results apart from processes, except for the mere purpose of abbreviation, is not to construct a science but to arrange a vocabulary. Thus it will not do to expound the scheme of ideas developed by logic as truths ready to hand and established for ontological purposes. If logical ideas are to be applied in ethics or in theology, they must be applied as logical ideas, in the light of their deduction, not as a metaphysical framework of things.

III. We are, therefore, forced to the conclusion that the general science of reality cannot be distinguished from the science of knowledge. Reality is the connection with the whole, and logic is the science of this connection in general, as direct science is in particular. But this conception will undermine much of what is propounded as metaphysics. Ontological speculation will assume a less rigid form; the thing in itself will appear as a phantom of existence projected into vacancy by the understanding in its zeal to explain everything by something else. Monads or atoms will not be demanded as metaphysical substrata, but will rest on their merits as objects of possible experience. Cosmological principles, e.g. the theory of space and time, and the wider laws that appear in nature, may come to be treated on the one hand in logic, as affecting the import of the entire scheme of knowledge, on the other hand, 'empirically,' in the simple inquiry as to what they are. And psychology, which now wavers between the mind's intellectual work and its more tangible conditions, would very well bear a similar division; the characteristic movement of thought, with distinctively human emotion, would fall into the range of logic, ethics, and anthropology, while the purely animal mechanism of thinking and feeling would belong to physiology. We do not mean by this distinction to block the path for contributions to philosophy from the inquiry into the mechanism of consciousness. That the action of reason is varied and limited in individual men by dependence upon an animal mechanism is a belief now almost inevitable, whether true or not. We expect inequalities and limitations in this matter, as in the matters of health and physical endowments, which indeed cannot be strictly distinguished from the mechanism of consciousness. It need not be imagined that philosophy has any vocation to protect the independence of reason and the will against the consequences of being mechanically conditioned. A far more difficult problem, and one that includes the former, awaits philosophy on its own distinctive ground; namely the assignment of a 'content' for the individual soul in determining its motives. Granting complete freedom to determine, from what source is any specific free determination to be derived? Such a problem as this dwarfs the difficulties of a mechanism of consciousness into insignificance, and presents itself in that direct consideration of the body and matter of thought which is the true province of mental science.

The view here indicated of the relation between logic and metaphysics is subject to well-known and formidable difficulties with which this essay cannot pretend to deal. The writer, however, cannot for his own part conceive any difficulties to be so formidable as those which attend the alternative method of a direct or uncritical metaphysic. By a direct metaphysic we mean any method which seizes on this or that element of experience as representing reality, guided only by some conviction as to the source (in or out of the intellect), or the character (universality, necessity, or the like) of the required element. That any such science is no better than a castle in the air is a proposition amply justifiable in theory: the limits of the present sketch and the triteness of the subject may perhaps be our excuse if we attempt an appeal to philosophical common sense. The tree is known by its fruit. In a sense, no doubt, we must admit the extraordinary vitality of direct ontological and cosmological speculation. We may point, for instance, to the curious precision with which Herbert Spencer illustrates his idea of the dependence of phenomena upon an unknown ground. Problems of the same class had an attraction for Lotze, and received from the genius of Professor Clifford a treatment as instructive as any of which they are capable. The point which strikes an observer in theories of this class is the absence of growth or development. One tendency indeed is clearly discernible, and that is, the tendency to assimilate the unknown reality to consciousness. But otherwise the ideas suggested seem otiose. They have no progressive control over experience, contain no substance and bulk of organised knowledge; they form a series whose last term is not distinctly more advanced than its first. These observations would be unjustifiable if they could not be brought to the test of history. But an appeal to history is always fair. The contrast with logic will show in what sense we make the appeal.

Logic, as also language, but in a higher sense, may be compared to the system of fortresses that secure a conquered country. It follows the march of knowledge laboriously but surely. The very aberrations and caprices of logic are owing to the vastness of its material. The great movements of culture and of science register themselves in periodical reforms of the theory of knowledge; every procedure and principle, from numerical computation to evolution in the realm of ideas, claims now and again to be *the* logical method. And there is room for all. After each ' reform ' the science recovers itself, and the new elements which were to turn the logical world upside down, fall so naturally into their place that we wonder how it was overlooked before.

The mention of a system of types or manifestations of the unity of thought (p. 72) naturally raises the question what the succession of forms can mean, and how it is warranted. Let us take as an instance the idea of cause as an antecedent in time, and as only one out of many possible antecedents, to which a certain effect or consequent in time may be due. To this idea corresponds the principle, ' The same cause will always produce the same effect,' and the idea may be set down as the idea of ' cause and effect,' *i.e.* of two things or events in a certain relation. No logical system can leave this idea as it stands. It cannot fail to be observed that cause is relative to effect no less than effect to cause, and that this relativity is expressed in the conception of a single necessary process, continuous in nature and grounded on some law or reason. In such a process it is clear that the given effect has always one cause, or rather ' ground,' just as the same cause has always the same effect. This idea might be described as that of convertible cause and effect; but the notion of cause and effect, as this and that, is gone when they are reduced to process or ground, because, in a continuous process, it is impossible to say where cause ends and effect begins. For the purpose of knowledge any part of such a process is sufficient to determine all the rest, and a modification of any part is impossible without modification of the rest, whether related to the former as effect or as cause.

But further; everything that acts in the real world is not only conditioned as cause by the receptivity of that on which it acts, but is also conditioned as effect by the activity of that other thing. In every moment the process branches out by reaction into several processes, so that if we restrict our attention to the single set of changes which first engaged it, we neglect an essential characteristic of our world. This characteristic is known as reciprocity or reaction; everything that modifies another is itself modified by the same connection. We might go on to insist that where action and reaction are in play we have *pro tanto a system*; but enough has been said for the mere purpose of illustration. Cause and effect, ground, reciprocity, system, are a set of ideas which can hardly help making their appearance in every attempt to systematise logic. In Mill we have an alternation, if not a confusion, between cause and effect proper, and the idea of process or reason in which cause is a conception that includes the occurrence of the effect. The further aspects of the idea are not specifically treated of by Mill, though implied in his account of causes. Not that his 'reciprocal' causation has anything to do with reaction; it only means cases where A gives rise to B, and B, subsequently, to A.

Why are these ideas to be arranged in a succession? If the initial form is incomplete, inappropriate to the formulation of experience, why introduce it into logic? Or if it is to come in because the individual mind passes through it in learning science, why not catalogue and arrange in order all the errors which a beginner may make in Euclid or in grammar? These mistakes probably have a family resemblance and a natural sequence. Or is there some section of rational experience in which it is best to regard cause and effect as separate events? In short, has the conception of cause and effect any place in knowledge which cannot be better filled by one of the subsequent conceptions, and if not, why do we let it appear in logic?

Whatever is a marked and uniform phase in the movement of reason belongs to logic. It would, indeed, be rash to deny that one or another well accredited stage of thought may seem to lose vitality, and thenceforward to belong only to history; and cause and effect have no specific province, as have, for instance, number and extension. Yet examples of such self-conquest on the part of reason should be accepted with great caution. And even where it does take place, it can only be effected by the substitution of some category that exhibits more clearly the nature of the old one. The imperfect or rudimentary logical forms have their various claims to their position. They have a connection both with the general movement of experience in science and history, and with the progress of the individual mind within each science. As long as the world presents itself to reason in 'things,' reflection will fix on concrete conditions as the explanation of changes that come after them. To say that 'the cause of death was poisoning by strychnine,' or that 'the cause of a railway accident was the breaking of a connecting-rod,' is a way of speaking which has its truth in the necessary abstraction of common life. It is as true as to say, 'that colour is *really* blue, but looks green by candle-light.' Cause, like reality, is a temporary fixed point to help in determining the bearing of something else. Even if a more advanced category were put in its place, an explanation of what was superseded would have to be given, or that new category would in turn be in danger of omitting what it should include. So much for the meaning of the logical succession as regards the value of those forms whose earlier place in the series seems to stamp them with incompleteness. Simpler instances are those in which the ruder form has an obvious use and an obvious limitation. Compare for instance the equation $A = A$ with the judgment 'man is animal.' The truth of every form is in its use, and its use determines its place in the succession.

But how is the arrangement or succession which we may adopt to be guaranteed? Are we proposing in a concealed way something that is not unlike the Hegelian dialectic? The first answer to all such questions must be οὐκ ἂν θαυμάσαιμι, εἴ μοι σκεψαμένῳ οὕτω δόξειεν. We do not indeed bind ourselves to any method, in the sense in which deduction, induction, and dialectic are styled methods, but if the examination of logical material leads us to a quasi-dialectical exhibition of its organism, we cannot help it. All we must presuppose is, as has been said above, the existence of knowledge or the possibility of necessary synthetic judgments in the sense there defined. Yet the censure of dialectic has been carried so far that this simple postulate requires defence, for in every synthetic judgment we have the phenomenon which has been held to be the essence of dialectic, the self-caused transition from idea to idea. ·Lotze's explanation of the Hegelian movement of an idea is too simple to be true; and is, we venture to think, inconsistent with the recognition of synthetic judgments. The notion that an idea may be such as necessarily to turn into its opposite is, according to this explanation, a mere confusion between the idea, which is fixed, and the things falling under it, which are variable. The criticism may be connected with Lotze's view of the relation between judgment and idea, which cannot be entered upon here. Now it may be conceded that the logical term 'opposite' in this context has little meaning, and may be taken to have much; and that the appearance of laying no weight upon verification rightly tells against such conceptions as this of dialectical movement. But if ideas do not pass into each other, each in virtue of its own nature being the ground of certain others, it is hard to see how a system of ideas is possible, or how any synthetic judgment can be true. The mental image of a triangle, as presented by the pictorial fancy, contains no movement; but the idea of a triangle consists of active thought, ranging between limits set by the elements of its definition. The processes of scrutinising our ideas, or of pushing a principle home, are the means by which knowledge is made real; and we all know what is meant by carrying an idea too far. It cannot seriously be objected that these are acts of the mind, and not of the idea; ideas in any genuine sense are acts or movements of the mind.

Perhaps we get to the root of the matter by admitting that if an idea on being pressed home turns into another, some condition has been supplied which was passed over in the first statement. If liberty on scrutiny turns out to be necessity, this means that in the first estimate either present conditions were neglected or absent conditions presupposed. A true or adequate idea of liberty would not turn out to be necessity. But is any idea, taken as we find it, properly i.e. completely, stated? Is it not the very postulate of knowledge that the whole is necessary to the definition of every part; or, as in Lotze's excellent logic, that the defect of each form is supplemented by its successor? That an idea which gives a new result under a new condition does not thereby turn into another, but only receives an addition, or is endowed with a relation to another idea, is a distinction that means nothing in the realm of thought. In no case is the original idea lost, but all additions which are proved of it must modify it in a greater or less degree. Experience moves every idea through perpetual new conditions, and this movement is the development of what the idea is, *i.e.* of the synthetic judgments into which it can enter. That a triangle, if the base is reduced to nothing, becomes a straight line, or that freedom to act, without a reason for acting, is blind chance or necessity, are considerations belonging to similar movements.

Experience, in short, forces thought along certain lines from partial to more complete notions. What name may be given or what cause assigned to such an advance is indifferent for our purpose ; but such a progress from idea to idea as expressed in synthetic judgments is all that needs to be postulated for a succession of logical forms, and its power to throw light on experience is the only guarantee that can be offered.

We have then to see how the proposed treatment deals with some of the main ideas of traditional logic. In this discussion great part of the idea is due to Lotze, though his view on the relation of judgment to concept does not commend itself.

3. The title of formal logic ' is objectionable as implying some other logic which is not formal ; *e.g.* a logic of truth, or applied logic. Following the conviction that the science of knowledge must, *quâ* science, deal with form, we shall eschew the title as tautologous. The following suggestions, however, start from the 'formal' logic of tradition as an outline to be filled up. They will not look very like a contribution to ontology. The writer's present purpose is only to show how the science may master some of the elements which at present make it chaotic.

We assumed that the subject-matter of logic was always the judgment, whether mediate or immediate. The object is then to exhibit the forms characteristic of these acts in a system depending on their respective value for knowledge. The direct judgment bears an exceedingly close relation to the mediate judgment or inference ; the distinction between them might indeed be treated as purely external. Every direct judgment that deserves the name must express an inference, *i.e.* a conclusion with a reason ; and it might be urged that the articulate expression of this reason in the

middle term of a syllogism makes no difference in what is
actually thought. The fact, however, that a single judgment may seem not to contain material for the subject of
the conclusion over and above the middle term, indicates, if
it does not furnish, the true distinction. It would no doubt
look ridiculous to analyse the judgment 'All triangles have
their 3 angles = 2 right angles' into the syllogism

    'All triangles have their 3 angles = 2 right angles.'

    'All triangles are triangles.'

    '∴ All triangles have their angles = 2 right angles.'

But the absurdity looks greater than it is : it is not so unheard
of to say, 'All triangles, just because they are triangles, have
their three angles,' etc. The meaning of the judgment is
precisely that, and though all propositions could not, yet all
judgments of the higher class could, be analysed in this way.
The true distinction between judgment and syllogism is indicated by this absurdity, and is one of a class which charac-
terises forms of thinking. The direct judgment retains the
professed structure and import of the simplest or most
empirical enunciation, e.g. 'I hear,' while capable of carrying
a precisely drawn inference like the above geometrical truth.
All the thought forms have this elasticity of application ;
it might almost be said that any of them can be forced upon
any matter. Their ideal import has a narrower range than
their intelligible use. But the express demand for a distinct
reason, as if in answer to the question, 'why?' is made by the
mediate judgment form or syllogism, thus bringing into
strong relief the inferential character which is latent in the
direct judgment.

The series of judgments would, perhaps, in a perfect
representation, be interrupted by syllogistic forms to explain
the transition from judgment to judgment ;[1] but for our
purpose it is better to arrange the judgments together and
observe upon inference later.

The categorical judgment is the real act of mind corresponding to a simple proposition, whether affirmative or
negative. 'The real act,' for the sentence is apt to disguise
the judgment, and grammar is often at cross purposes with
logical analysis, even if it uses a quasi-logical terminology.

[1] This conception may be compared
with the simpler dialectic of Lotze's
Metaphysic, Introduction, § xi. Lotze
seems, however, to be over-cautious
in refusing to recognise a natural or
necessary advance from notion to notion.

The grammatical subject, or any subordinate grammatical element, may often be the logical predicate. To interpret a sentence is to elicit from it the logical judgment which it is really intended to convey.

The sentence is the real unit of language; the word by itself, except when it has the power of the sentence by compound structure, or is used as a verb by help of sign or tone (a *true* interjectional use hardly comes under the head of language), corresponds to no act of thought. It is doubtful whether there is an exact Greek term for 'word.' Aristotle has to use a periphrasis when he wants to refer to it in a definition. No doubt he took his ὄνομα and ῥῆμα to have each its own meaning, but it does not follow that he thought of them apart from possible judgments. Apart from any sentence the meaning of a name could be nothing but a mental image; but we doubt whether even this exists in the human consciousness apart from ideas which would need a sentence to express them.

These remarks are introduced to illustrate the relation of the concept to the judgment. Because the sentence can be broken up into words, therefore it seems to be thought the judgment can be broken up into concepts. Now a concept has unquestionably a common meaning in all judgments that contain it; but it need not therefore have any meaning apart from each and all of these judgments. To think of terms or significant words is to put them into judgments or sentences; only the word, having an existence and history as a thing in sound and in print, impresses us as separable, but reflection shows that its function is really to set up an intellectual movement which it guides but does not include. In short, a judgment cannot be cut in two so as to give two fixed products like the printed words of the sentence; we may take 'the sun shines' and cut out the verb, but the truncated subject, when we turn the mind upon it, develops other predications out of itself, and breaks up again into a complete system of judgments. Nor are the original subject and predicate, apart from the original judgment, ever quite the same that they were in it. In 'the moon shines' and 'the sun is hot' we have, so to speak, not quite the same cases under the rules prescribed by 'shines' and 'sun' respectively, as we had in the original judgment, 'the sun shines.' The judgment then is a single indivisible act, though containing that distinction in identity on which thought and, ultimately, consciousness depend. Subject and predicate determine how predicate and subject are here and now entering into thought.

But it may be asked, ' Where is the import by which they determine each other, if thought is only in judgments, and there is only one judgment in question, viz. that which is being made ?' Have not the terms after all a fixed, separable import, like the shape or colour of a thing in space, which they bring to the judgment in which they are combined, as the phrase goes. There is a real difficulty in analysing the act of judging, because of its fugitive nature and its numerous grades of unity. To explain this question of the import we must think of such forms as relative sentences or as the syllogism itself. The unity is least, and the rigidity of subject and predicate greatest, in the judgment that compares pure qualities, without attaching interest to them by any further condition depending on either. ' Red is not green '; such a judgment, however, with no further import, is purely formal, and would never be made. If the judgment is taken as defining red to be the danger-signal, it unites the two qualities in a single and perfectly clear relation. Every judgment is really a conclusion, or at least a member of some context of judgments. This will be clear in the sequel. What has been said on the unity of the judgment applies equally to the syllogism, as appears sufficiently from the relation of the two. It is a corollary from this that they are not in time. The apprehension of a sentence takes time ; but a judgment, or proof *quâ* proof, is complete in the moment in which it is understood or ' seen through.' Consciousness is in many ways conditioned by time ; but *quâ* consciousness, *i.e.* as regards what is known or felt, it is the negation of time.

In scientific logic we ought to proceed at once to the theory of the judgment. The term or equivalent of a name has no place in logic apart from this theory. From quality to causation, and from cause to idea, all the matter of consciousness takes the form of the judgment.

One criticism must be made in this context on a conception which is usually treated under the head of terms. Aristotle observed that in one sense a genus contains its species, while in another, every species must contain its

genus.[1] The contrast thus indicated has since been developed
as the difference between the intension and extension of a
concept. What we have to observe upon this doctrine is no
more than a warning that it cannot indicate two co-ordinate
and separable kinds of import. We might say that the
denotation is a consequence of the connotation, if this does
not imply that the connotation can be thought without the
denotation. To think in denotation (extension) only, would
be to think of individual things without knowing what we
are thinking of; to think in connotation (intension) would
be to think of relations without knowing what subjects are
determined by them. The latter is the more possible abstraction of the two, but is only to be found by a strained
interpretation. In 'Goodness is praiseworthy,' the subject
is of course a quality that exists in instances, and though
we may sleepily pass over the term as a sound in its right
place, we cannot actively make the thought our own without
presenting to ourselves some sketch of the cases or forms in
which goodness is realised.

We shall see enough of this distinction in the perverted
forms of judgment which take a short cut to the logical ideal
by the route of abstract identity. We need only observe
before passing on, that in as far as the twofold meaning
represents more and less consciousness of number, both kinds
are often, perhaps usually, united in the same judgment,
the subject being emphasized in respect of number (though
it must be a number of something) and the predicate in
respect of content or nature, e.g. Some M.P.'s are Protec-
tionists. It is important how many M.P.'s hold the doctrine
in question, but less important what fraction they form of
the general Protectionist party. .

We spoke of a short cut to the logical ideal. The logical
ideal in its abstract form is simple identity. It claims to be
expressed in every affirmation, and as the barest expression
of this claim, the principle A is A has been set up as representative of the judgment. And at every step in the development of the thought form we are met by the temptation to
take a short cut to the ideal A is A. That is to say, instead of
justifying an affirmation, by finding out a real resolution of
the difference between its elements, the tendency is simply to
leave the difference, as a material difference, out of sight, but

[1] Cf. Trendelenburg's Selections from the *Organon*, § 24, *note*.

to save the assertion by making it identify a set of individuals with themselves.   All doctrines which put the
judgment on the level of an equation are of this nature.
They are attractive because they seem to furnish operations
of the mind in pursuit of truth which can be conducted
wholly on logical ground by the assistance of simple computation, or, perhaps, of the calculus of probabilities.   All
such processes, however valuable in themselves, have for
logic the character of arrested development.   The demands
of the ideal are only to be satisfied by a progressive material
determination of the judgment, which must bite deeper and
deeper into its subject as it passes into a larger system.   All
this, as we have amply seen, logic cannot do, but can only
follow the doing of it.

If it is assumed that to catalogue judgments after the
fashion of common text-books is insufficient, then two schemes
present themselves on which a series of judgments may be
based.   To trace the advance of thought from the synthetic to
the analytic judgment, beginning with the qualitative perception and ending with the definition or perhaps with the existential judgment, is in many respects the safer plan.   There
are grounds, however, which lead us to reject it, or at least to
modify it.   Every judgment is essentially both synthetic and
analytic.   The distinctions to be drawn could therefore be
nothing but distinctions of degree.   And even these would
be disturbed by psychological considerations tending to confuse the absolutely and the relatively analytic or synthetic
judgment.   Is not every new judgment synthetic and every
familiar judgment analytic, it might be asked.   Or again,
is not, as Sigwart ingeniously contends, the direct reading
of perception in every case analytic, while only the judgment
which involves an inference is truly synthetic?   What in
short is to prevent us from seizing any form of tautology as
the type of the analytic judgment?   Now that analytic character which justifies us in treating a thought form as genuine
knowledge is not tautology, but a thorough mastery of differences; not obtained by abstraction, but by organisation
of material.   In describing this process wholly in terms of
the categorical judgment, and subject to the above psychological difficulties, we should be neglecting a useful guide
which has been made serviceable by Lotze and others.   If
the forms of judgment are augmented by the inclusion of the

hypothetical and disjunctive, we obtain at least the support
of a definite scheme in tracing the influence of the logical
ideal. And in spite of the elasticity of thought forms, to
which we shall find certain limits, this scheme will be of
great service in marking the phases of knowledge.

i. The series of judgments begins with the impersonal as
appropriately as it might end with the existential judgment.
The impersonal approximates to a purely synthetic character ;
the existential is all but absolutely analytic. The former
has a predicate but no subject, the latter a subject but no
predicate. The difference between them therefore depends
on the different functions of subject and predicate. The
predicate determines ; the subject is determined. The empty
place of a subject, its mere abstract position before a realising consciousness, may be determined in predication by an
event which we cannot or do not care to define or localise.
' It is hot ' ; ' there is a sound.' Such a predication, floating
so to speak, attached only to experience in general, and not
tied down to any distinct relations, unless a simple ' now,'
might well embody the πρῶτον νόημα, the act in which
thought and sense meet. That is, the sense material appears
in it with as slight an investiture of defining thought as is
consistent with its presentation to a human consciousness.
Whether the impersonal judgment preserves any such
moment, or can be shown to have in fact ever corresponded
to it, is a question for philology. The impersonal sentence
of our own language seems to be for the most part a result of
artificial abstraction ; it might, however, be urged that without some genuine survivals there would have been no such
artificial products. But the result for logic is the same ; an
empty form, determined by a significant predicate, is, for
whatever reason, the scheme of the impersonal judgment.
Sometimes it is rhetorical, and little more than a grammatical device. ' There is a willow grows aslant a brook,'
throws the whole picture together, avoiding the break-up
that would be caused by treating any one feature as principal
subject. The true character of many such sentences is doubtful ; compare ' It is I,' Ich bin es, ἐγώ εἰμι. Is the English
form impersonal? Often the logical subject is supplied by a
side wind : ' It is hot out there ; ' ' It grieves me to say it.'
And the general reference of the subject form makes it an
effective vehicle of negation. ' There is none righteous,' ex-

presses the searching over experience and finding none, as contrasted with merely not finding them in some one place. It is
doubtful if any common trait marks the genuine impersonals ;
we hardly find, as we should expect, all the most indefinite
feelings represented in them, though some are, *e.g.*, heat, cold,
and the like. The weather has in several languages a special
right to impersonals, perhaps because a subject was specially
hard to frame, or possibly because it was divine and not to
be spoken of.

The 'existential judgment' in a complete work would
close the account of the analytic judgment. We may dis-
miss it here, observing that it sets itself to make an abstract
form of predication into something sufficiently determinate
to take the place of a predicate. This straining of the predicate form betrays itself in the tendency to change the
verb. Existence, then, as a predicate, borrows its meaning
from the subject. It determines the subject by the essentials of its own definition, those essentials which fix its
place and value in experience. The judgment of existence,
therefore, need never be false, for every subject has some
such predicates that will fill up the form. It is false, or true
in the negative, when it is guided by some interest to determine a subject with relation to a standard not its own. If
a bank-note which 'exists' in my imagination has been
alleged to be forthcoming to pay a debt, the answer ' it does
not exist' is justified—*i.e.* it has not the predicate which
belongs to such a bank-note as the context requires.

The predicate form in the ' existential judgment' is the
abstraction of experience used as a determination, and
therefore is the result of conscious reflection ; the subject
form in the impersonal judgment is also the abstraction of
experience, but only as what is to be determined, and therefore not a reflective but an unconscious abstraction, as near
as may be to the abstractness of feeling.

ii. When the floating subject-form of the impersonal
judgment becomes restricted to some point or mark in experience by the explicit distinction of a relation—*e.g.* of limit
as between thing and thing, we have as the result, it might
be urged, the singular judgment of ' formal ' logic. But it
is usual to treat that singular judgment as a case of the
universal judgment, on the ground that its predicate is
true of the whole subject. Now, apart from the artificial

contrast of intension and extension, it is plain that in the
rudimentary singular judgment we do not find the predicate
referring to the whole subject in at all the same sense as
in a genuine universal judgment. What is the subject in
'This stone is iron ore;' or in 'This man (for which a
proper name may be substituted) is the criminal'? The subject is in the one case 'stone,' the other case 'man'; for
when we have applied a name we have committed ourselves
to some general significance of the name. A proper name,
too, is nearly equivalent to a phrase like 'this man,' 'this
place.' The demonstrative pronoun, proper name, or other
purely formal limitation, supplies no universal link between
the subject so restricted and the predicate. We have, therefore, to find a form of judgment in which all that we really
know is a limited connection between the subject and predicate, and in which there is nothing to explain the limitation. Such judgments may best be treated as 'particular,'
under which term should be included as its cases the singular and the plural judgment, the latter having the sign
'some' or any indication of the plural. The plural judgment amounts to nothing but a summing up of singulars.

It is easy to make allowance for cases in which a proper
name (usually, as such, a mere 'chalk mark,' that *minimum*
of connotation which is a *sine quá non* of denotation) has
attained by adoption into language the rank of a significant
word. Compare such a phrase as 'the Rupert of debate.'
In 'Socrates was a martyr' the predicate is thoroughly in
unity with the subject and grounded in it, and therefore the
judgment may rank with the universal, like the singular of
formal logic.

The particular judgment then is limited but not determined. The limitation, being accidental or external, interferes with the movement of thought in the act of judging,
and so interferes with the logical ideal of complete unity in
its differences. However we describe its defects, it will be
admitted that such a judgment as 'Some combinations of
tones are discordant,' cannot be left where it is; it impera-
tively demands explanation.

From this point, besides the true road of logical determination, there are two divergent short cuts to the logical
ideal. First, we have the unfruitful attempt to exhibit an
identity in the judgment by placing an unexplained quanti-

tative definition on its predicate, with the help of logical symbols of precision. This is the quantification of the predicate; it does not share the practical certainty of numerical computation, while it surrenders all attempt to strengthen the grasp of thought upon its matter.

Secondly, we have a somewhat similar abstraction pursued with method and success, when the repetition of similar judgments is recorded by the help of number, and we either tabulate the unexplained limitation precisely in statistics or a ratio, or, if possible, remove it by the substitution of an empirical 'all.' In the former case we are dealing with statistics and the calculus of probabilities; in the latter we are applying, in the strictest sense, 'induction by simple enumeration' to the formation of a general judgment. The general judgment, 'All A are B,' considered as an empirical result, is not more than a statistical proposition, '100 per cent. of A are B.' To this outgrowth of the particular judgment belongs the 'numerically precise argument,' which is a device for getting a conclusion out of particular judgments by a simple computation. 60 per cent. of A are B, 50 per cent. of A are C, at least 10 per cent. of A are both B and C.

All these operations with the limit of the particular judgment, having no bearing on its material determination, are outside the true path of logic. It is to be observed, however, that we are here at the root of no less a system than the system of number, which arises out of two conditions: repeated judgments about distinguishable things comprehended under a single character, and indifference to these distinctions beyond or within this character. Such are precisely the conditions of the process from singular to plural and general judgments. 'This tree is mine, this tree is mine, and this tree is mine,' form a set of judgments to note the repetition of which is to count. Number is distinction without a difference, and such is the distinction embodied in the particular judgment, whether singular, 'This man' (why 'this'?), or plural, 'Some men' (why only 'some'?). Notice that the use of number to mediate between subject and predicate is different from its function where it enters into a material relation as an essential note, e.g. in a table of specific gravities, or the like.

iii. The general judgment[1] obtained by simple enumera-

---

[1] Not Lotze's 'generelles Urtheil,' which more nearly equals 'generic' than 'general.'

tion is the formal goal of this method; it has really nothing but a statistical value, and is not in a logical sense any advance on a precise particular. Both imply ratios, and whether the ratio is 100 or 50 per cent. makes in itself no logical distinction. ' Half the books on that shelf are German;' 'All the books on that shelf are octavos,' are judgments of just similar import.

We may now take up the thread from p. 88 and ask how else we can develope a particular judgment of the form, ' Some combinations of tones are discordant.' Instead of counting how many combinations or what proportion of them are discordant, we may obviously ask under what conditions, as yet unspecified, the predicate attaches. That is to say, the limitation demands to be replaced by a determination. From this point of view the particular judgment may, as Lotze has pointed out, be taken as modal (a tone combination may be discordant); the transformation seems verbal, though no doubt it has a certain merit in guarding against the quantitative interpretation.

iv. The judgment which professes to be a completion of the particular by introducing a determination adequate to the limit may be called a universal judgment. All judgments naturally tend to *claim* this character. The purely statistical proposition demands so forcible an abstraction from the ordinary habits of thought that it may be questioned whether we were right in admitting it to express a single judgment at all, and whether it should not rather be analysed as a succession of predications attached to an abstract and slightly defined subject. ' All English Euphorbiaceæ are without petals ' may be merely a rapid linguistic expression for ' the plants observed are such and such (naming all the species); and the plants are all without petals.' The judgment as first given undoubtedly claims, in common usage, that the subject somehow explains the predicate.

All natural judgments claim this ideal unity, whether they have it explicitly or not. Common sense interprets the subject of a judgment as the ground of the predicate, and resents, at least in extreme cases, the superfluity of determination such as Aristotle would censure, *e.g.* in ' All isosceles triangles have their angles = 2 right angles.' But to be thoroughly strict in applying such a principle would require us to surrender the natural freedom of the judgment, *i.e.* to make every universal judgment convertible, as a definition is. For if no more is made explicit in the subject than is essential as the ground of the predicate, we have Aristotle's commensurate predication, 'All organisms breathe,' not 'All men breathe.' It is well to remember that such are the only predications which completely fulfil our ideal of the universal judgment, viz. that the determination which is constituted by the subject name should be the ground of the predicate; but we may admit, in accordance with custom, and having other forms to fall back upon, that any judgment is universal which justifies its predicate by a cause or classification. Causes which are not yet analysed out of plurality, and the arrangement of genera and species [1] cover a wide extent of scientific ground. They are the province of the universal proposition which is not commensurate.

v. The form of the universal judgment is, strictly speaking, empirical; it is the mere direct relation or intuition (perception) of a simple synthesis, 'It is so,' weighted with inferential meaning by the inevitable tendency of thought. It has therefore been suggested that the more appropriate form for a true universal law or grounded relation is to be found in the hypothetical judgment. There is, of course, no doubt that whatever can be said in a hypothetical judgment can be said in a categorical judgment, and *vice versâ*. But this elasticity of the thought form is not to deter us from examining the conditions of use which are indicated by its structure, and assigning it an ideal or proper significance according to them.

In the first place, we may put aside the form, 'If A is B, C is D,' on the ground that it is only suited to express a mark, and not a true reason or logical antecedent. The connection between the two clauses is disguised by the change of subject; and if the disguise is only accidental, the judgment is easily remodelled; if essential, then the judgment cannot be self-explaining. Of the former case we may take as an instance, 'If the barometer falls suddenly, coal-mines are likely to be set on fire,' which on removing

---

[1] Even here it is obviously the ideal not merely to say *Orchis maculata* is one of the Ophrydeæ, but to say *Orchis m.* is such a one of the Ophrydeæ as has come to exist in this or that way. But this ideal is far off.

the disguise turns out to mean, 'If the air suddenly presses less, it is likely to let gas escape.' An example of the latter would be, 'If a curtain-shaped cloud is seen, a storm will take place within thirty-six hours.' This is an empirical prognostic which seems not easily reducible to the manifestation of any one cause or principle; its disjointed form is therefore appropriate, but it does not come up to our ideal of a hypothetical judgment.

In the second place, of course each of the terms is meant to contribute to the result. It is an abuse of the form, 'If A is B it is C,' to fill it up with, *e.g.*, 'If anyone is a man he is mortal.' The type we look for is rather, 'If water is heated under one atmosphere it will boil at 212° Fahrenheit.'

The hypothetical judgment thus understood is a pure expression of the interdependence of laws or relations. The condition on which a new relation follows is explicit, not, as in the categorical judgment, implied in a concept. Nevertheless, within these limits, the relation of antecedent and consequent may take various shapes.

They are, naturally, not convertible, and so far correspond to the relation of cause and effect (friction to heat, poison to death); or in simultaneous relations to any special condition that carries a general consequent, *i.e.*, 'If two triangles are on the same base and between the same parallels, they are equal to each other.' But obviously, if the relation of dependence is quite pure, the antecedent and consequent must become *de facto* convertible.

What connection is there between the relation of dependence here in question and the actual facts of causation? Of course antecedent and consequent in the hypothetical judgment are in no way dependent on succession in time. The logical antecedent is often later in time: 'If a rock is of vitreous texture it has passed through a state of fusion.' But because knowledge is not in time, and can even make time run back for purposes of inference, it does not follow that conditions of time must be neglected in knowledge. The system of interdependent truths which is the ideal of science, aspires for itself to eternal validity, but this is not to say that what they contain can take no account of the order in time. Causation is just as well represented by the *nexus*, 'If a body has traversed such and such a space in a certain time, it must have traversed so much space in an equal time immediately preceding,' as by the converse connection. It is a trite remark that the order in time could only exist for a consciousness out of time.

Logical antecedence then primarily embodies the idea of a necessary interdependence between truths or laws, of which connection the causal relation is only one case; the case of process in time. The idea of reciprocity or reaction is equally well represented by antecedent and consequent when the time relation is reduced to a logical present.

vi. The disjunction, of which the true form is always ' A is either B or C, or &c.' not, ' Either A is B or C is D,' is in part an advance upon the hypothetical judgment and in part a divergence from its type.

First, it is the completed form of knowledge in respect of its property of giving value to the negation or limit which every judgment implies. Sigwart has maintained at length that denial is secondary to assertion ; and he is right as long as denial is restricted to that formal abstract negative which corresponds to no real relation. Formal or pure negation is, as he says, merely a judgment about a judgment, the enunciation that a certain affirmative judgment cannot be made. But we have to ask whether in actual living thought this characteristic does suffice to prove a priority of affirmation over negation. And we must reply that every judgment is a judgment about a judgment (or about several) ; though it may be granted for the sake of illustration that the ideal judgment of quality approaches asymptotically to a simple or primary relation, whose limit, or negative character, has little or no interest. We do not say ' that is red ' simply in order to deny that it is green ; at least we do not as a rule, for of course it may happen that we do. Still every judgment has a limit, i.e. involves a negation of other judgments, and so is a member in a tacit disjunction. As the interest which occasions any categorical judgment is progressively gratified, the disjunction under which it stands comes more sharply into consciousness, till with the satisfaction of the logical ideal it is made explicit in the two degrees with which we are familiar, first as an exhaustive and secondly as a mutually exclusive disjunction. Negation thus acquires a more and more definite positive import; and with the completion of a true disjunctive judgment, involving mutual exclusion, the difference of import between affirmative and negative is formally and actually abolished. And in living or actual thought all negation is of this type, for it is fair in logic to assume that every judgment is charged with an interest; so that the denial which is not in favour of any affirmation has no place in knowledge. On the other hand, negation under a tacit disjunction is the genuine outcome of thought. 'That tower is not vertical.' There could be no more direct expression of a positive truth. 'Vertical' expresses the line in which gravity acts. The denial of verticality to a tall structure generalises all directions in which it can diverge from the line of gravity. The tacit disjunction is that the tower is either vertical or has a tendency to instability.

The negative element in disjunction may be illustrated by its equivalent hypotheticals. The exhaustive disjunction is equivalent to a hypothetical with negative antecedent, or to a repetition of such hypothetical if the members are more than two. (This assumes that all the disjunctive members are to be affirmative.) That is to say, the negation of B must be known as the ground of C.

A disjunction, in order to be both exhaustive and exclusive, requires the hypothetical with negative antecedent to be supplemented by another with negative consequent. The affirmation of B must be known as the ground of the negation of C. In short, the elements of the hypothetical must each condition the other by its negation as well as by its affirmation. And this amounts to requiring complete reciprocity between antecedent and consequent, which is only *de facto* and not *de jure* in the form of the hypothetical judgments.

This latter is the true disjunctive form; for it is the form prescribed by the logical ideal as embodied in the interest which guides us in every judgment. The interest demands that the negative of the judgment should be made explicit in comparable predicates; a review of comparable predicates necessitates a ground of disjunction; and a true ground of disjunction must give mutually exclusive judgments.

We may notice in passing that we have nothing to do with the negation *of* a disjunctive judgment. All intelligible negation is *under* a disjunction, and in tracing the negative from its implication in the categorical to its expression in the disjunctive, we have exhausted its real import.

Secondly, however, the disjunctive members are strictly co-ordinate. Each of them conditions all the others, and *vice versá*, but the *positive* relation of condition to conditioned which thought seems to need, is here lost. Indeed the equivalence of hypothetical judgments to a disjunction may, for this reason, seem artificial. The reciprocal antecedent and consequent to which we referred are related by negation only, not by mediation of one positive principle through another. But the fact is that the mediation of the whole set of members is thrown back on the common subject, which is drawn out into a system of judgments whose precise relation is known. Thus each judgment is really mediated by the entire system, not only its limits but its positive ground being made thoroughly transparent. Here we have the idea of a system, of whose possible states, whether simultaneous or successive, each excludes all the others; and yet all alike go to constitute the system.

Such a system in the fullest sense is a notion, though here again the form may be filled up with the most indifferent empirical matter; even if the technical rules are in fact complied with, there may be no true self-explanation, and so no mediation of the individual judgment. *E.g.* zoology and all the concrete sciences of classification are only beginning to hope that their generic arrangements may one day be justified on intelligible principles. But the ideal is what has been . described, and might be sufficiently illustrated either from abstract knowledge or more concrete embodiments of the notion.

Lastly, it has been observed that the calculus of probabilities rests upon the disjunctive judgment. Nothing but a disjunction can provide what the calculus demands, a specified number of alternatives, such that (granting the existence or occurrence of the general subject) one of them must occur, and only one can. This is true, but not the whole truth. Number, we said above, is a distinction without a difference, and it is by such a distinction, *i.e.* as simple units, that the given alternatives must be contrasted if the method is to apply. This postulate is expressed by the calculus in the requirement that there should be no ground for anticipating any one alternative rather than any other. Such a postulate is directly in contravention of the ideal of the disjunctive judgment, which implies a necessary know-

ledge of the conditions which govern the realisation of each
alternative.   Here then we have an arrested development of
knowledge ; what the calculus really needs is a disjunction
grounded on counting.   Knowledge need only go far enough
to assure mutual exclusiveness, and in different matters
different grades suffice for this.   But otherwise it must
retain the character of the particular judgment, which as
we saw tends to the expression of a ratio.   Such a ratio
takes stock of our existing knowledge ; it does not attempt
an addition to its matter.   Counting is an operation which
presupposes a disjunction, but a formal and empty one ; and
this is the type of disjunction to which that must be reduced
on which the calculus rests.

Before concluding this essay with some short observations on the process of inference, it will be well to indicate
the standpoint to be adopted towards the main axioms or
principles employed in logic.   The writer agrees with Mill's
comments upon abstract principles regarded as the foundation of science, though he differs from Mill in his interpretation of that experience from which they are drawn.   Logic
is not founded on the laws of thought. They are abstractions
which express with more or less felicity the nature of that experience whose systematic working is the warrant of their
truth.   Perhaps the most convenient treatment of these
principles is to exhibit them in some kind of series as supple-
menting one another.

The import of the three 'formal laws of thought,' and
their defects, are a very trite subject.   Formulæ so abstract
in expression may be interpreted much as we please ; but if
we are at all strict it can hardly be denied that they are
limited to guaranteeing some kind of unity in the judgment,
and a purely empty reference to all things but the thing
denied for the negative.   That virtue is either square or not
square may be true, but certainly is not interesting.

The postulate or principle of the ' uniformity of nature,'
developed by Mill into a recognition of the world as knowable in various processes whose interaction constitutes it, at
least recognises the objective character of knowledge ; which
is further specified by order of time in the law of causation,
introducing the reflective conception of antecedent [1] and in-

_____

[1] There is a curious uncertainty attaching to Mill's use of the phrase
' invariable antecedent.' If analogous
to invariable consequent it should mean

variable consequent (*in time*, not in the pure logical sense). Finally, the relativity of cause to effect results in placing the process in time on the same footing of a law with the system of simultaneous relations. After this it only remains to point out the ideal of knowledge as a system of interdependent laws, in Mill's language the fewest assumptions, which being given, the whole course of nature (and we add, experience as a whole, including the higher world of art and religion), can be deduced from them; or rather explained by help of and in accordance with them.

In passing to the discussion of inference, we are first met by the theory of induction. What relation is to subsist between the inductive methods or 'methods of observation and experiment,' and the traditional forms of reasoning? These methods are properly and adequately designated by the second of these titles. They are strictly and essentially methods of verification. The only postulate which they need is little more than the laws of identity and contradiction furnish. Every set of changes is what it is, and not what it is not. In order to separate what it is from what it is not, we must begin with a hypothesis as to what it is. Mechanical or simply progressive generalisation is a chimera, except in as far as it consists in attaching predicates by analogy to existing class conceptions, which then do the work of ready-made hypotheses.

In testing hypotheses we may deal with judgments of any degree of generality or reflective structure. The methods of experiment and observation in their simplest form deal with framing and limiting the judgment of perception; even in this process the constant rectification of hypotheses may be readily traced. In every case, however, the function of the positive or affirmative instance is to suggest causes or confirm them, that of the negative instance to suggest limitations of the cause, or to confirm them. The positive instance is read off into a judgment A is a; A is the cause of a; the negative instance into the judgment 'What is not a is not caused by A,' the contrapositive converse of the affirmative. The object

an antecedent A, which is never absent where a consequent a is present, just as invariable consequent means a consequent a, which is never absent when the antecedent A is present. But he seems to employ it simply as emphasizing the invariability with which the conse- quent is found where the antecedent A is found, so that the antecedent is invariable only in respect of always having that consequent. There is independent ground for assuming that he felt at times the untenability of his plurality of causes.

of the methods is to bring these two judgments into agreement as to the precise nature and limits of a and A.   In all
judging there is such a limiting function, but in scientific
judging it grows into a whole process of analysis, directed to
finding the essence or law of a thing or process, and is of
preponderating importance.   But the principle is always the
same : what is separable from a set of changes does not belong
to them, and what is not separable does belong to them.   In
the first place then the methods of experiment and observation are guides to the judgment of perception, and appear
in inference only by the precisely determined judgments
which are obtained through them.   But beyond this, the
principle that parts of the same process are inseparable will
often appear in reflective reasoning.   It then takes the form
of an idea that regulates the consequences to be expected
from any hypothetical cause ; such consequences as belong to
that cause will be inseparable from it or vary with it (*i.e.*
follow it more and less), such as do not, will not.   An argument of this reflective class is Mr. Darwin's, that variation
under domestication depends more on the nature of the
organism than on the conditions to which it is subjected,
because the variations are not, with any degree of regularity,
like under like conditions, and unlike under unlike conditions.
That is to say, the presumed effect of the conditions according to the principle of which we are speaking is not that
observed ; the result does not vary with the conditions, and
therefore is to a greater extent attributable to the only other
cause in operation.   It is separated from the conditions,
does not belong to the process which they, as conditions, set
up.   There is no method of ' induction ' that will apply to
arguments like this.   The special results to be presumed
from the conditions, and with them the probability that
the observed results ' belong ' or do not ' belong ' to the conditions mainly, are material questions to be settled by deductive reasoning ; the principle of the ' method ' has here
a regulative function ordering us to eliminate from each
causal process what cannot be deduced from it, and to find a
cause from which it can be deduced.

We are here brought face to face with the relation of
induction to deduction, and a few words on this must close
the present essay.

Sigwart and Jevons are agreed that induction is essentially deduction regarded inversely. Not that it is the inverse of deduction in the sense that we rise from particulars to universals by induction, and descend from universals to particulars by deduction. This is just what they do not mean. And so far they seem to be in the right.

All induction is, according to this view, to be assimilated to Mill's 'Deductive Method,' only that for the first step, which, according to Mill, involves or may involve 'direct induction,' the framing of a hypothesis will always, and in all cases, be substituted. It must strike the reader of Mill that his treatment of direct induction contrasts unfavourably with the clear account of the use of hypothesis. Perhaps the *crux* of generalisation, as distinct from observation and experiment, was never thoroughly faced by him. Though even in observation and experiment we cannot really escape the demand for framing and testing hypotheses; few intellectual occupations involve making, testing, and rejecting so many hypotheses as microscopical observation with a high power.

Induction then is the process of coming to understand or see through causal and all synthetic relations, and those more obscure analogies which constitute natural kinds. Multiplying instances does not increase evidence, except by decreasing the probability of error, and providing the wonderful facilities of suggestion which belong to a complete conspectus of phenomena. But the principle which we see in the instance is a hypothesis; and it is verified by the agreement of its deduced consequence with observed facts, though only established in proportion as we are convinced that the verified results could not be deduced from any other principle.

True as this explanation appears to be, it may be doubted whether its authors perceive its full importance for logical theory. We have here a form of deduction in which the truth of the premisses follows from the truth of the conclusion! The whole context of conclusions is, indeed, required for the purpose; no one is sufficient alone. But all this is opposed to our ordinary ideas of deductive knowledge. In that, we are accustomed to suppose, the premises must be taken as certain and the conclusion must receive its certainty from them. And it is true that any one conclusion would be given by almost any premisses, and can therefore do little to substantiate the truth of those premisses that do give it. Still, it is absolutely clear that every verified result is *pro tanto* a confirmation of any principles from which it is deducible; and those principles are finally established from which alone all verified results allow themselves to be deduced.

Thus, that is true which will organise experience as a system, and the organisation is always in form deductive; but this does not mean that certainty is derived from generals to particulars. It is their systematic union that gives certainty both to premisses and to conclusions. The hypothesis, with its tentative deduction, soon begins to add probability to unverified results ; true or false, what has explained so much is likely to explain more. The deduction of the purest kind, say geometrical for instance, seems almost beyond winning a practical increase of trustworthiness for elementary principles by new applications, even if verified ; yet if we proposed to cut off all verified conclusions from geometry, we should find that there are no premisses so necessary as not to gain certainty, as they gain significance, from their application. Thus, the hypothetical doctrine of induction after all only appeals to what is the essential character of knowledge, in induction and deduction alike ; and every syllogism whose conclusion is verified gains certainty for its premisses by that verification, as every set of premisses that has stood a series of applications, has some certainty to confer on its further conclusions.

One word more on verification. The facts by which we test conclusions are not simply given from without. The confirmation of a deductive result by experience means its confirmation by certain determinate standards of measurement, and the like, all of which are themselves of scientific origin, and owe their fixed value to some province of systematised experience which has been brought to bear on them. Where, for instance, is the measure of time, the *sine quâ non* of the most elementary verifications ? How can the earth's rotation be compared with itself, and tested for uniformity ? The only answer is, that a capricious variation of motion is excluded by the congruence of our whole system of recorded motions, in clocks and in everything else. Such trust do we put in this system as a whole, that we venture to criticise the motion of our chief time-keeper, the earth itself. Such a criticism is implied alike by asserting and by denying that the time of daily rotation is uniform. The extraordinary reliability and precision of our measurement of time, for which we have no one absolute standard whatever, is an excellent type of the nature of the system of knowledge. And verification by observation and experience always means a reference to the standards of some such system. This is the best illustration of what we mean when we say, that truth and reality are to be looked for in the whole of experience, taken as a system.

B. BOSANQUET.

IV.

THE HISTORICAL METHOD.

THERE is no more striking characteristic of recent science and philosophy than the extent to which the historical method has taken the place of the methods of direct observation and reasoning. The comparative method, which has revolutionised natural science, created the science of philology, and is now profoundly modifying scientific psychology, is in essence identical with it; and it was becoming evident, even before the time of Comte, that it was only through the systematic application of this method that sociology could ever become a science. This historical treatment of the sciences has grown up in the present century side by side with the more scientific treatment of history. The tendency in the preceding century had been to look on truth as needing only the application of enlightened reason for its discovery, and to make history a mere recital of erroneous views or meaningless events. But the conception of the evolution of man by interaction with his environment has filled with life an otherwise aimless record, and shown the meaning and purpose of history by emancipating our views of the past from their bondage to the ideas of the present. And as history has in this way assumed a scientific character, its scope and application have been extended to all departments of investigation: the sciences have become historical.

But while every science has its history more or less closely connected with it, the historical part is in some cases merely a new department of investigation added on to the old without exerting any modifying effect upon it. This is the case with all those sciences whose subject-matter is definite and unchanging. There is a history of the science of mathematics, for instance, but mathematics itself is quite independent of that history. In this sense every science has or may have a history. But the historical method cannot be spoken of as used in the science unless the theoretical part is modified by the historical. And it is only in the simplest way, and to a very slight extent, that such modification can take place here, namely, by pointing out the lines on which the science has advanced hitherto, and thus suggesting the course of subsequent progress.

In other cases, however, the theoretical part is directly affected by the historical. If the subject-matter of which the science treats has itself undergone an historical development, the science will largely consist in tracing the beginning, successive stages, and ultimate form of the phenomena under investigation. It is through the employment of this genetic method that the natural sciences have ceased to be merely descriptive, and advanced even beyond the stage which seeks to trace mere causal sequences. In technical language, it has led them from the categories of quantity and quality to those of cause and reciprocity.

But the case may be still more complicated. For we shall find that the categories of cause and reciprocity themselves are no longer sufficient when we have to deal with self-consciousness and its phenomena. The customs, conduct, and relations of which the social sciences treat are in many ways modified by the theories about them held by those whose relations to one another and to circumstances are being traced. Nor can the complex question thus arising as to the part the internal and external factors respectively play in the formation of any given law, custom, political theory, or political constitution be got rid of by the assertion that the internal or ideal factor is itself the result of the external or real factor. For, even could this assertion be proved, the facts are so involved as to make the conclusion of no practical use. In the words of Mr. Mill, 'So long a series of actions and reactions between circumstances and man, each successive term being composed of an ever greater number and variety of parts, could not possibly be computed by human faculties from the elementary laws which produce it.'[1] And if we admit as a fact—whatever its explanation may be—that social phenomena are affected by the ideas of men, we are compelled to place the social sciences on a

[1] *Logic*, II. 513, 10th ed.

different level from the natural. In the latter we have to trace a sequence or an interaction of factors which are strictly observable and calculable, whereas in the former, the subjective factor modifies its objective environment in a way which cannot be traced by the ordinary methods of natural science. Hence the application of the historical method to the social sciences has a difficulty of its own, and the historical prediction which Comte claims for sociology can only belong to it to a very limited extent.[1]

But a further and still more important distinction requires to be made. Hitherto we have spoken only of special sciences. But the application of the historical method really involves two questions of different kinds : a scientific question which takes many forms according to the nature of the science discussed, and which must be decided for each science on its merits, and a philosophical question, which is one and an ultimate question as to the final method of philosophy. In the former case the question is simply as to the way in which ordinary scientific methods are to be used in certain departments of investigation. When, for example, the question is put as to whether political economy is or is not an historical science to be treated by the historical method, we have obviously to deal simply with a question of logical procedure to be settled by the nature of the subject-matter and the kind of evidence it admits of. But when the question comes to be one as to the ultimate nature and significance of our intellectual and moral ideas, the discussion must evidently be raised to a different platform; for the categories quite properly assumed in any investigation of the special sciences cannot be taken for granted in that science which professes to be final and self-explicative. The question here is therefore not as to the way we are to set about inquiring into this or that special department of investigation, but as to the ultimate method of philosophy—whether it is to be realistic and historical, or idealistic and speculative.

For the historical method is in this case but a branch of the realistic or experiential method. And this, indeed, is the sense in which the term is often used when applied to the special sciences as well as to philosophy. Not only must we distinguish various forms of the historical method accord-

_____
[1] *Positive Philosophy*, Miss Martineau's translation, II. 121.

ing to the subject matter to which it is applied: the term itself has a double meaning. As generally used it connotes two essential characteristics. In the first place, it seeks to arrive at its conclusions by tracing an evolution in time, and it thus takes the name 'historical' in the strict sense. But it is also in most cases equally characteristic of it that it is realistic not idealistic: it traces a development of circumstances and external conditions, not one of thoughts or ideas, or the latter only by means of the former. In ethics it seeks to show how our present moral customs have been gradually arrived at by the development of previous social conditions, and how moral beliefs and laws then and now have been formed by these. In jurisprudence it exhibits the process by which present legal institutions have been produced by the past history and needs of the people; in political economy, how the industrial condition of the country is at each epoch the result of preceding states, economic laws being but the expression of that condition. Through all these various phases the social organism is represented as having grown up in time by a natural process of evolution from its rude and simple beginning to its present complex state, with all the delicate adjustment of parts that state involves. And for the spring or pulse of this historical movement we are referred to no ideal end or final cause gradually realising itself in life, but to outward circumstances, and the selection and development of the organisms that can best adapt themselves to the external order.

The criticism of the historical method thus really involves two questions: (1) Are we, in the various departments to which it is applied, to look for our scientific theories to the order of things and their sequence in time rather than to the logical order of thought which our perception of things may be shown to imply? that is, is our method to be realistic? (2) Are our theories to be formed from an observation of the past history and progress of social and other human conditions rather than from a study of their present position? that is, is the method to be historical in the stricter sense of the term? For the most part, it is the second of these questions that has to be examined in considering the method of the special social sciences, while the former question has still to be asked of the 'first philosophy.' In the former case, since experience is assumed and left to philosophy to be

accounted for, it is obvious that the adoption of an experiential method creates no difficulty of its own, and the
question of method may therefore be thus put : granting that
it is to be experiential, is it to be from the facts of history
or from those of present experience that we are to start?
Even thus, indeed, this question is often mixed up in a per-
plexing way with the other.   For the problems belonging to
the social sciences run into, or at any rate, have not yet been
definitely marked off from those belonging to the ' first
philosophy.'   It is difficult, for example, to say even in
general, in what respects ethics is a part of philosophy, and
in what respects it is to be treated as one of the social
sciences, and it is still more difficult to draw the line in the
detailed discussion of ethical questions.   A similar difficulty
meets us in the sciences of law and politics, while empirical
psychology has only begun to be separated from the theory
of knowledge.   There is thus a danger—not always obviated
—of our assuming the applicability of a realistic method to
questions to which it may turn out to be inappropriate.   It
is difficult always to bear in mind—though the truth of the
proposition cannot be denied—that the method suitable
to one class of questions may imply a constant *petitio
principii* if applied to other questions which yet stand in
close connection with the former.   For in the case of
philosophy proper we cannot take for granted that our
method is to be experiential, seeing that the first business
of philosophy is to give a reasoned account or justification
of experience itself.   The question of the applicability
of the historical method to philosophy may be thus said
to resolve itself into the question, how the adoption of the
historical method in place of that of direct observation
or reasoning alters the fundamental dispute which exists
between philosophic systems according as their methods are
realistic or speculative, or whether it affects that dispute at
all ?

By the realistic school the historical method is regarded
as a bond connecting all the special departments of investigation with the ultimate and co-ordinating science called
philosophy.   It enables us to rise to the ideal of a system of
knowledge interconnected in all its parts, and one alike in
its highest generalisations and in the method by which
these generalisations are reached.   A new aspect, it is con-

tended, is thus assumed by the old controversy between realism and idealism, and a decision arrived at in favour of the realistic view of things. The extent to which this contention is justified will become more apparent when the character of the historical method has been made plain by noticing its application to the mental and social sciences. It is to the controversy on the method of jurisprudence carried on towards the beginning of the present century that we must turn for the fullest account of the meaning and use of the historical method afterwards applied by Comte to social science generally.[1] Theoretically, the modern historical method of jurisprudence was a protest against the theory of a law of nature which, descending from the Roman jurists, was indiscriminately applied to legal topics by the theorists of the eighteenth century. But it had also a practical origin in the resistance made by the States of Germany to the imposition of the Code Napoléon and the controversy that arose among German jurists as to the codification of their law. It was in these circumstances that, in 1814, Savigny published his pamphlet 'On the Vocation of our Age for Legislation and Jurisprudence.' He objected to the proposed codification, because it would not really further the national unity it aimed at, and contended that the cause of the evil resulting from conflicting systems, was not in the laws, but in the people themselves, who were therefore not qualified to frame a code. Unity, he thought, might be best attained, not by a code, but by 'an organically progressive jurisprudence common to the whole nation.'[2]

In speaking of 'an organically progressive jurisprudence,' Savigny seems to have two things chiefly in view. In the first place, he means that law is not something arbitrarily imposed by an external ruler, but a living embodiment of the spirit of the people. 'This organic connection of law with the being and character of the people,' he says,[3] 'is also manifested in the progress of the times, and herein it is

---

[1] Montesquieu seems to be regarded by Comte (*Positive Philosophy*, II. 56, ff.) as the founder of the historical method, and Sir Henry Maine speaks of his work in similar terms (cf. *Ancient Law*, p. 86, 8th ed.). On the other hand, Professor Flint holds (*Philosophy of History*, p. 97) that Montesquieu made no systematic use of '*the expedient* of historical philosophy, the comparison of co-existent and consecutive social states'—an assertion which seems justified of the greater part of the *Esprit des Lois*, though scarcely of such a discussion as that in Book XXVIII., with which may be compared the remarks on method in Book XXIX. chap. xi.

[2] *Vom Beruf unserer Zeit*, p. 161, 2nd ed.

[3] *Ibid.* p. 11.

to be compared to language. For law, as for language, there is no moment of absolute cessation. . . . Law grows with the growth and strengthens with the strength of the people, and at last dies away as the nation loses its individuality.' In the second place, Savigny holds that the historical method, by tracing laws to their source, will ' discover an organic principle whereby that which still has life will separate itself from that which is already dead and belongs only to history.'[1] In this way the historical study of law and custom will show us when any particular legal institutions are the product of conditions which the nation has outgrown, and may thus become a method of ascertaining when laws have outlived the circumstances under which they were appropriate. Beyond this Savigny does not go. He does not seem to look on the historical method as competent to settle the distinctively theoretical questions of jurisprudence, and, in his ' System of Modern Roman Law,' published in 1840, he goes so far as to say that ' the reasons which first gave rise to the name of an historical school have as good as disappeared with the prevailing errors which it was then necessary to attack.'[2] Nor does Sir Henry Maine, with whose name historical jurisprudence is chiefly associated in this country, expressly apply the historical method to the solution of other than historical questions, though he is so far from agreeing with the opinion just quoted from Savigny, that he looks upon the ' philosophy of politics, art, education, ethics, and social relation which was constructed on the basis of a state of nature ' as ' still the great antagonist of the historical method.'[3] Yet, even Sir Henry Maine himself is more successful in vindicating the claims of the historical method against old abstractions than in making clear the extent of its applicability. The ' law of nature ' of the dogmatical jurists was merely an unreal figment of the understanding got by stripping actual laws of their distinctive content, just as the ' state of nature ' to which Rousseau advocated a return, was not so much a positive notion as a mere negative of civilisation. And we are therefore not at liberty to assume that Sir Henry Maine, in opposing the historical method to the ' law of nature '

---

[1] *Vom Beruf*, u.s.w., p. 117; cf. Von Maurer, *Einleitung zur Geschichte der Mark-, Hof-, Dorf-, und Stadt-Verfassung* (1854), p. iv.

[2] *System des heutigen Römischen Rechts*, I. p. xvi.

[3] *Ancient Law*. p. 91.

intends it to do the work of theoretical jurisprudence, or would even exclude from that function the law of nature when more correctly interpreted. 'Nature,' properly conceived, is a concrete not an abstract conception, does not exclude history but necessarily includes it, being itself an evolution in time towards ever-increasing complexity. The fault of the old theorists was not in taking nature as their standard, but in identifying that nature with the simple beginnings of history to the exclusion of its complex and co-ordinated results, and in constructing its initial stage by a fiction of the imagination instead of arriving at it by historical research.

The historical study of law has been so rich in positive results as to divert attention from its possible limits, and to create the impression that this method covers the whole field of legal science. Yet it would seem that even its most important results are closely connected with questions the decision of which lies beyond its range. That law had its origin in *status* and not in *contract*—that it began with custom only afterwards formulated into command—is a conclusion of modern jurists which has shed a new light on legal history. But it is an historical conclusion which does not do away with the necessity of clearly distinguishing between legal ideas and legal customs and leaving room for their possible divergence. In any community in which there is no divergence between these, there is at the same time no scope for progress; while in any community in which they do diverge from one another, either custom tends to mould the ideas into conformity with it, or the ideas to reform and modify custom, or both forces act together. It is in this way that change and progress become possible. Primitive societies and undeveloped races are more prone to be governed by external circumstances than to reflect upon their nature and tendencies, and hence their ideas of legal relations are for the most part the mere reflection of customs inherited from a previous generation or necessitated by outward events. In this lies the explanation of the fact which historical investigation has established, that law arose from *status*. But in developed and civilised communities, where men have learned the lesson of reflection, the tendency is in the opposite direction: custom has to justify itself before the bar of reason, and conduct comes to be guided by a definite conception of its end, instead of by a vague belief that it is usual. Thus ideas begin to have a power over custom corresponding to that which custom previously had over ideas. Herein partly lies the rationale of the theory that law began with contract, a theory developed by the unhistorical reflection of Hobbes and Locke and Rousseau. As an account of the origin of law this theory seems to us now almost ludicrously wrong. Yet, apart from its historical inaccuracy, it had hold of an important element of truth—the truth that reflection upon action and a conception of its end produce modifications upon conduct and upon the customs in which conduct tends to become fossilised.

From the varying elements of which advanced societies are composed, it follows that a broad distinction must be drawn between the legal ideas of the educated and expert on the one hand and those of the community generally on the other. Thus when Savigny speaks of law as expressing the common consciousness of the community, he must be understood as referring only to its essential elements, not certainly to the finer details which are the work of professional jurists. Savigny indeed says that in this—which he calls the technical as distinguished from the political element of law—these experts 'represent the community.' [1] But they represent it not by expressing its ideas, but by expressing their own at its command and within certain limits. The ideas of the community at large only extend to certain leading principles, the development of which is left to experts, while there is often a considerable want of harmony between the ideas of the expert and those which find favour amongst the rest of the community. Now, even supposing that the floating legal ideas of the community are the mere reflex of existing legal customs and institutions, the same does not hold true of the ideas of the thoughtful and the expert. I do not think indeed that any such sharp distinction can be drawn between one class and another as to justify us in saying that the ideas of the one are entirely moulded by outward circumstances, those of the other independent of them. Rather it would seem that the share the external factor plays in their formation differs only in degree between the opinions of the expert and those of the

[1] *Vom Beruf*, u.s.w., p. 12.

vulgar. But even though the ideas of the vulgar be entirely moulded in this external way, it is obvious that the ideas of the expert are not so formed; for while his surroundings in the way of legal institutions and customs are for the most part the same as those of the ordinary man, his legal conceptions are different. Can then the method of historical realism give a sufficient account of the formation of legal ideas or conceptions such as those of the jurists and legislators who modify law? This, it should be noticed, is a question which concerns not merely the history of legal ideas, but also the history of legal customs. For these ideas, however arrived at, tend to form new legal institutions and modify old ones. The question of the formation of these legal ideas thus becomes a crucial one for the historical method. Of course it may be said that as it is a 'deficient imagination' which is largely the cause of slavish adherence to custom,[1] so the formation of conceptions which pass beyond the actual to the ideal is the result of an efficient imagination. But while this answer may be true so far as it goes, it is certainly insufficient. The conditions implied in forming conceptions by the scientific imagination still remain to be investigated. And it is this analysis of the process by which these conceptions or ideals are formed which is one of the chief problems to be dealt with in considering the claims of historical realism to be the ultimate philosophical method. The question thus leads beyond the mere application of the historical method to jurisprudence or other social sciences, and can only be properly discussed when the conditions implied by its use in philosophy have been first of all investigated.

The application of the historical method to jurisprudence has had a result reaching far beyond the limits of the science immediately affected by it. Its historical treatment made law cease to be looked on either on the one hand as a system of arbitrary enactments, or on the other hand as approximations to a natural code common to mankind at every stage of development and only obscured by human institutions. Laws and the customs they sanction were seen to be an expression of the national life, the result of its past evolution, indicative of its present position, and modified at each stage of its progress. In this way jurisprudence

[1] Compare Miss Simcox's striking essay on *Natural Law*. p. 22.

came to be regarded as a part of that comprehensive science
that treats of social relations; and, in the positive philosophy,
sociology, as an historical science, had its definite place
assigned to it in the circle of knowledge.

The preceding account of the historical treatment of
jurisprudence has shown us the grounds on which the application of the historical method to the social sciences
generally is to be discussed.   We have seen that the introduction of the new method was partly a protest against the
imaginative constructions of history that formed such
theories as that of the social contract, and partly also supported by the positive assertion that present facts and
circumstances can only be properly understood by studying
the process by which they have come to be what they are.
In both these claims the new method is justified.   It is
indeed a matter for separate discussion how far we must
inquire into the history of each different class of social facts
and relations before laying down the laws of their present
action, though there can, of course, be no question that it is
absolutely necessary to do so before speaking of what they
were in the past.   But we have also seen that the claims of
the historical method do not stop here.   Perhaps the only
branch of the social sciences in which these claims may be
said to extend no further is political economy, the reason for
this being that the scope of this science is now generally recognised to be much narrower than it was looked upon as being
in the days of Adam Smith.   But in those questions of
statecraft which were formerly mixed up with it, and in
theoretical politics and jurisprudence, the historical method
has a further application, or at any rate makes a more
comprehensive claim, which it is harder exactly to determine.
The reason of this difficulty is that we here pass beyond
actual events past or present, and approach the philosophic
confines of these sciences, thus raising the whole question as
to the significance of the historical method in philosophy.
For both in jurisprudence and in politics we have certain
ideals which we wish to realise, though our efforts to attain
them are necessarily limited and conditioned at once by
their own nature and by the material we have to manipulate
and to elevate to the ideal.   In such sciences the material we
have to deal with is the actual legal and political relations
of the nation in connection with the whole character of the

people and their historical position. In all such cases, therefore, our attempts to realise the ideal must be conditioned by the position and character of the people as determined by their historical antecedents. So far as practical, these ideals are dependent on the actual state of affairs, but in their nature as ideals they pass above and beyond it. Hence arises the question as to the manner of their formation and the possible functions of the historical method in this reference as well as in the former.

Again, in psychology and in morals the same question meets us, and here in an even more fundamental form, applying to the bases of the sciences not merely to their further limits. Anthropology may show us how the present mental and moral condition of men is the result of an historical evolution. But are not cognitive categories, however crudely held and ill-applied, presupposed in the germinal knowledge of man? are not ethical ideals, however indistinctly conceived and blindly followed, implied in the rudimentary moral activity of the lowest races? The question thus comes to be whether the historical method which exhibits the development of knowledge and morality can also account for their existence. Does the process history presents us with itself afford sufficient explanation of all the facts to be explained? What, in fine, is historical explanation worth when quest is made for the meaning of the whole of things?

The most attractive thing about historical realism is that it is a unity, an organic system. The ordinary scientific but unhistorical realism of an earlier date was without any such bond of unity. It conjured indeed with the term experience, but only with the term; experience itself was for it a mere haphazard external somewhat, standing in no necessary relation to consciousness. For knowledge, for morality, for æsthetic and religious ideals, we were referred to experience : they arose there; it accounted for them; each individual, coming in contact with nearly the same set of external circumstances, received much the same kind of mental filling-in in the way of knowledge, morality, &c. But in this way the different parts of his experience were only externally connected with one another, *his* experience only arbitrarily connected with that of other individuals. The historical method has brought unity and life into these *dis-*

I

jecta membra. The principle of hereditary transmission has enabled it to connect the experience of each individual man, as an organic part, with that of the race. And when experience is thus no longer broken with every individual, but maintains its continuity through an indefinitely long period of time, we are able to see how its different parts are not the mere chance associates of a complex aggregate, but members of an organised system in which there is no part but is connected with the whole, and through the whole with every other part.

Realism has thus become pre-eminently a *system*, in which an attempt is made to explain the totality of things, and to explain them by the same method of historical evolution, beginning with the simplest elements and working upwards to the most complex results. The physical, the chemical, the organic, the sensitive, and the self-conscious are thus regarded as so many stages in the development of the universe, in which there is no absolute break between the different members, and in which—if the theory is to be fully made out—each member gives birth to, and, along with surrounding modifying circumstances, contains in itself an explanation of that which succeeds it. As we pass from one division to another we are indeed obliged to make use of different and additional categories for the explanation of our facts. But from the standpoint of historical realism it must be held that, although we rise from the categories of quantity and quality with simple causal connection, or at most reciprocity, to design and life, and from life which is merely sensitive and animal, to that which is conscious of itself, yet each step of the process originates in and arises from what precedes, and we are never guilty of leaping from *terra firma* into the empty air of speculation. If the speculative school begin with self-consciousness which they hold to account for all the categories, but to be itself accounted for by none, the historical school look upon it as but the latest and most complex product of time. Their chief working category is that of causality, and all the others are explained as but more complex and closely interwoven cases of the causal connection. They perhaps concede that, in our present limited knowledge, there is still a hiatus in experience between the inanimate and the living, and again between the merely animate and the self-conscious. But the contention is that we can bring the two sides so close together as to see that the gulf is not impassable, and that it only needs proper material and a link of connection to enable us to throw a bridge across. The category of design, for example, has been thought to be explained without the assistance of conscious or intelligent purpose, simply by the organisms whose undesigned modifications make them the fittest to live, surviving in the struggle for existence, and transmitting to descendants the qualities which enabled them to wage successful war against the hostile forces in nature. In a similar way it is contended that even self-consciousness may be an historical result of the unconscious. And just as the reduction of the category of design to that of causality is no reason why we should not make use of the former in science (remembering always that it is not an ultimate category), so self-consciousness itself—no longer regarded as the source of the categories—will have its place in the systematic theory of things, but for its ultimate explanation must be traced to its historical source in the unconscious.

The point of greatest difficulty for this theory is the passage from the unconscious to consciousness. For even the theory of historical evolution—superior as it is in unity of conception and in philosophic breadth to any other realistic theory—ignores the very question with which philosophy begins, the nature of knowledge. So long as it remains on purely objective ground the value of historical realism must be tested by the ordinary scientific canons. It is only a science, though a science of the most generalised kind. But when it attempts to make the transition from the object known to the knowing subject, it forgets the obvious fact that this subject of knowledge has been all along assumed, and that it can be no longer safely ignored now that it is being turned from objects back upon itself. At this point, at any rate, the question must be raised as to what is implied by the subject having knowledge, and a transition must therefore be made from objective science to the theory of knowledge. So long as we kept to the sciences it was not necessary to refer to this fact of knowledge, for the sciences do not profess to justify their own existence. But the explanations of philosophy are only philosophical explanations in so far as they are ultimate; and it therefore belongs to philosophy to inquire into the nature and conditions of that knowledge which all particular sciences assume.

It thus becomes evident that to identify this question with some special point of psychological or moral analysis is to mistake its central meaning. The question is not, for example, the same as, however closely it may be connected with, the question whether perceptions of space and time can be shown to have grown up in the human mind through the accumulated experiences of many ages, or whether sympathetic feelings and moral ideas can be shown to have their roots in early social institutions. The question is much wider and more fundamental than these, for it involves the justification not of any special doctrines merely but of a point of view. The fact that Kant's analysis of space and time was placed at the opening of his great work has led to the critical importance of that analysis being greatly over-estimated, and the central point of the ' Critique '—the necessity of a reference to self-consciousness for all knowledge—being sometimes overlooked. The arguments by which Kant supported his view of space and time are entirely of a special kind, and their sufficiency and correctness have little or no bearing on the rest of his theory. What it was essential for him to show, and what he really showed, was that experience implied the conceptions which it was made to account for by the individualistic empiricists of his day, and which it is now made to account for by the historical realists of our day. His contention was that thought or self-consciousness makes experience, not experience thought, whether the experience referred to be limited to the brief span of an individual life or extended to the indefinite duration of the race. In short, the detailed analysis of space and time given in the 'Transcendental Æsthetic,' is only an outwork of the system. What is fundamental in the discussion is the doctrine that these perceptions are not generated by unrelated feelings but require a mental construction, and can only be unified through the synthetic action of the self-conscious subject. Kant himself no doubt laid greater stress on his special arguments than he would have done had the ' Æsthetic ' been written after instead of before the ' Analytic.' And it is thus not to be wondered at that the analysis of space with which Mr. Spencer, on the basis of the modern evolutionist philosophy, attempts to supersede the Kantian analysis, should be put forward by him as an integral part of a theory which tries to account by a natural process of development for knowledge and the self-consciousness which Kant regards as its supreme condition. Mr. Spencer's discussion of the subject is also one of the best examples of the method of accounting for knowledge by showing its genesis. And as it is further a typical case of the application of historical treatment to a question connected both with the theory of knowledge and with the analysis of mental states, it may repay a fuller consideration. Mr. Spencer has, of course, this advantage over Kant's earlier opponents, that he has an unlimited time at his command in which the results of individual experience can be consolidated and transmitted. But however long a period of time may be granted him, however many generations the evolution of the nervous structure may have occupied, the difficulty of passing from the perception of that which for the perceiving subject is non-spatial to that which is for it spatial must still be met at some point or other. Even granting a sufficiently developed nervous structure, the perception of space implies the reference to things outside one of the sensations to which this structure is organic, and the crucial difficulty—the conversion of the non-spatial into the spatial—is only apparently surmounted in an analysis which presupposes that the distinction between various parts of our organism is already a distinction for the percipient subject before there is any spatial perception, and then evolves the perception of space from the consciousness of this distinction. Yet it is evident as soon as stated that, so far from originating the perception of space, this known distinction of organic parts really presupposes it.[1] This difficulty seems to be obscured rather than overcome by Mr. Spencer's method of treatment, in which the perception of (extended) matter is discussed before that of space or extension, while the admission is made that, on his theory, the perception of space implies that of motion—a perception left to be explained subsequently,[2] but afterwards found to be not what we ordinarily call the perception of motion, but simply the 'muscular sensations'[3] which are said to accom-

---

[1] Cf. *Principles of Psychology*, 3rd ed., §§ 327, 239 ; vol. ii. p. 168 ff. ; vol. i. p. 549.

[2] *Principles of Psychology*, II. 176.
[3] *Ibid.* II. 218.

pany (the objective fact of) motion, and from which the (subjective) perception of motion is said to be built up. The perception of space on the evolution-theory is thus reduced to the same terms as in individualistic psychology : a series of touches concomitant with a series of muscular feelings, and recognised as similar to a number of simultaneous touches.[1] The resultant association of the series of muscular feelings with these simultaneous feelings of touch is thus made to constitute our germinal perception both of space and motion. By speaking of these simultaneous sensations of touch as ' a series of co-existent positions,' the genesis of the perception of space appears easy enough. But when we keep them strictly to what they are—a number of sensations which require to be successively attended to in order to be brought into distinct consciousness—and then associate them simply with another series of sensations which physiology has since taught us to call muscular, the transition to the spatial still remains to be made. Once given his ' notion of relative position' in space, Mr. Spencer's evolution-theory enables him to show how the definite conception of space as we now have it has been built up by the experiences of previous individuals being handed down in the form of modified structure to their descendants ; but it has not in any way solved the difficulty of showing how sensations which *ex hypothesi* are not in space can yield the spatial perception.

It is on this account that Lotze's hypothesis of ' local signs' as the original elements of the space-perception has been admitted with such great unanimity by recent scientific psychologists. The adoption of this hypothesis does not indeed necessarily imply an acceptance of the Kantian view that space is an innate form of intuition, but it is an acknowledgment that it cannot be built up merely from passive

---

[1] *Pyschology*, II. 224: 'What it now concerns us to notice is this:— *that as the series of tactual feelings A to Z, known as having sequent positions in consciousness, is found to be equivalent to the accompanying series of muscular feelings; and as it is also found to be equivalent to the simultaneous tactual feelings A to Z, which are presented in co-existent positions; it follows that these two last are found to be equivalents to each other.'* I cannot help thinking that the phraseology of this important passage is misleading. 'Position,' Mr. Spencer would admit, is either in space or time. If, then, the ' co-existent positions' in which the ' simultaneous tactual feelings' are presented, are spatial positions, the presentation of space is already there, and does not need to be got at by any combination of ' equivalent' feelings, or series of feelings. If, on the other hand, the ' co-existent positions' in which the ' simultaneous tactual feelings' are presented, are positions in time, the statement simply means that the simultaneous feelings are—simultaneous.

and muscular sensations, but necessitates a further condition. This condition is the assumption of an element of distinction between the sensations coming from different sensory circles of the skin, or different fibres of the retina— an element which prevents the coalescence of the qualitatively similar sensations originating at different quarters, and is thus in germ that out-of-one-another-ness which we call space. According to Lotze himself, this condition would be inoperative did there not first of all exist in the mind an original and innate *tendency* to form the perception of space.[1] But even those investigators who do not admit this innate mental tendency, have adopted his suggestion of local signs as the element which gives distinction to sensations qualitatively alike; so that modern scientific psychology, if no longer content with Kant's analysis of the spatial perception, is yet far from endorsing the derivative view he was opposing. It must be allowed to psychology to analyse, so far as analysable, the perception of space, like any other mental state. But historical psychology has been no more successful than individualistic psychology was in resolving this perception into elements of mere tactual and muscular feeling. For the germinal perception from which our present complex perception is built up is found to have already implied a differentiation of sensational elements which are not qualitatively distinguishable. How this germinal perception has been worked up into the various forms in which it now appears can be traced by the evolution-theory in a way which the older psychology could not rival. But the extended time which that theory puts at our disposal does not make it any the easier to pass from mere sensation to the perception of spatial distinction.

The failure of the empirical analysis of space, even when aided by the doctrine of heredity, is due to no mere temporary defect of psychological analysis, but to its attempting the impossible feat of getting out of unrelated sensations a relation which mere sensation could never generate, since it implies the distinguishing and relating function of the conscious subject. The so-called historical basis of ethics is open to a similar objection. The theory which traces the growth of the moral feelings and the widening of moral ideals has still left undiscussed the conditions of moral

[1] *Grundzüge der Psychologie*, p. 30.

action, has given no solution of the question, What is implied in that identification of self with an end or course of action, on which morality is based? No competent inquirer is likely to deny nowadays that moral ends and the feelings accompanying moral action have differed in different races and participated in the general development of mankind. And in drawing attention to the share morality has had in this development, the historical school has undoubtedly done good service. But we go beyond our record when we assert that moral action has been developed out of merely natural action. The action to which alone moral value can be ascribed is that which is consciously determined, in which an end is seen and pursued. Morality is thus, we may almost say, a kind of knowledge, or rather both knowledge and morality are kinds of consciousness. In this respect, as well as in its more obvious meaning, Spinoza's doctrine of the equivalence of action and intellectual cognition [1] holds true: we act only so far as we know; otherwise the action is not really ours. If knowledge implies an activity of the subject in receiving and relating the data of sense, so does conscious action imply a distinction and selection of the end pursued. Hence, the first point which a complete evolution-ethics has to explain seems to have been practically overlooked; no account has been given by this theory of the distinction between merely natural actions and those which as self-determined can have moral predicates ascribed to them.

It lies with the historical method alone to trace the growth of altruistic and other moral feelings, and to exhibit the development of ethical ends in connection with that of social and political institutions. But there are two questions which it fails to touch, or at any rate to decide. The first of these is the point just mentioned, the differentiation of moral or consciously determined action from that which is merely natural or determined by conditions independent of consciousness. This may be called the fundamental question of ethics. And as the historical method has failed to touch it, so neither in the second place has it shown its competency to decide what may be called the final question of ethics, to decide, namely, between various ethical ends, and to determine that which 'ought' to be followed. It is one thing to trace the modifications which

---

[1] *Eth.* iv. 24: 'Nos eatenus tantummodo agimus, quatenus intelligimus.'

moral ideals have undergone, and the results in conduct of these various modifications; it is quite another thing to pass from this merely historical ground of what has been, and to set up an ideal for present action and future striving.

We are thus brought back in ethics to the point where the historical method of jurisprudence left us in uncertainty. How do we form the ideals which regulate scientific progress or govern practical conduct? To this question, there would seem to be two imperfect answers. According to one of these the ideals are presented to us in history and fact, and we have neither need nor right to go beyond experience in framing them. It is some such answer as this, I think, that is given by those who hold that the historical method is able to decide what have been called the final philosophical questions into which we are led. But it is a matter of no little difficulty to give an exact statement of this view, chiefly because, so far as I am aware, those who seem to adopt it as a consequence of the historical method have never fully worked it out or even defined it with sufficient clearness. It is only when the claim thus made for the historical method shall have been put forward with greater precision and supported by appropriate argument, that it will be possible fully to estimate its value. At present it is hard to tell whether it is meant (a) that the historical evolution of outward circumstances and institutions contains in itself a sufficient explanation of all theories as to the end of conduct, or (b) that the development of opinion is such that each successive view is determined and fully accounted for by those which preceded it, or (c) simply that we must be guided by history and fact in the formation of our ideals. The first view seems to be a moderate expression of the opinion not seldom met with, that we had better give up altogether the inquiry after an 'ought,' and rest contented with the 'is' and the 'was.' But this is merely cutting the Gordian knot the historical method itself has tied. The test of this method as the final method of philosophy is its competency to determine ends or ideals, and for solution of the question we are told that ends cannot be determined. This answer can, however, only be taken as a frank acknowledgment of the limits of the historical method, hardly as a proof that what it does not extend to is therefore unattainable by any other means. Rather, having already seen that this method implies conditions which it cannot itself account for, we need not be surprised at its leading up to questions that lie beyond it, though they do not lie outside the field of consciousness. To say (a) that opinion follows external circumstances, is to make an assertion founded only on the broad correspondence existing between the two, a correspondence which may be equally well or better accounted for by the supposition, not that one is cause alone, and the other effect alone, but that their mutual action has a tendency to bring one into harmony with the other : so far as experience goes it shows us opinions modifying circumstances as often as modified by them. Again, the assertion (b) that each new opinion follows from those which preceded it either leaves no room for the mutual influence of opinion and outward customs or institutions, or, if it does admit both factors, neither of them altogether independent of, and neither of them altogether dependent upon, the other, this is an admission that the mental element in the evolution both modifies and is modified by its surroundings. It may of course be said that it is just this interaction of organism and environment which the historical method has commonly to trace in natural science. But the difference is that our internal factor here is not an organism like a plant or an animal, but self-consciousness and the mental states which follow from or depend upon it. And if, as in a previous part of this paper I have attempted to show, self-consciousness stands apart from historical evolution, and can only be evolved from it when it has been already assumed in it, it follows that the ideals we form are in part at least dependent on a source which stands above the merely temporal succession traced by the historical method. It is indeed still possible for us to assert (c) that history and fact must be our guides in the formation of these ideals, but supposing this proved, it only shows that their material content must be got from external events and institutions, while the various elements composing this content will still be selected and unified under the guidance of an idea supplied by the self-conscious subject. It is the use of these regulative ideas which makes it possible for the scientific imagination to frame conceptions which pass beyond actual experience.

The other theory referred to as imperfect recognises, but in a one-sided way, the truth that the formation of these ideals passes beyond actual events, though not beyond the range of consciousness. According to this theory our ideals are formed independently of facts or experience, and the aim of morality, of politics, and of law is said to be the realisation of some such abstract principle as that of equality, justice, liberty, or it may be happiness. It was as a protest against this abstract way of looking at practical ideals that the historical method came into prominence, and by a natural revulsion tended to ally itself with a one-sided empiricism. Ideals of this sort, separated from experience, and often unconnected with the spirit of the time, have more frequently hindered progress than furthered it. As Bluntschli justly remarks,[1] 'Napoleon was not far wrong when he said "the metaphysicians, the ideologists, have ruined France." For the "ideological" conception of liberty and equality left the land in ruins and drenched it with blood. So, too, the *doctrinaire* elaboration of the monarchical principle repressed political freedom in Germany and impeded the development of its power, while the abstract principle of nationality has been so applied as to endanger the peace of Europe. The truest and most fruitful ideas become pernicious when "ideologically" conceived and developed with narrow fanaticism.'

Both the empirical and abstract theories just mentioned may be said to be true in what they affirm, false in what they deny. The former theory is right in so far as it asserts that all our ideals to be fruitful must be founded on experience or history. The end we seek must in all cases be, as Aristotle says in his 'Ethics,' ἀνθρώπινον, a human end, and built on the foundations already laid. In ethics the first duty which lies before the individual is to fill his place as, and to perform the ordinary functions of, a member of the family, of the community, and of the State, and any ideal which conflicts with this is in so far discredited. In politics the first aim is to conserve the constitution of the State and to regulate international relations with respect to its historical place and action, while in legislation regard is had to the continuity of established custom, and each proposed change is jealously weighed. But if we are to pass beyond the duty of the good neighbour and honest citizen to higher and more comprehensive ends, if the State is to develop and laws to be improved, we need to pass beyond

[1] *Lehre vom modernen Stat*, I. 6, 5th ed. (1875).

history.   Only through the ideal of a condition better
than the present, and still remaining to be realised, have
previous improvements been made or is further progress
possible.   On the one hand, therefore, from the historical
side, we must guard against an ideal unsuitable to present
circumstances, while on the other hand, the reason that
'looks before and after' passes on towards a unity of
knowledge and a perfection of practical ends which experience cannot yield.   How these ideals of science and life
are formed is a question for philosophy itself, not for
methodology.   The materials of the ideal may themselves
be traceable to experience, but they are formed anew by the
reflective reason.   Thus the conception of humanity as the
end of conduct which forms the high ideal of the positivist
philosophy is one which could never have been reached on
the merely positivist or historical ground.   For it sets up as
the moral end a conception which passes far beyond actual
experience, which looks upon that which is past as part of a
whole along with what has as yet no actual existence.   It is
only a metaphysical theory which, by virtue of its function
of examining the conditions of knowledge and action
wherever found, can thus pass both beyond the individual
and beyond the race as a mere part of experience.   It is
true, as Comte remarks,[1] that the science of the individual
cannot advance to this conception ; and if the science of the
individual can be metaphysical, as Comte supposes, this
individualistic metaphysic is under the same limitation.
But it is only on account of the unity of conception—itself not
a product of experience—which underlies Comte's historical
method, that even the science of the race can attain to it.
Metaphysics, which necessarily transcends the individual in
considering the conditions essential to thought and action,
is thus able to reach an ideal for knowledge and conduct.
It is true, indeed, that in all the practical sciences—in
morals, law, and politics—ends of conduct may be conceived
and followed which do not rise above empirical ground.
But these ideals, through their own limitation, carry in
themselves a reference to higher ideals.   And it is to the

[1] *Positive Philosophy*, II. 509. When
Mr. Stephen (*The Science of Ethics*,
p. 453) asserts that the metaphysician
cannot reach the 'ought,' he seems to
be looking upon metaphysics as an
abstract science without necessary relation to experience. Only as such is
the metaphysic of morals what he calls
it, ' a transfigured bit of logic.'

presence and power in human life of these higher ideals—not yielded by experience itself, since they imply a principle of the harmony and tendency of experience—that progress is to be ascribed.

The examination of the historical method has thus led to the conclusion that its applicability, however wide, is necessarily limited. It implies categories of which it can only trace the historical manifestation, leaving the investigation of their logical position and nature to the theory of knowledge or to the theory of action; and it leads up to problems which pass out of the range of the chronological sequence to which it is restricted. Yet, between these two limits, its application extends to the whole field of development in time. The result thus arrived at by analysing the nature of the historical method might also be confirmed from another point of view. The logical and ethical postulates with which the theory of knowledge and the theory of morality have to do find their realisation in an experience which is in time, and our metaphysics thus needs to be supplemented by an account of the historical process through which these conceptions have been manifested in the human mind and in society. But this speculative justification of the historical method does not seem to be called for now. It would almost appear an impertinence to vindicate a place in philosophy for a line of study which has won its own position by its positive achievements: it seems sufficient at present to have restricted attention to the method itself, showing the range of questions to which it is appropriate, and the limits beyond which it ceases to be of any avail.

W. R. SORLEY.

V.

THE RATIONALITY OF HISTORY.

IN ARISTOTLE we find the first attempts at a history of
philosophy as an essential part of a philosophical system;
and in him, too, we find some faint recognition of a philosophy of history. He gives a historical, instead of a merely
logical, account of the origin of political society;[1] and he
seeks to show the inner necessity of the actual order in which
the constitutions of Greece succeeded each other.[2] But here,
as in many things, the wide domain claimed by Aristotle was
left unoccupied until after Kant. In the intervening period,
such ideas as there are about the philosophy of history must
be sought (apart from the isolated speculations of Vico[3])
among theologians, poets, and in general literature, rather
than among the philosophers. It is the great merit of
Hegel—a merit which even those who most disagree with
his dialectic cannot dispute—that he has attempted to regain
for philosophy the whole province of the work of spirit, and
that, above all, he has occupied himself with history in every
department. And if philosophy is to be taken seriously as
an effort to explain the world of thought, nature and man,
it must not shrink from the interpretation of the facts of
history.

While a philosophy of history is necessary if philosophy
is to be adequate to its task, it is equally necessary if history
is to attain its end. The student of history, if his interest
in his subject is anything more than the curiosity of the
antiquarian, the zeal of the polemical critic, or the enthu-

---

[1] *Pol.* I. 2.
[2] *Pol.* III. 15, §§ 11-13.
[3] 'Pendant que la foule suivait ou
combattait la réforme cartésienne, un
génie solitaire fondait la philosophie de
l'histoire. N'accusons pas l'indifférence
des contemporains de Vico; essayons

plutôt de l'expliquer, et de montrer que
la *Science nouvelle* n'a été si négligée
pendant le dernier siècle, que parce
qu'elle s'adressait au nôtre.'—Jules Michelet, *Discours sur le système et la vie de
Vico.*

siasm of the rhetorician, is always struggling to win from the particular details of past events some new help for the better understanding of a nation or a period as a whole. Thus, a true historian of Rome should not merely be occupied in fixing the dates of the Agrarian laws or determining the procedure in the senate, nor in overthrowing this or that hypothesis of Niebuhr or this or that assertion of Mommsen, nor in giving picturesque descriptions of battles or elegant reflections on the decay of morals—as if any of these things, by and for themselves, were his real object: he should always be seeking to grasp better, and put in clearer light, what was the spirit of the Roman people—the same in all its different manifestations, in internal struggles, in conquest, in legislation, and what is its significance for the whole human race. Of course, as a scientific inquirer, the historian has primarily to do with particular facts. Ulterior aims should not interfere with his care and impartiality in getting at these; but, at the same time, these facts can never be in themselves an end. What the good historian does for a particular period is to arrive at the meaning, or underlying principle, or 'idea,' of that period. Suppose that could be done for *all* history, we should have a philosophy of history, or at least a certain proof that a philosophy of history was impossible; for the philosophy of history seeks to discover the 'ideas' of different periods in their relation to one another.

The philosophy of history can hardly be regarded as identical with universal history. While the philosopher does something less than discover the facts, he must do something more than epitomise them. History is a science. Some ancient writers seem to have regarded it as a branch of rhetoric, aiming rather at flattering national vanity than at the discovery of truth. Even if we feel that history is more a department of literature than chemistry, we yet regard the scientific interest, the desire for truth, as the most essential. Again, history is a science of the higher type. It has not merely to collect and classify phenomena, but to explain them by their causes. The historian is more than the chronicler or annalist. In the great historian must be united the capacity and industry of research, the disciplined imagination, which will lead him to see events in their connection, and the literary ability of presenting them correctly and vividly to the reader.　The absence of any of these qualifications detracts from the merits of a historian. Beyond all these we demand some appreciation of the deeper significance of the time and events with which he is occupied, in their bearing on the history of mankind as a whole —*i.e.* the greatest historian must also be something of a philosopher.　But this is a demand which, though raised by history as a science, is yet a demand for something more than a science, as such, can satisfy.　The philosophy of history is thus distinct from history as a science.　The philosophy of history would be included in an ideal universal history; but it is less and more than what we ordinarily mean by history.

Again, though covering to a great extent the same ground, it is not to be identified with a so-called ' science of history' or ' sociology,' which, from a collection and comparison of particular facts, draws generalisations as to the course of human events, and the test of whose perfection would be the power of foretelling political and social changes—a sort of human weather-wisdom.　Whether or how far such a science is possible is not our present question. Whether possible or not, it would not be a philosophy of history, which attempts less and more.　For (1) philosophy should make no pretence at prophecy.　It is concerned, properly, with what is or has been, not with what will be or may be.　At the same time it must not be denied that the desire to read the future in the light of a true understanding of the past is irrepressible and not unjustifiable and not wholly irrelevant to the philosophy of history.　(2) The philosophy of history is not an inductive science.　It is an attempt to construe the phenomena of history *à priori*. The phrase need not cause alarm or derision.　*À priori* is, perhaps, an unfortunate expression, because it suggests primarily an idea of time; but it is so much sanctioned by use that it can hardly be avoided.　The philosopher can make no pretence to know the Egyptian dynasties without studying the hieroglyphics, or the writers who have studied the hieroglyphics, nor to understand the early history of Rome better than Niebuhr or Mommsen.　He must accept the facts as reported by the best authorities available.　They are the ' matter' with which he has to deal.　His business is to interpret them in terms of thought—*i.e.* to show their rationality, their significance as part of that one great process which he as a philosopher, along with most unsophisticated persons, *assumes* history to be. For he who attempts to interpret anything assumes that it has a meaning.

An illustration will perhaps make clear what is here meant by 'philosophical interpretation,' as distinguished from 'scientific explanation.'[1] Suppose it is said, as it constantly is, that the French Revolution is the outcome of the Protestant Reformation of the sixteenth century, this assertion, if understood as implying that the Protestant Reformation was the *cause* of the Revolution, may justly be combated by the historian. It might very well be said that the Revolution was in great part due to the failure of the Reformation in France. The presence of a strong Protestant element would have supplied a liberal, and yet conservative, opposition to royal despotism, and a check on the corruptions of the Church. But though the statement may not be true as an expression of a fact of causation (as that is understood in inductive science), it may very well be true as meaning that the principles (of private judgment, individual freedom, &c.) involved in the Protestant position were carried out to their logical (*i.e.* abstractly logical, and therefore, in great part, practically illogical) result in the Revolution.

Using Aristotelian phraseology, we may say that the scientific historian and the sociologist are occupied with the *material* and *efficient* causes of events and institutions, while the philosopher or philosophic historian is occupied with their *formal* and *final* causes—*i.e.* with the spirit and meaning of them, as shown by the end to which they are tending. The philosophy of history implies a teleological view of phenomena. Thus the philosophic way of regarding history is more akin to the religious and artistic than to the scien-

---

[1] Of course it must be noted that we are here using 'scientific' in a narrow sense, which many scientific historians, and these the very best, would be the first to repudiate. The truly scientific spirit never does narrow itself to that abstract view of causality to which the inductive logician seeks to bind it down. True science, and therefore true history is always striving to become philosophic, *i.e.* to escape the abstract formalism of the logical understanding.

It is to be regretted that Professor Flint, in his very learned book on the history of *the Philosophy of History*, has made no distinction between 'scientific history,' 'science of history,' 'philosophy of history.' It is true that the first writer on the philosophy of history called it, 'scienza nuova.' But science and philosophy have distinct meanings by which it is best to abide.

tific (in the narrower sense). The pious mind believes that
God is causing all things to work together for His own
glory and is bringing good out of evil. 'Surely the wrath
of man shall praise Thee.' The poetic soul sees in the tur-
moil of the passions and struggles of mankind, in the rise
and fall of dynasties and empires, the elements of a Divine
poem—a great tragedy with plot and purpose. And in
gloomy periods the cynic or satirist, using a sort of Satanic
teleology, can find a tragic-comedy in the 'ups and
downs' of the world, and can mark with Tacitus the 'ludibria
rerum humanarum.'

If the scientific historian is right in occasionally ignoring
final causes in order to avoid prejudgment in his researches,
neither the ordinary man who thoughtfully considers public
events nor the statesman who helps to make them believes
that history moves without a purpose, or that that purpose
is wholly unknowable by man. Their belief, which is already
a sort of half-conscious and unformulated philosophy of
history, is generally a religious or quasi-religious faith in
Providence or Destiny. The conclusion that 'all is vanity'
implies more reflection than the unsophisticated, practical
man can exert himself to undertake, and is only a passing
phase of educated thought. The healthy spirit works not
only or always for the satisfaction of immediate personal
wants, but also for the future, at least of his kindred, his
nation, perhaps of the human race. This implies some
belief in a system underlying events. Cæsar's trust in his
'fortunes,' Cromwell's 'Providence,' and Napoleon's 'destiny,' were not merely subtle forms of self-conceit, but implied their recognition of a plan of which they were counted
worthy to be the instruments. If even the private citizen
has his views about the course of events and the mission of
his country, to the statesman or public man it is a duty to
have such views and to see that they are right. The man
or nation who misunderstands or ignores the 'spirit of the
age' must pay the penalty of blindness. Charles X., sup-
pressing the freedom of the press, has been aptly compared
to the peasant who put his hat on the source of the Danube,
saying, 'Won't the people at Vienna be astonished!' If
Metternich were living now he would have to admit that
Italy is something more than 'a geographical expression.'
Diplomatists nowadays can hardly deal with the feeling of

nationality as did those who framed the Holy Alliance. Surely most statesmen believe that some age is to reap fruit from their labours. The only consistent political pessimists are the defenders of despotism or anarchy.

'Final causes,' like ' à priori,' has an alarming sound ; it suggests those bugbears, the Schoolmen ; and 'teleology' is apt to remind us of Paley's Almighty watchmaker. But, if we are philosophers, a word should not frighten us, even were it as badly made as 'Sociology.' Mr. H. Spencer says, 'We must interpret the more developed by the less developed.'[1] This is quite true ; but it is at least equally true that we interpret the less developed by the more developed. We explain a thing not only by its origin, but by its end. To understand what anything really is, we must look at it in the completest and most perfect form of it that we can find. The ceremonial usages of early times will not explain adequately the political constitution of a civilised nation ; nor will the marriage customs (euphemistically and proleptically so called) of primitive man account satisfactorily for its social structure. Rather these remote ages and rude manners only have their value for the scientific investigator because he looks at them in the light of what they come to be. No anthropophagist savage is himself an anthropologist savant. The later and more complete is latent in the earlier and ruder form, and grows out of it ; but it is latent and is only seen in the light of what it, as yet, is not. We only understand the egg by thinking of the chicken. But this is no external and artificial teleology, such as would explain eggs by omelettes.

All the elements do not make the real thing. The biographer examines the descent, education and surroundings of a man of genius ; yet the genius with its originality remains—the man himself, who can only be known by what he did. Similarly we may analyse Greek civilisation into its materials, Phœnician, Egyptian, Phrygian, Lydian, &c. : yet how different do all become when mastered by the Greek spirit ! *That* we can only understand by looking at its own work. So, again, if Christianity be explained as the result of the meeting of the Hebrew with the Greek spirit in the ' medium' of the Roman Empire, such a formula, even if complete (which it is not) as an expression of the elements

[1] *Data of Ethics*, p. 7.

in the *origin* of Christianity would still be quite inadequate philosophically; because it says nothing of what Christianity in itself *is*, *i.e.*, what it is in its perfection, in its end.

The true meaning of historical actions must be sought to a great extent in their issues, not merely in their antecedents, the motives of their doers. By the philosopher, therefore, who should see things in their totality, the nature of events must be looked at as determined by and revealed in their ends. Of course this does not mean that he should confuse motives with results—a very common fallacy of historians, but that he must look at events as having a farther meaning than could be seen, except very faintly and dimly, by those who were partakers in them. But this implies that he must regard events as parts of a plan which is manifested in them —that history is the work of reason. The philosophy of history is not a method of getting miraculous glimpses into the future, nor does it profess to disclose the past to those who are too lazy to undergo the trouble of historical research. It is rather an attempt to read the plan of Providence, to unravel the plot of the great drama that is played throughout the centuries.

But is such an attempt possible? That there are real difficulties it would be absurd to deny; but it is equally absurd to imagine difficulties which do not exist.

It is said, in the first place, that such an attempt is presumption. This objection is made equally by those who wish to defend theology, and those who wish to defend science against what they regard as the dangerous encroachments of metaphysics. 'God's ways are not as our ways, nor his thoughts as our thoughts.' 'Our human reason is not capable of comprehending the plan of the universe.' 'If history has a meaning at all it can be known only to God. *We* can only see the acts of individuals.'

Now, of course the limitation of time—the fact that we can only know a small part of the world's history—that we do not know the beginning of the play very well, and cannot see it out to the last act—is a very real limitation. The objection as coming from those who try to reject alike theology and metaphysics, is intelligible enough, whatever we may think of its validity; and to the Agnostic we can only answer by making good our profession of knowledge, and showing that his no-metaphysics is only a bad meta-physics after all. But one would like to ask those who are always pointing out the difference between human and Divine intelligence, whether they think they exalt the Divine nature by undervaluing what they regard as likest to it, and what they mean by repeating that 'God made man in his own image,' and by calling the guidance of Providence 'wise' and 'good'? If a person professed to believe in a perfectly irrational Deity, then he might be justified in deny-ing that anything of the plan of history could be intelligible to reason. It is possible for the professed believer in an intelligent Deity to deny that a *complete* solution of the mystery of human toil and suffering can be found in this world (however the antithesis of this world and the other be explained), but not to deny that there is *any* revelation of God in history. That would be giving over the earth to the rule of unreason, it would be making the Prince of Darkness Prince of this World—a creed not quite un-known to mankind, but which, if really believed, and not merely professed, is a creed of political and social despair. It might befit a Stoic Republican of the Roman Empire or a hermit of the Thebaid, but is not worthy of any good citizen of a free country. But, if it is once admitted that the world is governed by reason, it must be admitted that that rational government must be intelligible to reason : else the talk of rational government is a mere phrase, and might as well mean irrational government. An intelligent Providence can hardly be an unintelligible Providence.

In any case we are not here concerned with the general question 'Is philosophy at all possible?' but, assuming that philosophy is to some extent possible, we have to ask, 'How far is it able to construe the phenomena of history?'

Leaving the strange objection that history is unin-telligible because its plan is Divine, let us consider the converse objection that it is unintelligible because its phenomena are human. 'The sphere of history,' it is said, 'is the sphere of human freedom, and is therefore not subject to general laws such as govern nature. Historical events are always in the last resort determined by the volitions of this or that individual, and to try to reduce them to general laws or to find for them a universal formula is to ignore alike the freedom and the individual diversity of mankind.' This is an objection made against a science of history as well as against a philosophy of history. The answer given by the empirical psychologist is, however, hardly sufficient for an idealist. If—or, rather, so far as—human actions are simply of the same kind with natural phenomena, subject to the same law of cause and effect, they of course admit the same methods of study and can be brought under the same sort of generalisations. The average number of suicides in a country is equally capable of scientific discovery with its average rainfall. But philosophy is not needed to defend the value of statistics. That is obvious enough to the practical man. The absence of individual freedom, in any sense in which it would render impossible general inductions about human conduct, is known to every enterprising shopkeeper. To the philosopher freedom means something other than unaccountable caprice, and individuality something more than unlimited unlikeness.

The antithesis between nature and history is often wrongly stated, as if it were absolute and exclusive. We know from the examples in the elementary books of logic that 'All men are *animals*,' and nobody ever thought of opposing to that proposition even a particular negative, though many persons seem to think it very shocking that the same theories should be applied to man and pigeons. But we are also told that 'Man is a *rational* animal.' Man is a part of nature, but he is not merely a part of nature. He knows that he is such, and therefore he is more than a mere part. He is not either a beast or a god, but a curious complex of the two. It is because and in so far as man is rational that he is free: and in so far as each man acts more under the guidance of reason and less under that of blind, *i.e.* merely natural, impulse, or passion, he is more of a free agent. But freedom in this sense is the very reverse of unintelligible caprice. Now history is man's constant struggle to rise above merely natural influences—to escape the tyranny of nature and make it his friend and servant. And just because history is this struggle towards rational freedom and not occupied with merely natural causes, while it may be less easily studied than nature by the methods of inductive science, it admits better of philosophical explanation.

Individuality therefore and freedom, so far from being

incompatible with national and race (*i.e.* general) development, are only rendered possible by the latter. As civilisation grows and becomes more conscious and more rational, and therefore more capable of being understood as a rational movement, the individual has a better sphere o realising his true freedom than in the ages of merely natural impulse and unintelligent childish caprice. The savage, roaming solitary like a wild beast in search of prey, is more a mere part of nature and less a free individual than the citizen who lives along with others in a complicated political society whose ends are rational and the development of which it is possible to trace.[1]

If we were not allowed to speak of any other unity than the individual, history would resolve itself into a complicated tangle of biographies, and would become impossible to study or to write. It is true that historical events can always in theory be traced to an origin in the volitions of individuals; but these volitions and these individuals can never be understood apart from their antecedents and environment. The individual with his particular volitions cannot indeed be analysed away into the combined influences of nature, race, education, and circumstances, but, apart from these, he is a mere abstraction, about whom we can predicate nothing except negatively—'He is not anybody or anything else.' Individuals live and act in a physical, political, social, and moral environment which determines altogether the occasions and, at least to a great extent, the character of their volitions and actions.

Man is a part of nature, but he is more. The splendid climate of the Mediterranean has had a great deal to do with the character and work of the historical nations of the old world; but climate alone cannot make a civilisation or preserve it. To geographical are often opposed *race*-influences, as if our choice lay between one and the other. Both play their part—sometimes the one more than the other—in determining the character and consequent history

---

[1] If this be understood and carried out in thought, it should serve to explain and reconcile two *dicta* of Hegel's which seem to have caused much trouble. (1) That history is the realisation of freedom. (2) That the object of history is the State. Of course by 'State' is meant not the abstract formula of a paper constitution, but that complex reality (including religion, culture, &c.) which the Greeks meant by πόλις; by 'Freedom' is meant not the negative idea of 'being left alone' but the condition and actuality of highest and fullest development.

of a people. They are the conditions, or, as Aristotle would say, the 'material cause' of a State. But their importance is greater in the less advanced stages of a people's political development: and they alone are not enough to explain a nation. To understand the spirit of a people we must consider most of all their political constitution and their religion: and to understand these we must know their history. We only know what the spirit of a people (or of an individual) *is*, when we know what it *does*.

In estimating the probable, or explaining the past, conduct of an individual, still more of a number of individuals, it is impossible to leave either country (province, town) or race (tribe, family) out of sight. And to these we must add the particular period of time. There is not only a national feeling, but a 'spirit of the age.' The Crusades—that strangest product of the earthly unworldliness of the Middle Ages—could only have happened *when* they did. That there is such a thing as a '*Zeitgeist*,' or 'spirit of the age,' no one will deny. The extent of its influence over individuals may be made matter of dispute; but the controversy will really turn upon what is included in the 'Zeitgeist.' It is possible to recognise its character, at least to some extent. To do so is one of the chief aims of the man who thinks. If we were seeking to sum up the *public* duty of a man (beyond the determinate duties of his position in life) we might do so by saying: 'He must strive in the *first* place to understand the spirit of his age, and in the *second* place to improve it.' The attempt to perform the second duty first leads to much well-meaning mischief. Of course the person who understands is often, unfortunately, for that very reason less capable of acting: and by the very fact of his understanding the spirit of his time, it is clear that he has already got beyond it. The spirit of an age (or of an institution) is healthy in proportion as it trains up those who can see beyond it; for so, and so only, is *progress* possible. No one living at any given time can *fully* understand that time. Only when an event (or person) has become matter of history can it be fully and fairly appreciated. But this limitation does not prevent the clearer heads from seeing the tendencies of their age. Even those who are in the stream and carried with it may have some consciousness of the direction in which they are moving—of the relation in which they are to their contemporaries, to the past, and to the future. We must not think that people are unconscious of everything which they can find no formula to express.

These considerations should serve to refute the objection [1] that we cannot explain history as the development of an idea, unless we can show that people in general are conscious of their stage in that development. (1) We must not limit consciousness by power of expression. (2) We must not suppose an ideal process to be unreal, because not consciously apprehended *at the time.* The effort and struggle, which issue in some great action, first clearly reveal their meaning to the thinker in after ages; but are not therefore without a meaning. In religious phrase, the actors, with their passions and aims, are only 'instruments in the hands of Providence;' and there can be no objection to the phrase, if we avoid the superstition that only the unusual is providential. When some Greeks were defeating Persians at Salamis, and others were defeating Phœnicians in Sicily, these events together were the triumph of European ideas over Eastern. Yet only a few of the Greek leaders appreciated the enormous significance, even to their own country, of resistance to Asia: its significance to the world they, of course, could not comprehend. In the English Rebellion of the seventeenth century, the bulk of the Puritan party only wished to substitute a covenanted king or a theocratic republic for a monarchy of divine right. They wished to be as intolerant of dissent as their antagonists. Only a few, like Milton, understood that they were really fighting the battle of liberty.

But it will be said, 'The great things of history are done by *great men,* and it is generally against the spirit of the age and its tendencies that the hero is struggling.' This is true, but we must not be misled by a phrase. (1) One formula will not express the spirit of an age. The period of the high Renaissance is not to be summed up in the elegant Paganism of Pope Leo X. That was only part of the movement that brought mediæval Europe to an end. If it be said, then, that Luther, as hero of the Reformation, struggled against the spirit of his time—this is only partially true. Other and stronger elements were with him. (2) 'Hero' we can truly

[1] Cf. Lotze, *Mikrokosmus*, III. p. 39, ff.

call him who struggles against his age, and perishing, is
enrolled in the 'noble army of martyrs;' but the great men
of whom history, as distinguished from biography, must
specially take account, are *representative* great men. Sa-
vonarola, Wycliffe, Huss, may be as interesting personages
as Luther, but they were 'before their time,' and it is in
him that the spirit of the age—at least one great element in
it—became incarnate; he is the symbol of a whole movement. We call those who die for a cause its martyrs—
witnesses, that is, for some truth, which, because it is such,
ultimately triumphs. Most sensible people have given up
applying the name (unless in inverted commas) to the unsuccessful champions of lost or evil causes. Charles I. and
Louis XVI. make rather sorry martyrs, now that most
persons have ceased to accept as an article of faith the divine
right of kings to govern badly. Cato, who chose to remain
on the side which the gods had deserted, may move the
admiration of the republican formalist, but, apart from any
judgment on personal character, he is, what Mommsen calls
him, 'a political Don Quixote,' living as much as the Knight
of La Mancha in a dream of a dead world, incompetent to
understand his time, and unable to help it. Of course what
is clear to us, who can look at events in the light of what
came of them, could not be fully seen by the clearest vision
of the actors in them. Our judgment on a historical action
or person is very different from that of a contemporary. It
may be right, and his duty, for an individual, judging by
what he can see, to resist a movement which to him appeared
unjust, and led by wrongdoers, but which has vindicated
itself afterwards at 'the bar of history.' [1]

Far from ignoring the importance of great men, the
philosophy of history might be charged with giving itself
over to a blind and immoral hero-worship, exaggerating
the significance of a few not altogether admirable individuals
and calmly contemplating the sacrifice of the welfare of
mankind to the selfish ambition of a Cæsar or a Napoleon.
But even the ambition of the representative great men of
the world can never be adequately explained by calling it
'selfish;' or, if we call it 'selfish,' we must imply that the
'self' has become to a greater or less extent identified with

[1] 'Die Weltgeschichte ist das Welt-
gericht.'—*Schiller*, in a poem called 'Re-
signation.' Cf. Hegel, *Phil. das Rechts*,
§ 340.

the wishes of many others. One might call both Pericles and Alcibiades ambitious; but the ambition of Alcibiades was merely selfish, whereas that of Pericles was identified with the ambition of the Athenian people.

'World-historical individuals are those in whose aims a general principle lies;' but they are not necessarily conscious of that general principle, or are so only to a slight degree. Cæsar's success meant the welfare of the provinces as opposed to the selfish interests of the senatorial oligarchy; but we should be going beyond the facts of history if we made the result of his conduct its *motive*. His own safety, his private ambition, might be a sufficient motive for his acts. But in these acts there was something more involved.

When Alexander, Cæsar, or Napoleon are called great men it is by no means implied that they are models for ordinary men to imitate. The supposition is really absurd; but it is made by those who are always protesting against the immorality of hero-worship. Looked at from the stand-point of universal history, even the evil passions of great individuals may have a meaning and a worth. That does not imply that they are to be imitated. The judgment we pronounce on the morality of a man is distinct from that which we pronounce on his historical significance. But does not that mean that we apply different moral standards in judging great men and ordinary men? There is a tendency to do so, or, at least, to express our judgment as a judgment by a different *moral* standard, whereas we are really apply-ing not a moral but a historical standard. But is not that to make history immoral, or at least, to remove politics from the sphere of morality? So far it is true that we do make history *non*-moral, and that political questions cannot be judged by the standards of personal morality, partly (1) just because they are political questions and not personal, and partly (2) because, in some respects, political morality must stand in the rear of personal morality. (1) The claims of morality are certainly supreme; but irrelevant moralising produces the most mischievous historical and political judg-ments. Pompey was not therefore preferable to Cæsar as a political leader because he was a respectable family man; he might be considered by his contemporaries a better poli-tician because he was loyal to the constitution; he can hardly be considered such by us, because we see the constitution was dead and Pompey knew it not, or if he knew it, knew not what to do. Charles I. was not therefore a good ruler and Napoleon a bad one, because the one was a good husband and the other not. (2) A higher morality, or at least a higher ideal of morality, is possible to a few individuals in every age than is conceivable or possible in the conduct of public affairs where compromise is unavoidable. Of course, as we said already, historical events may always be traced to volitions of individuals, and therefore, though we say ' good comes out of evil,' this is true only when the phenomena are looked at from outside ; volitions which are merely evil can never issue in good ; the passions of great men, when they bring about good results, are not mere evil passions, and great representative men often embody even in their passions the good ideas and good volitions of many forgotten individuals. Similarly, when it is said that the worst results often follow from the best intentions, it is not from the good in men that the evil comes, but from the defects (e.g., in knowledge, foresight, &c.), that are mixed up with it. People often talk as if a man, even a public character, were sufficiently excused when it is shown that he was mistaken. Modern ethics have been apt to forget the ' intellectual virtues.'

The objection of immorality takes another and wider form. ' If you justify the conduct of individuals or nations by results, is not that to confuse might and right ? ' In a sense it is—and, in a sense, might is right. If individuals or nations are able *permanently* to succeed in influencing the world, we must regard their conduct as justified by their success. To deny this is to deny the rationality of history altogether—to deny that God reveals himself in history. ' If this counsel or work be of God, ye cannot overthrow it.' To convert the proposition is certainly a logical fallacy ; but the permanence and success of any ' counsel or work ' is the test of its divine sanction. When some one indignantly denies that might can ever be right, the might of which he thinks is mere external force. Bayonets can do a great deal in the world ; as Talleyrand observed, ' you can do anything with them, except sit on them ; ' and that is just the important limitation. The might which can turn itself into right must be a spiritual as well as a material force.[1]

[1] Cf. Arist. *Pol.* I. 6, § 3. . . . Τρό- πον τινὰ ἀρετὴ τυγχάνουσα χορηγίας

Alexander's armies overran Asia, but his empire broke into fragments when he died. What really conquered the East was the civilisation that came from Hellas, and especially from the vanquished Athens. Rome's legions defeated the world; but her law ruled it.

With the sad spectacle before us of so many fair civilisations overthrown before rude invaders or perishing through internal strife, of the horrors and crimes which accompany war even when the cause is just, and victory on the side of the higher race, it is, indeed, difficult at all times to hold fast by our faith in the ultimate rationality of history. We are apt to look on the world as the scene of a confused and perhaps picturesque melodrama which may excite the imagination, but can have no deeper significance. For this impression the way in which history used to be presented to us in school-books is in part responsible. Battles and royal persons are supposed to be more interesting to the youthful mind, which is passing through the semi-savage state, and occupy a disproportionate space. The less striking work of constitutional growth and industrial progress falls into the background. Even great original historians are partly to blame for the blood-stained appearance of their pages. The events and persons that strike a contemporary are not always those of the most real importance. Some of us would be glad to exchange even Thucydides's account of the Peloponnesian war for a good description of the political, social, and artistic condition of the Athens of Pericles. After all, battles, and massacres, and assassinations, and court intrigues are only the accidents of a people's life : if they are more, the people's life has hardly begun, or it is already near its close, and it is well for the world that it is so. The order and patient drill which enables an army in the end to conquer, the skill which directs its movements, the enthusiasm which is with it in victory and in defeat, counts for much more than the blowing of trumpets and the clashing of arms. These are only outward signs. The Roman Senate commending its defeated Consul because he had not despaired of the Republic, had more of the force which can make itself real, because it is spiritual, than the victorious army of Hannibal,

καὶ βιάζεσθαι δύναται μάλιστα, καὶ ἔστιν ἀεὶ τὸ κρατοῦν ἐν ὑπεροχῇ ἀγαθοῦ τινός . . .; which we may paraphrase, 'Spiritual excellence, if provided with sufficient external means, is most able to turn itself into force ; and conversely, might always implies a superiority in some good quality.'

aiming only at conquest, and unsupported by his countrymen. Military success is only the symbol of strength in one of the elements in a people's spirit. It is often, indeed, besides religion, the only element in which, in a rude age, the nation can find expression; but the order which military training requires is an essential preparation for a higher political life —it is a prerequisite of freedom. Of course what is only a means may be made an end; what is only a condition regarded as essential. If so, the nation will surely wear out its energies in external struggles, or decay, because its soul is dead. As Aristotle said of the Spartans, 'they could fight, but in peace they rusted.' The Turks could take Constantinople and nearly took Vienna; they cannot govern even themselves.

When the conquests made by civilised nations over barbarous are traced to lust of gain and brutal force, a truth is stated, but it is only a half-truth. It is not right to explain the Spanish conquests in America (it is as well to take a non-British instance), horribly cruel as they were, as the result simply of evil passions. They implied the victory of the more enterprising, the more civilised, the relatively higher race. If the 'better morality' of native races be pointed to, it must be remembered that their morality is on the whole of a lower type. A simpler state of life is free from many of the vices, but is incapable of most of the virtues, of a more highly developed condition. Even the pretext of spreading Christianity must not be regarded in such cases as a mere piece of hypocrisy. Whatever be thought of the Christianity spread, or however inapplicable missionary justifications of murder may be now, it was then a quite honest belief, as in the days of the Crusades, that the Cross should conquer by force or fraud.

The long and wide prevalence of slavery, condemning so great a proportion of mankind to a hopeless and miserable life, corrupting the slave and not less the master, is often brought forward in protest against our pictures of the splendour of the past. But this again is an objection which implies an ignoring of historical perspective. It implies a reading of the moral feelings of a modern citizen of a state which forbids slavery into the mind of the member of a slave-holding community. Slavery was the basis of ancient society. Only on such a basis was Greek and Roman political and social life possible. Slavery mitigated the horrors of ancient warfare, which otherwise would have had no check. In Athens, though the slave could never hope to become a citizen, he was generally well treated and regarded as a part of the family. In Italian slavery there were horrors enough, especially as the slave was often more cultured than the master; but the Greek slaves were not as a rule wasted in the 'ergastula,' and the slave of a Roman might become a Roman himself, and his son sit down at meat with a Cæsar. It is often said that Christianity abolished slavery. This is true as an interpretation of the facts; it is not true as a literal expression of them. Among Christian writers the abhorrence of slavery is very recent. On few points have theologians, Catholic and Protestant, been less divided than in approving slavery—until after the French Revolution. But none the less the proposition is true, though centuries had to intervene between the implicit acceptance of an idea and its realisation. The equality of men in personal rights was already implicitly contained in the spirit of the religion which proclaimed their equality before Heaven.

Because the individual, with his special interests, cares, suffering, and destiny is *irrelevant* to philosophical history, that does not mean that the significance of the individual is overlooked by the philosopher. He is overlooked where he is not the subject studied. The individual, according to *our* ideas of morality, has a worth independent of his position as a member of a particular family or a particular state. This is just the great step which practical ethics have made in advance of Plato and Aristotle. Whether there is any sense in saying that the individual has a worth independent of humanity may be doubted; but this is a question which may be left for the present. When the philosopher or historian calmly contemplates the sacrifice of individual happiness to what he calls, with most men, the greatness of a nation or a period, he must not therefore be taunted with hardheartedness. His 'calmness' comes from his point of view, and that is necessarily removed from the scene of private interests, unless he is to have a distorted image of the significance of events. History is not concerned with the destiny or the happiness of the individual as such. It is therefore no valid objection to a philosophy of history that it does not justify the order of events by showing that the well-being of each individual is thereby attained. Nor, again, is it any argument against our ' justification ' that the life even of nations, after fair promise and brief splendour, has gone down into darkness. Mere duration is no real test of strength or of greatness. Can we say that Athens was a failure ? She failed, it is true, to establish an empire ; she failed to keep alive on her own hearth the fire she had kindled for the world. But many of the very causes of her decay were the conditions of her glory; and she did not fall before she had offered to mankind the gift of her heroism, her art, her literature, and her philosophy. We feel that these are not mere phrases. There is something in a great deed of an individual, or a nation, which is independent of the permanence of its external results. Permanence may only mean stagnation. When a people has fulfilled its ' mission,' by realising its portion of the potentialities of the human spirit, its powers are often exhausted, and it sinks quite as much through internal weakness as through the strength of its destroyer. But the political fall of a people is often the very means by which the best portion of its spirit can become the possession of the world—at least of the succeeding world-historical people. The Hebrew race made their highest contributions (which who can fully estimate ?) to the religion of mankind, after the overthrow of their political independence. Their captivity and suffering taught them more than the old glories of their monarchy. Hellenic civilisation spread over the world through the Macedonian conquests, which had first destroyed Hellenic freedom. The Romans in order to rule had themselves to lose their liberty, and the great fabric of their law was raised on the ruins of their political constitution. Yet Hebrews, Greeks, and Romans have surely done more and failed less than the Chinese, with their torpid civilisation, or the wandering tribes of the desert, who have never fallen because they never rose.

History, because it describes the character and writes the life of a people, presupposes that a people has a unity, we might almost say a personality, and is not a mere aggregate of individuals. Universal history, and therefore a philosophy of history, presupposes that there is a unity of mankind, that the human race can be looked at as not merely an aggregate of peoples : it presupposes that humanity has a history. But if we look at the actual history of the world, and at the attempts to show its rationality, we find that only a very few of the peoples who have lived and live on the earth are taken account of. The savage races, and the vast periods during which what are now civilised races were in the savage condition, seem to be ignored altogether. And among the civilised or semi-civilised peoples there seems to be an arbitrary selection. Thus, akin to the objection that philosophy of history ignores individual interests and rights is the objection that it ignores periods and races. An abstract justice might indeed require that all individuals should be taken account of, or, if we have given up the individuals, and admitted that not they but peoples are the object of history, that all peoples should be recognised. But this is a demand which—quite apart from philosophy—no scientific historian, no practical politician, for a moment concedes. Within each people the politician concerns himself with those only who are representative; in the world, with those races that are prominent. We talk, intelligibly enough, though not with abstract correctness, of 'the whole world,' when we mean only civilised nations, and perhaps only a few persons in them. We regard these persons as speaking for the others, these nations as representing the true interests of the others. So, too, the historian must perpetually make selection; otherwise he is giving us a mere collection of materials for history. He must pick out certain events and persons as historical, i.e., as historically important, and the rest he must reject as unhistorical. To do this well is no easy matter. Yet not merely as literary artist, but as scientific historian, he is obliged to select. What is true of particular portions of time is true of the world's existence generally. There are unhistorical races and unhistorical periods.

Of course the historian finds himself met by the practical limit that he can say nothing about times about which nothing is known. When a people has left no record of itself, then it cannot, even in its best minds, be said properly to have attained to any true consciousness of itself as having a history at all (of course, even this would be very much less than a consciousness of the meaning of its history for the world). A tribe may have defeated and dispossessed another tribe; but unless it has expressed itself in some way, by some definite religious belief, by something we can call a

constitution, by poetry, by buildings, by institutions which
have influenced some portion of the world, it can hardly be
said to have a history. Something, perhaps, of its dim
spiritual life may be gathered from its language ; but, if that
be all, it is relatively an unhistorical people.

But it may be said 'the Greeks had no written history,
no definite chronology even, long after they must have been
in a more advanced stage of political and intellectual
development than many other peoples.' As if the ' Iliad ' and
the ' Odyssey ' [1] were not better memorials of a people's life
than genealogies of kings and lists of priests !

Where a race has left memorials, and these have to a
great extent since perished or become unintelligible, it is of
course more difficult to estimate its historical significance.
Thus opinions will differ very much about the Etruscans,
and their place in European history. But even if we knew
as much about the Etruscans as about the Greeks, it would
not make them of equal historical importance. The Byzantine Empire has more historians than the age of Pericles,
yet no one would compare the significance of the two
periods.

All this is recognised by history as a science, and need
cause no trouble to philosophy. That some people are
' elect ' to carry on the civilisation of the world, and that
others are unable to assert themselves and are rejected, is an
indisputable fact. The same is true of individuals within
any nation. Only those who do assert themselves and make
good their claims to be leaders of men can be regarded as
historically important. The villager might have been
a Milton or a Hampden ; but history cannot deal with what
might have been. The civilisation of Mexico or Peru may
interest the antiquarian, but is hardly a part of universal
history.

Why this should be so is a question of the same kind
with the question raised by the waste which appears in
Nature—questions which are partly the result of abstraction,

---

[1] Vico devotes the third book of his
Scienza Nuova to the ' discovery of the
true Homer.' The *Iliad* and *Odyssey*
(anticipating Wolf) he regards as not the
work of one man, but as the product of
the Greek race through several centuries, and in different places ; and
this sense he calls Homer 'the first
historian of the Gentile world,' and his
poems 'the great treasures for the antiquities of Greece.' The *Scienza Nuova*
appeared first in 1725. How many
elegant comparisons of Homer and
Virgil were made after that date !

partly of impatience, partly perhaps unanswerable. At any rate we must judge the plan of the world—if it has a plan—by its successes and not by its failures. And when we are looking at things fairly, and not in some cynical mood, we do judge everything by the highest type of it. We do not suppose every Athenian to have been a Pericles or a Phidias, every old Florentine a Dante or a Giotto, yet we take these great men as the *types* of their people. And so it is in universal history.[1]

It is quite obvious that the civilisations of Greece and Rome to which we can directly trace the civilisation of modern Europe must be taken account of when we are trying to find what history means for us. It is more difficult to see how China and India are to be dealt with. There we have two remarkable civilisations of a high, if not the highest type, still continuing to exist, not far enough below European culture to perish before it, not near enough, and too old, to submit easily to its ways. Both countries have abundant history, in the sense of written records, and yet both must be regarded as relatively unhistorical. In the relation of Egypt and Persia to Greece, of Greece to Rome, of Rome to the nations of modern Europe, we see a continuity and a succession which we do not find in the remoter East They have handed on to one another the lamp of civilisation; Egypt, Persia, Greece, and Rome have perished, but each in dying has given life to its successor. China and India neither die nor live.

The part of Hegel's ' Philosophy of History ' which is most unsatisfactory is that which deals with the Asiatic countries. In the relation of China, India, Persia, he is unable to find a real historical connection. For this he substitutes a geographical succession. The sun rises in the east and moves westward; so does the history of the world. That there is a general truth in this we cannot deny, but the geographical succession of India to China is a very in-

---

[1] To the objection that the philosophy of history takes account of only a small portion of the human race may be added the more sweeping objection, that even if we did take account of the whole inhabitants of our earth, that is only a small part of the universe, and that wo cannot therefore read a Divine plan with so small knowledge. This objection is in part the first objection (see p. 132) in a new form; partly the result of an exaggerated admiration of mere space parallel to the admiration of mere time, which leads to the objection we have discussed. If there are inhabitants in Mars, they cannot be supposed to interest us.

adequate counterpart to that of Italy to Greece, where the real historical relation is so much more important than the geographical. Then what is to be made of Egypt, with a civilisation older than India ?[1]

The succession in *time* seems more easily intelligible and interpretable than the succession in geographical position, but is not without its difficulties. The development which philosophy seeks to find in the world is primarily a development of thought. Aristotle had already recognised the distinction between a prior in thought or nature, and a prior in time, and he generally regards these as in antithesis to each other. Thus the State, in thought or nature, precedes the family, but the family in time precedes the State. But we cannot rest satisfied with the mere antithesis, because we soon find many cases where the logical and historical developments fall together, especially if our development in thought is from the more simple to the more complex, and not *vice versâ*.

(1) In the unfolding of ideas in time we must not expect to find the regularity and symmetry of a logical system. The division of history by centuries is illogically symmetrical. In the life of the individual we count the time by days and years; but everyone feels that more is often lived through in an hour than in years. And so it is in the life of the race. Sometimes a year counts for more to the philosophic historian than a century, so crowded is it with significance : on the other hand he must avoid impatience at slow progress. 'One day is with the Lord as a thousand years, and a thousand years as one day.'

(2) When we talk of the 'spirit of a generation,' or the 'leading ideas of a period,' we are selecting only what is

[1] It may be objected that no account is taken of one of the greatest nations of the world—the United States of America. But to this we can answer that as yet it is too new; in spite of its immense achievements in the *material* elements of civilisation, it has contributed little as yet, except a few eccentric religions and some startling experiments in literature, to the spiritual existence of mankind. It is performing a gigantic political and social task; but the task is not nearly completed. Its population is constantly increasing by immigration, and its best culture is still an echo of the 'old world.' Yet, even apart from the doctrine that 'westward the course of empire takes its way' (Berkeley), the American can certainly feel that to him belongs the future. Whether the Slavonic races of Eastern Europe have an equally great future before them is more doubtful. In any case America and Russia are not old enough to belong to philosophic history. All study of their development is too much that of contemporaries.

Those who wish to see a history of the future written from a philosophic point of view will find such in the end of C. L. Michelet's *Philosophie der Geschichte* : but one would hardly like to stake the credit of the method on the success of his prophecies.

most typical of the time. At any given date one portion of mankind will be far in advance of another; and, within any given nation, while a few chosen spirits may be in advance, the great mass of the people may be a long way behind what we yet quite rightly regard as the stage of the nation's progress—meaning that of the bulk of its representative members. Thus we might say that England had got beyond the proverbial stage of morality, in spite of the admirers of Martin Tupper. Again (without raising any question of ' higher' or ' lower,' the only point being ' farther '), we can call the style of one building later than that of another, although it may have been built at an earlier period, meaning that it belongs to a later stage of architectural development. Gothic architecture had a short life in Italy, and a very long one in England, and so a Florentine palace of the fifteenth century may be later than an English college of the sixteenth. The philosophic historian of any special period or nation feels this, and thus is often obliged in his narrative of events to depart from the strict order of their occurrence by which the mere chronicler or annalist is bound to abide. This necessity is still more pressing when an attempt is made to view the history of the world as a whole. We must not look for a symmetry and a uniformity which is alien to the complex material with which we have to deal. Nor must the philosophy of history be blamed if it fails to make the order of ideas exactly fit the order of time.

So far as we have gone we have *formally* only discussed the *possibility* of a philosophy of history. But a great deal has already been necessarily anticipated which properly belongs to the discussion of its *character*. . Thus our treatment of the latter may be brief. 'Everyone,' as Hegel says, ' brings his own categories with him.' No one who thinks about the past or about his own time, can avoid having some philosophy of history of his own, more or less unconsciously held, more or less based on knowledge or prejudice. We can distinguish six main ways in which history may be and has been regarded.

1. Even he who denies that in history we can find anything beyond *Chance*, has made of chance a conception by which to explain to himself the phenomena. The denial of a plan in history is as much an interpretation of the facts by

an intellectual conception as the assertion of a plan. The only true sceptical attitude would be to refuse either to assert or deny a plan.

2. The religious recognition of a divine *Providence*, guiding human events, implies the introduction of a teleological conception into the material. But the religious recognition generally refuses to go into any detail, or it does so only in some special instances, and not in others. This is to make Providence either irrational or partial.

3. It may be, and has been said that the world, in a sense, is not ruled by God. 'In history we have a *Decadence* from early innocence. The rule of God can only be restored by the overthrow of the dominion of man.' If this only meant that the evil in the world should perish before the good in the world, no objection need be taken; but as the 'evil' is usually made by the defenders of this view equivalent to the State, and the 'good' to the Church, we are brought face to face with an absolute dualism which cannot so easily be accepted by either the statesman or the philosopher. Of course this reading of history does find in it a restoration, and therefore a progress, but its keynote is 'a regret that there should be such a thing as history at all,'[1] and this is an implicit denial that history is rational. This mediæval way of regarding political institutions and worldly progress as *in themselves* antagonistic to the kingdom of God, is an anachronism now. It is the philosophising of romanticism which is really a protest against reason, and it can only be carried on at the cost of perpetual inconsistencies.

No vision of childhood is so surely refuted by science as the dream of a golden age. All historical and anthropological research proves that, in Grote's famous phrase, it is 'a past that never was a present.' When the savage is talked of as 'degraded,' this only means that he falls below our ideal of what man ought to be, not that he has necessarily sunk from some better condition. There are indeed cases of real degradation and retrogression, but these are exceptional, and do not represent the normal condition of things. We know of a pre-political age: we can speak of the 'age before morality': and that is the only age of innocence— the innocence of the infant or the beast. Yet to put our

---

[1] Gans, in Pref. to 1st edit. of Hegel's *Philosophy of History*, criticising F. v. Schlegel.

ideals in the past is a natural habit of mind, and often a convenient way of speaking. Reformers profess to restore primitive purity, and innovations are introduced with the seeming sanction of antiquity. This idea of a purer religion and a better life in ancient times has stimulated research into the early condition of society, much as the hope of reaching the half-fabulous countries of the remote East described by Marco Polo, led Columbus across the Atlantic to discover a new world.

4. In extreme antithesis to this last view is the 'rationalistic' tendency and wish to see in history a continuous *Progress*. The attempt to make this real has led to 'progress' being narrowed down to intellectual advance. Even if we accept this, it cannot be strictly maintained that the sum of knowledge has always grown. And we should be obliged to regard the first fourteen centuries of our era as a period of nearly entire loss to mankind.

5. A consideration of the fluctuations in civilisation led to the wide prevalence of the idea of *Cycles*;[1] an idea which commended itself also by reconciling filial piety to past ages with a recognition of the fact of progress. But it is an idea which implies an unhistorical and unscientific way of looking at history. History seems to repeat itself: but it never really does. It repeats itself always with a difference. A philosophic, *i.e.* a not-abstract, way of regarding history has done a great deal towards dispelling the fallacies of historic parallels.

6. And thus we come to the recognition in history of a *Progress by antithesis*. Progress cannot mean merely 'going forward,' for that might be in a wrong direction. Again, to explain progress (or development) as 'differentiation of function,' is right but inadequate, as it gives only a negative characteristic. If we see in history a progress, we must explain it by what man *comes to be*, and not merely by what he ceases to be. We may call it the struggle for freedom (in no merely negative sense), the liberation of man from the domination of nature and fate. Or we may say that it is humanity making itself, or coming to a consciousness of it-

---

[1] An idea shared by Vico, but which can certainly not be used to sum up his philosophy of history. The return of his 'divine age' in the Middle Ages is no literal return in the sense in which Plato and Aristotle speak of a cycle in events.

self—*that* is implied in freedom; or we may call it the 'education of the human race.' None of these formulæ need exclude the other; each is inadequate. But in any case we must recognise that the movement is not uniform: it is a *struggle*, with loss and gain. What is a blessing to one age may, for that very reason, be a curse to the next; and, on the other hand, those who have advanced less far may, for that very reason, be able to go on afterwards beyond those who had outstripped them. Some elements of the spiritual life of man are realised by one period or nation; but just because they are *some* elements only, they are realised in a one-sided and exaggerated, and therefore self-destructive way. The next step is, therefore, in a contrary direction. Then comes an attempt to bring the two sides together. But because spirit is infinite and its temporal manifestation finite, this must always prove incomplete; and thus the world must proceed again through a new antithesis to a new reconciliation. In the concrete world of human action 'the straight line is not always the shortest distance between two points.'[1] We get from one point to another through a third.

It must not be thought that the number 'three' is adopted for any magical or superstitious reason. It is inevitable when we have to express a rational process. If a syllogism be formulated in less than three propositions, something is suppressed; if in more (as in the Indian logic), something is repeated. Whenever there is real inference, real movement forward, we must pass from one to another through a third. This is not, as Mill says, a mere marching up hill and down again—at least it is marching down on the farther side. Unless we are content with a theory of the universe of being and knowing which makes it a mere aggregate of particulars, we must admit that we can only pass from particular to particular through a universal. And, if the process we are dealing with be a real progress, we shall certainly expect to find that we are passing from abstract universal and particular to a more concrete form which is at once universal and particular.[2]

---

[1] Lessing, *Erziehung des Menschengeschlechts*, § 91.

[2] Of course there is no special virtue in the terminology. The three stages may be called abstract unity, difference (multiplicity), concrete unity, *i.e.* a unity of the manifold, a living unity: and this is often the best formula. It recalls Aristotle's εἶδος: ὕλη : τὸ σύνολον.

People have a suspicion of such formulæ, because they think that thereby facts are ignored or perverted. And the suspicion is wholesome, because this is often the case. Only let us be sure whether it is the case with this formula of idealism, if we apply it wisely; and whether it is not far more the case with the apparently simpler, because more abstract, formulæ of the understanding which are constantly being applied by empiricism.

That our formula can only be applied with great limitations in history must be at once conceded. As Aristotle says, the exactness of our method must always be proportioned to the subject matter. Therefore, in the first place, we must not expect a logical formula to fit exactly the complex material of human affairs; secondly, we can see the process of thought most clearly in those countries and periods which have attained more of self-consciousness, more of freedom, *i.e.* in which nature counts for less and spirit for more— perhaps hardly at all among African savages, dimly in the Oriental nations, more clearly in Greek and Roman history, less clearly again in the Middle Ages. We cannot add, ' most clearly in modern history,' for here another difficulty meets us—we are too much immersed in the events themselves to see clearly their full meaning : we cannot see the forest for the trees. Again, in any given period, the presence of reason is most manifest in the development of those elements which are more spiritual, less in those which are more 'natural' or more dependent on matter. Thus we should look rather to the history of a people's philosophy (if they have any), religion, art, and institutions, than to their external growth, which depends more on external circumstances than on the spirit of the people themselves. The development of the national spirit, especially in early races, is generally best traced in the history of religion. At a time when political *ideas* have scarcely dawned, when what we call political history is chiefly a personal struggle of kings and nobles, in their religion, with which the beginnings of art and literature are closely connected, we can find the spirit of the people.

We must constantly recognise the exceeding complexity of human characters and actions, and not regard one interpretation as excluding the possibility of several or many others. In seeking to read the meaning of history we are

obliged to make formulæ which, just because they are formulæ, must be abstract, and therefore we must constantly
recur to the realm of particular events to correct their abstractness. The philosophic study of history, as of everything
else, is thus a constant struggle neither to ignore facts for
formulæ, nor to lose sight of reason among a mere chaos of
particulars which need a formula to explain and hold them
together. We may be sure that we are misapplying a formula if we are interpreting complex material in only one way.
The great epochs of history, if we study them fairly, present
at least a double aspect. Thus, if we regard the Greeks in
their relation to the preceding world-historical people the
Persians, and to the succeeding people the Romans, they
represent the element of difference, of the manifold, not only
in their political character, but in the rich diversity of their
culture. On the other hand, if we oppose them to the
mediæval or modern world, they represent the wholeness of
spirit—spirit at one with nature, and therefore at one with
itself. Yet, while each of these expressions has a general
truth, we feel in presence of the Greeks the inadequacy of
any formula to their significance in the life of mankind.
But after all, when we speak of Hellenic civilisation, it is
chiefly Ionian, and especially Athenian, civilisation that we
mean. We rightly judge them by their highest type : and
it is only in the intellectual Ionian races that the Greek
spirit becomes conscious of itself, and finds its full expression in literature and art. Yet again, we must not narrow
our view to Athens, for Sparta represents more fully than
Athens the strength of the civic *bond*, though Athens shows
the highest intensity of city *life*. Again, what is most
characteristic of Greek religion, the worship of Apollo,
belongs specially to the Dorian races. Indeed, the better
position of women at Sparta than at Athens might be urged
in favour of the claims of the former to represent the higher
type; but this is only one illustration of what we find everywhere, that progress is not in a straight line, and advance
in one direction generally implies a certain one-sidedness
and neglect of other elements. Athenian philosophers looked
with longing on the better discipline of Sparta; but their
master, Socrates, whom Athens put to death, could not
possibly have been produced in Sparta. The Hellenic spirit
realised itself more freely through having many channels,

especially the two, Ionian and Dorian. But this very severance—this antagonism between Ionian and Dorian, brought about its political ruin. The political disunion of Greece was the external cause of its fall; the internal 'break up' of the wholeness of Hellenic thought may be traced in Athenian philosophy. In Plato's 'Republic' we find a picture, not only of what the Greek State (especially in Sparta) tended to be, but of the stages through which Greek thought (especially in Athens) tended to pass. The old Cephalus and his son Polemarchus represent the conventional unreflecting morality of old days. Thrasymachus, Glaucon, and Adeimantus in different forms typify the critical and rationalistic spirit of the Sophists. Socrates attempts to reconcile the 'reason' of the second with the 'custom' of the first stage. The ideal State is intended to be the rule of reason made customary. But this reconciliation was attained by the Greeks only in thought; in their practical life they did not get beyond the antithesis of a disciplined Sparta without philosophy, and a philosophic Athens without discipline. Later Greek philosophies were compelled to seek a home for morality independently of the shattered fabric of the State, and they sought to find it in the larger but vaguer unity of a brotherhood of mankind.

To pass from Greece to Rome is to turn from poetry to prose. If we try to express the Roman spirit in one formula we can find no better word than Hegel's 'abstract'—of course not in any sense which would suggest 'intellectual' as opposed to 'practical,' but in the meaning of 'narrow,' 'one-sided.' With a true instinct Hegel rejects Niebuhr's fiction of an early Roman 'epos': the Roman legends are not material for poetry, however suitable for rhetoric. Her deities are not brilliantly human like the Greek, but cold abstractions of moral qualities. Though Venus Cloacina appears *not* to mean 'our Lady of Drains,' but 'the purifier of marriage,' this, if a more moral, is certainly a less artistic conception than Aphrodite rising from the sea-foam. Rome's own national poet recognises that art is not her sphere, but conquest and legislation. The Roman was no mere conqueror: *Cives vocavit quos domuit*—'She made her subjects her citizens.' Her colonists were not, like those of Greece, the founders of new political units, which might come to rival the mother city, but the outposts of her empire. The

Greeks were scattered over islands and the shores of many lands, united, but separated by the sea. Rome was the centre of a network of great military roads.

But Rome, in bringing different nations and races under her uniform law, broke up the old unities. And in her own history we have a similar twofold aspect—in extending herself over the earth she lost her own liberty, and the unity of her empire proved a dead lifeless unity, which gave a long peace to the world, but allowed its energies to decay. We must not look on the uninteresting Roman Empire as a period in which nothing was done for mankind. It was not a time only of corruption, but of preparation for a new movement. The Athenian had his activities exercised in the struggles of the Agora. The citizen of the Roman Empire had no political career : he was thrown back on his own self, to find there the emptiness of this world, contenting himself with it as a sensualist, or fortifying his soul against it as a Stoic, or seeking escape from it as a mystic. The Roman Empire which gave the 'form' of legal personality to its subjects, but could give no satisfactory 'content,' was thus the 'material cause' of Christianity.

To the Greek and Roman religion had been a part of the State. Christianity, finding the State such as it was, held aloof from it. And thus began the antithesis between Church and State, which even when they are united, remain distinct spheres. This antithesis gives their chief characteristic to the Middle Ages. There are now two ideals before men, and these are at war with one another. In their extreme forms they take the shape of the chivalric and the monastic ideals. No period has been judged so differently. To some the Middle Ages have appeared as 'the ages of faith,' in bright contrast to the preceding corruption of the Roman world and the scepticism of Hellenic culture on the one hand, and on the other to the succeeding sensualism of the Renaissance and the rationalism of the Revolutionary epoch ; to others as a picturesque and romantic dreamland, dispelled by the hard realism of modern life ; to others as a time of barbarous ignorance, superstition, and cruelty—a dark night from which the Renaissance was a welcome deliverance. The diversity of judgment only shows that the phenomena are too manifold to be summed up in one formula. If we contrast the Middle Ages with the ancient world (especially

with what is most typical in it—the Greek world) they
represent a period of alienation of the human spirit from its
surroundings—a period of discontent—a negative period.
On the other hand, contrasted either with the wreck of the
Roman Empire, or with the age of criticism which follows,
they are a 'positive' period—a period in which the life of
man was regulated by an established and accepted order of
things, in which nothing was left to subjective caprice.

So, too, if we contrast the Renaissance with the Middle
Ages it is a reconciliation, or rather an attempt at reconciliation, between the old and the new—an attempt to join
'Christ and the Muses.'[1]   Looked at in the light of what
follows, the Renaissance is the beginning of a revolt, the
proclamation of a humanist ideal which has not yet been
reconciled with the ecclesiastical ideal of the Middle Ages.

To interpret our own time is the hardest task of all.   It
is impossible to avoid the influence of our wishes.   Hegel
has not escaped this difficulty and may easily be charged
with unfairness.   His national feelings lead him to exagge-
rate the Teutonic in comparison with the other elements in
the formation of the mediæval and modern world ; he even
puts himself to the trouble of defending the Lutheran
against the Calvinist view of the Eucharist, and he speaks
as if all political wisdom were summed up in the Prussian
monarchy as he knew it.   He has fallen into the temptation
of 'finality.'   But his own method is independent of his
particular applications of it.   His recognition that the freedom of *all* is the mission of the modern world should prevent contentment with a narrow bureaucracy.   And surely
representative government, especially representative democracy, against which he shows a decided prejudice, is in its
ideal the truest reconciliation we yet know of the rights of
the many with the wisdom of the few, the best realisation of
a 'concrete' freedom as opposed to the abstract freedom of
immediate democracy which issues only in such instruments
of tyranny as the 'plébiscite.'   In reference to present and
practical questions Hegel's method has received very different applications.   It has been used by defenders of the
Roman Church, and out of his school have come most of the

[1] In its architecture—often the best
index to the spirit of an era—we have
the attempt to unite the reserved, uniform classical forms with the fantastic
variety of the Gothic spirit.

intellectual leaders of socialism.[1] The number of its sects does not prove the truth of a religious system nor of a philosophical, but is no argument against it; while the incapacity of admitting of more than one application is a sure proof of the narrowness of a formula and a sign of its want of vitality.

The idea is certainly 'in the air' that we have reached a time whose principal end should be positive construction rather than destructive criticism. This idea is often made to sanction reaction in politics and religion. Such an interpretation ignores the fact, that a return to the past is strictly impossible; 'restoration is always revolution'; and that, in real progress, the third or reconciling stage, though it looks most opposed to the second or critical, must take up the truth of the second into it as well as that of the first. Different views will unavoidably be held about the character and issues of the democratic tendency whose existence no one can deny; different views about the economic future of society, though most people feel that 'Laissez-faire' is not the final word to express the relation of the State to its members;[2] the conflict raised in most European countries by an irreconcilable Ultramontanism, may make the immediate future of religion seem very uncertain, and the destiny of Protestantism must depend on the victory of letter or spirit. In external politics, the coexistence of separate and independent nations will be more generally accepted, though opinions will differ whether the abstract conception of a 'balance of power,' which has caused more strife than it has prevented, is still the only link between them, or whether the feeling that there is an international morality may some day render possible the fact of an international law. In any case we must recognise that the civilisation of the world is not now entrusted, as of old, to one keeper only ; and history should teach us that no nation has the right to say, 'Surely we are the people : and wisdom will die with us.'

D. G. RITCHIE.

[1] In Lassalle's *Arbeiterprogramm* will be found a brilliant application of the Hegelian method to economic history. Yet Lassalle also has fallen under the temptation of finality. He expects his third period, which is to reconcile the fixity (Status) of the old world with the freedom (Contract) of the new, to follow quite soon and quite suddenly through State agency.

[2] No one who carefully studies the change in English Liberalism in recent years can doubt that it has ceased to make the negative formula 'freedom of contract' its ultimatum. See a lecture by the late Professor Green, 'Liberal Legislation and Freedom of Contract.', Oxford, 1881.

VI.

ON THE PHILOSOPHY OF ART.

PLATO in the 'Protagoras' makes Socrates say that conversation about poetry and the meaning of poetry should be left to people who have not completed their education and are not able to converse freely. The vulgar like to dispute about the interpretation of the sayings of poets, who cannot come into the company to answer for themselves; men who have been well schooled prefer, in their conversation, to go on without the help or the distraction of poetry, ' each one in the company taking his turn to speak and listen in due order, even though they be drinking deep.' To turn conversation into a wrangle about the interpretation of poetical passages is hardly less a sign of want of education than to bring in flute-players in order to save the banqueters from the sound of their own voices. Socrates, before making this contemptuous speech, had criticised and explained a passage of Simonides in a way that shows how possible it is for a critic to maintain his freedom and speak his own mind while professing to draw out the hidden meaning of his author; how the sermon may be made a different thing from the text. The whole passage is characteristic of an age which has grown too old for poetry, which is determined to work out its own problems with its own understanding, not expecting much help nor fearing much hindrance from the wisdom of bygone ages. The belief that is the centre of all Plato's theories of art is expressed here. Stated rudely, the belief is this, that art has lost its authority, that the poets and their followers are well-meaning men who would have to-day rule itself by yesterday's wisdom, whereas to-day has its own light to which yesterday's light is an impertinence. Enlightened men speak the thoughts that are in them, free from bondage to the letter of ancient wisdom ; the philosopher knows clearly what the poets knew vaguely and confusedly. Plato's various theories of art are all expansions of this speech in the 'Protagoras.' At the worst, art is a false semblance; at the best it is an education. The philosopher knows what beauty is better than they do who listen to the singers in the market-place. There cannot but be a quarrel between poetry and philosophy; poetry is weak, imperfect, and ignorant, pretends to be strong and all-seeing. Philosophy secures its own position by showing how poetry in its proper place may be the servant of truth, and how dangerous to truth it may be in its light-minded pretence of omniscience.

This dissatisfaction with art is not mere puritanic bitterness, not the caprice of a sectarian who sets himself against the common belief of the world. Plato is speaking for his age, not against it. He has no innate spite against art, he has the sincerest reverence for it, yet he cannot choose but bring it down from its height, because the age for which he is speaking knows that there are results to be gained which cannot be gained in the old ways, that the philosophers are working towards new ends of which the poets and image-makers have never dreamt. This is the way in which the attitude of Plato towards art becomes intelligible. It seemed to him that art with all its excellences was not enough for the needs of a new age, and that it should not be allowed to claim more than its fair share of respect from men who were in search of truth, who were minded to try what they could make out for themselves, 'speaking and listening among themselves' without superstition or bondage to idols. Yet no one more than Plato recognised the value of poetry, of imagination, in the progress of the mind towards pure truth. He did not contradict himself in so doing. He denied that poetry was the whole of wisdom; he did not deny that it was the beginning of wisdom. It is the positive side of his theorising about art which has been best remembered. The polemic against the teaching of the poets was forgotten. The belief that the beauty of sensible things is in some way the image of an unseen beauty remained as an element of many later philosophies, the creed of not a few poets. There is something in it which wins an assent that is not altogether founded on a critical investigation. The theory that the youth are to dwell in a place of pleasant sights and sounds, and to grow up unconsciously into the image of reason, that when reason comes they may welcome it as not alien—all this is heard at first as a story which ought to be true, which overcomes prejudice at the outset. The difficulty is to fix the details of the story. The listener wants to know more about the beauty and more about the reason, and to know where, if anywhere, there is anything like this progress from the half-conscious life among beautiful things to the awakened life in reason.

This theory in the 'Republic,' and the similar theories in the 'Symposium' and the 'Phœdrus,' are the first attempts at a philosophy of beauty. They describe in dark language a relation of the manifold beautiful things to the one unchangeable idea of beauty, and describe the progress of the soul from the beauty of the manifold things of sense to the unity of reason or of the idea of beauty. If there be such a progress, it is obviously in it that the secret of beauty lies. But how are we to conceive this progress? what is the idea in which it ends? The education which begins in art and ends in philosophy, how does this resemble or differ from other progresses of mind; for example, the progress of any mind, however ill educated or uneducated, from the unreal world of childhood to the more or less real world of common sense, or the historical progress of nations from myths to rationalism. Everyone knows that there are some progresses in which the mind rejects old fancies for new truths, turning in revolt against its old self; are there others, like this one of the 'Republic' or this one of the 'Symposium,' in which the old unreal things which are passed by are not falsehoods but images of the truth? And supposing that art stands in some such relation as this to philosophy, will it not be of some importance to know what is to become of the images when the reality is attained to, of the pleasant places of art when philosophy is perfected, of the manifold shapes of beauty when the one idea of beauty is revealed? Are they to be rejected as Socrates rejected the wisdom of the elder moralists, as Plato rejected the art which was an imitation? Plato's own attitude towards art is a continual wavering between two opinions, which are both based on the one sure opinion that the poets do not at any rate contain all wisdom. Admitting this sure opinion, there are still two alternatives to Plato; sometimes he is for expelling the poets altogether; sometimes he speaks more gently of them, as servants of the

M

Divine Wisdom, who say more than they know, more than
sane men are able to say.   The difficulty which he finds in
explaining art, and the poet's character, and the beauty of
sensible things, arises from his opposition to them.   He is
the first philosopher to attempt to make a philosophy of art,
and the sum of that philosophy is that art and philosophy
are different.   It is the imperfection of art, the imperfection of
visible beauty, which he emphasises.   To be content with art
is a fatal mistake; it is to prefer opinion to knowledge.
Thus Plato's philosophy of art was almost wholly negative.
It could not help being negative to begin with, could not
help asserting its superiority as critic over the matter criticised.   The first thing of importance to be said about art
is that there is a science which goes beyond it; and Plato
said this, and described in many ways the movement of the
mind from the scattered things of sense to the unity which
they reflect.   But he never succeeded in teaching anyone
that science of unity; what he taught was that science of
the unity was to be sought after.   And so long as this science
was unattained, the unity, the universal, was simply an
abstraction of which the only thing that could be said was
that it is a negation of the many, of the particulars—including them in some way, but in some undefined, unknown
way—including them as a limit outside of them.   Plato
recognised that the relation of the many to the one was not
explained simply by being stated; he recognised that the
many were not a mere negation of the one—that wrong
opinion was possible—that knowledge of the inexact line
and the inexact circle have their place in the world for those
who wish to find their road home.[1]   He apprehended that
the ideal was not always the truth.   The criticism of
Simonides in the ' Protagoras ' succeeds in showing that the
ideal is often much respected by bad men who find their
actual circumstances irksome: that the duty of a man often
compels him to leave the ideal alone and be loyal to his
kinsfolk, *accepting* the particular circumstances in which he
is placed.   This apprehension of the value of particular
things is never elaborated by Plato into part of the science
of the universal; so that at the end there is little more
said than that there is one idea, and that there is a progress
of the mind from particulars to this universal through

[1] *Philebus*, 62 B.   Compare πρὸς τὸ ἀνθρωπεύεσθαι.

successive stages of subordinate universals. So the end of his philosophy of art is that there is one idea of beauty, eternal, the same with itself, not in any likeness of anything in heaven or earth, and that the earthly beauty is a stage on the way to this. That is the end, that is the philosophy of earthly beauty—that it is nothing in comparison with the one idea of beauty, that it passes away as the thought goes beyond it to reach the idea of beauty. Plato praises art, regarding it as a step on the way to true knowledge, and blames it, regarding it as without life in itself, as without any principle in it which can give it permanency or authority; but whether he praise it or blame it his view of it is always this, that it is valueless in comparison with philosophy. At its best it is a makeshift, at its worst it is a makeshift pretending to be the chief good. This theory of art is unsatisfactory because of its meagreness, its abstraction, but it is necessarily the first philosophy of art. The first point in the creation of a philosophy of art is the separation of art and philosophy—the hostility of philosophy to art. Philosophy comes in a time succeeding the time of the flourishing of art, and to justify its own existence has to prove that art is not the whole of wisdom, not the summit of man's history. Philosophies of art, to begin with, are either puritanic ἔλεγχοι of art, proving that art is vanity, or theories of the fitness of things according to which fitness art leads the way to true knowledge, to enlightenment. The view of art as an education is the natural one for enlightenment to adopt. It has an appearance of justice, because it admits the value of art, and it does justice to enlightenment itself by making it the end to which art is an instrument. There is and must be an enmity of philosophy towards art, because it is in opposition to the past, which art represents, that philosophy arises. Criticism is enmity, to begin with. The first step towards reconciliation of this enmity is to show that the matter criticised is not really hostile, but really exists for the sake of the critic. It is this step which is taken by any theory which regards art as an education — as existing for the sake of something higher, namely enlightenment, accurate and self-conscious insight. This reconciliation is imperfect because art, the subject criticised, the instrument existing for the sake of the end, which is enlightenment, maintains its separate existence in spite of the critic, pursues its own ends without regard to

the existence of any enmity against itself, or to any disputing in the Schools about the end of art.

Ella s' è beata e ciò non ode.

The theory that art is an education does not make art
much easier to be understood.   That art exists for the sake
of something else may be a fact about it, but does not
reveal anything of the laws of art itself, of the end which
it realises for those unfortunate people who have not yet
passed beyond the stage of art.   That is to say, that however true it may be that art is an education, or a step to
something higher, it is still impossible to explain art fully
by reference to the something higher, because for the artist
art is not this education, not this step, but an end in itself.
And it is a reasonable claim that art should be considered as
an end in itself—as an activity following its own laws.   If
it be not this, then the opinion is wrong. But wrong opinion
is not nothing.   Wrong opinion is as complicated as right
opinion, is as much a *positive fact* as right opinion.   So in
this case, art, as it is for the artist, is not explained by the
statement that art is not the goal of the mind, that it is not
an end in itself.   If art be an education leading to philosophy, and the philosophy to which it leads be worth anything, then it ought to be possible for philosophy to regard
art not merely as an incident in the development of philosophy, but as a form of activity with its own laws and its
own history.   Art may be a king to whom it has been given
to be the nursing father of philosophy, but in his own kingdom that title is not ascribed to the king openly, and it is in
no case the whole truth of the kingship.

The theory that art is an education is of very doubtful
value if taken by itself.   Art is certainly an education for
the artist : with other men it is less certainly an education.
And it is seldom an education whose pupils can boast that
they have done with it.   It is true that there are cases of
great artists withdrawing themselves for a time from art
into the sphere of pure thought, making art for a time
external to them in place of being the spirit of their life and
work.   But these periods of abstraction lead not always to
a renunciation of art, and sometimes lead to a higher kind of
art, to perfection in art, so that regarding the lives of individual artists it is impossible to arrive at any certain for-

mula. Sometimes it seems that art is the porch of philosophy, sometimes that philosophy is for the individual artist only a passing phase in his life, a centre of indifference, not fruitless, but leading to the production of different beauty, from the incorporeal beauty which Plato wrote of in the 'Symposium.'

Dante describes a change in his life which is like that which Plato related of the favoured children of his 'Republic.' Dante tells in the 'Convito' how, after the death of Beatrice, when the fantastic world of his youth was broken in pieces, he went to philosophy (in Boethius and others) for consolation. There, he says, seeking silver he found gold; he found not only remedy for his grief, but clear knowledge, whereas his mind before had seen many things but only as in dreams, which things were written of in the 'Vita Nuova.'[1] This confession of Dante about himself and the way in which he came to the knowledge of philosophy is of some value. It describes a progress of the mind in a way which may enable us to understand what is meant by saying that those who are brought up among fair sights and sounds will find when reason comes to them that it is no unfamiliar thing. But the parallel does not hold absolutely. It is dangerous to force the resemblance between the prophetic utterance of Plato and the actual life of the man who was not suffered to become a guardian of his earthly city. The world of imagination in which Dante spent his youth was a world in which poetry was not a natural growth, but in great part philosophy disguised—idealism and symbolism which owed a good deal to the Schools. And the progress of Dante did not end with his entry into the Schools. The clear vision in which Dante ended his progress was not a vision of abstract ideas, or not of them only. The 'Vita Nuova' is more removed from actual life than the 'Paradiso:' the vision of the Highest is at the same time the vision of the narrow streets where the unrighteous dwell, the Monna Berta and Ser Martino who pass infallible judgments upon sinners. Dante at one time, he tells us, read till he grew nearly blind, trying to unravel the mystery of First Matter; but he did not end in these abstractions. He gathers together into one vision all things and all men that he had ever seen or

[1] *Convito*, II. 13. 'Per lo quale ingegno molte cose quasi come sognando giá vedea.'

heard of, and in the vision of them he finds his wisdom—of them and of the unseen ruler, in whose mind all things are determined, the meanest chances of earth no less than the highest self-proven truths.   Such art as this is not to be explained by the ready formula that fair sights and sounds are good for weak minds that have hope of becoming stronger.   We can understand how the youth of Dante was educated by the world of symbolism and mysticism in which he lived, by the pure enthusiasm of the poets : we can understand how this corresponds in some measure to the place of beauty in which Plato's fosterlings were to be trained.   We can understand how the abstractions of philosophy were welcomed as expressing what had before been dreamt of. We can understand also in part how the abstractions were discovered to be abstractions—how the memory of visible things and the knowledge of them in their particularity, as having value of their own, became the end of his philosophy. We can see that however true it may be that art is an education, it does not necessarily mean that it is an education for some end different from art. All artists are educated in this way, in this half-conscious apprehension of beauty. The history of almost every great artist tells how his life begins in vague enjoyment of beautiful surroundings : he lives in a world of beauty, of which he is part and which he only half understands.   He conforms to the fashion of the world in which he lives : his early works are no better than those of his fellows, not at least in the opinion of his own age. As he grows older he asserts his freedom : he works no longer as a mere natural outgrowth from his nation and his time, but as a free man walking his own way in the world, seeing things as they are, valuing them for himself, not as others have valued them before.   Chaucer in his later life is not merely part of the pageantry of the English court : he is a spectator, not merely a singing man in the show. He is *more immediately* part of the life of the time when he is with the English army in France, learning to rhyme fashionably about cruelty and pity.   He has made his place for himself, gained for himself his freedom, when he sets down his own view of his age in the prologue to the Canterbury Tales.   He is not less but more an Englishman of the fourteenth century because he belongs to his age, not simply as the trees that grew and blossomed according to the fashion of these years, but as a free man who, while not ashamed of being a child of time, does not hold that 'thought's the slave of life, and life time's fool.' He is not the less the brother of the Englishmen his contemporaries because he in a manner withdrew from them for a time, and set down their outward appearance in his book. But he did withdraw from them, he did refuse to be bound by laws of art which were not true for him, to see things with other men's eyes. In this refusal is the end of his apprenticeship.

The creative memory of the artist is as different as abstract philosophy from ordinary experience which grows unconsciously. There is a difference between the unconscious manner in which beauty of art or nature influences the mind of the pupil, and the manner in which the perfect artist works in full consciousness of the end at which he is aiming and the means by which he is to attain it, if not always with perfect consciousness or developed curiosity concerning the sources of his power.

The problem for the philosophy of art is thus not merely ' how is philosophy to indicate its claim to supersede art, as being perfect science of that which art feels after blindly ? ' but ' what is the kind of end which the artist attains ? how are we to analyse the relation of works of art to the mind ? '

Art and science are very much alike at the beginning. Science does not know anything *about* things at the beginning; it simply perceives things—or rather, simple perception, to perceive things clearly, is the ideal which early science aims at—which it does not always attain. It is here that art begins its services to mankind. The bone knives found in the caves of the Dordogne show that the artists who engraved them saw reindeer clearly, and were ingenuously interested in them, having reached a stage of civilisation and wealth in which they were not simply ravenous for reindeer, but could afford to contemplate them with self-restraint, like gentlemen. Their contemplative leisure employed the keen eyesight, no longer that of a beast of prey, and the interest, no longer of the stomach, in engraving a clear outline of the interesting animal on the handles of their hunting knives. Other early engravings show how the mammoth might be made, by untrembling hands, into a lasting ornament. The idols that stand in the porch of the

British Museum show that some long-forgotten dwellers in the Easter Islands grew one day to be *securi adversus deos*, and employed their security in making images of the beings they worshipped, in order to know what sort of beings they were.   When it is said that the makers of such images had reached a certain degree of civilisation, it is not meant merely that they had attained some technical skill in shaping materials, but that they had so far raised themselves above the level of the beasts, so far withdrawn themselves from sensation and appetite, as to be able to make permanent for themselves the objects of their interest and their worship. This defining of the perceived or imagined object is the great triumph of early art, and it is at the same time the beginning of science, of clear knowledge.   Thus early art is sometimes extremely realistic, and seems to accompany wonderful powers of perception—of combining various particulars in one intuition.   The Esquimaux, who draw the things they see with some skill, are said sometimes to show a talent for remembering locality, the relative positions of places, so as to be able to make fairly accurate charts of a coast after a short acquaintance with it. The artistic faculty of clear apprehension of details here has to do duty for science.

How does completed science differ from completed art? For science the particular visible object is unimportant, or important only as an example of a general law, or as material for an experiment to lead to the knowledge of a general law, or as a member of a species, interesting and intelligible, not in itself but as a member of the species—the species itself being interesting and intelligible only as having a definite place in the universe, as standing in a definite relation to other things.   Things are interesting to science not for what they *are*, but for what they *are not*, that is, for the other things to which they are related, or still more, for the relation—for the general formula of relations which sums up the truth about the particular things.   Science is thus an endless process.   It is perpetually busied with certain things of the outward world, but interested in them only as they point to other things.   The particular things with which science deals are instruments, not ends in themselves. The particular member of a species is of little more importance to science than the particular chalk triangle drawn on a particular slate. The triangle is merely a perceptible repetition of one type, the truth about which type is quite independent of the particular chalk triangle.   The particular member of a species has no importance, unless it has some individual peculiarities which make it different from its species, in which case it may be important as one of a new species.   But in no case has it any importance in itself.   It has importance either as being an example of a species in which the characteristics of the species may be known and demonstrated ; or as a link in a chain of causation, and it is the chain, not the link, which is important.   Even individuals, having from one point of view value in and for themselves, may for science be simply instruments and specimens to demonstrate the working of a law, or particular phenomena, whose importance is not in themselves but in their causes or effects.   Mahomet or Columbus may be considered by scientific history not as individuals interesting in themselves, but as single terms in a series.   History is not interested in any single event, or in any individual man, but in the *relations* of men and of events.

In art the case is altogether different.   There the particular thing exists with a being of its own, as a thing which can suffer nothing else to stand in the place of it, as something which cannot be exhausted by any formula or expressed in words, as something whose relation to other things, to causes or effects or laws, is altogether a subordinate matter—not the true essence, but an accident which not even inadequately can express the nature of the thing.   Both art and science have for their end to make things clear to the mind.   But science makes things clear by perpetual reference to other things.   Its activity is an endless process; its kingdom of light is rounded by the darkness of the unknown on which it encroaches, but which it can never conquer.   Art does not make things clear to the understanding which asks the reasons of things and their connection with other things.   Its creations do not prove anything; they have no reference to things beyond themselves, they add nothing to knowledge, they do not throw light upon the natures of things, they are themselves clear and definite objects, that is all.   The things which art makes are interesting to the mind with an interest quite different from that which belongs to the demonstrations of science.   Science throws light on a portion of the object world; clearing it up, showing the secret of it, the unapparent law of its being; using particular perceptible things as instruments to demonstrate the law. Art makes a thing which is not an instrument by which to demonstrate the general law of a class of objects, but is free, serving no law but its own, revealing itself, and nothing but itself, to the mind. Science is face to face with an object world, which is a system of related classes of things, and explains certain classes of those things, regarding each thing as an example of a class, and each class as explicable by formulas more or less fixed. Art makes new things, whose value is that they explain themselves in a way with which science is unacquainted. Art satisfies the mind not by affording it new examples for experiment, from which to arrive at new truths of the objective world, but by presenting to it objects which have that freedom from dependence on other things and other laws, that unity in themselves, which is wanting in all the objects of science— in the object world which for science is never a whole complete in all its parts, and is *one* world only *ex hypothesi*. The work of art is an object which is only partially or accidentally subject to the laws of the object world; which is in the world but not of it. A statue is a perceived object, a particular thing in the object world, but it is not to be explained scientifically, like other objects, like natural things, as a member of a species, as standing in particular relations to the universe. It is not to be explained by reference to other things; its nature is that it explains itself. It is not a problem to be solved; or rather it is both problem and solution, both the secret and the revelation of the secret. This does not mean that works of art are exempt from the law by which the universe is one and all the parts of it correlated; this is not to say that there can be no science of art things, or that they can be *understood* apart from their history. But all histories or explanations are inadequate— not as in other cases because the relations of any one thing to the rest of the universe are inexhaustible—but because they regard works of art *only* as phenomena to be explained, and forget the main point, that they are phenomena which explain themselves.

The work of art is separate from the world in which it exists. It is a contradiction to any theory which would regard each thing as a point in an endless series of relations. The work of art is a thing which will not be explained, like other things, by a natural history or a statement of its relations to other things. It is in one sense finite, because it has had a history, because it stands in relation to other things that are finite. In another sense it is not a finite thing, because its nature will not yield itself to analysis; it cannot be dissected. There is a point at which its history ceases, and *only then* does it exist; before that it is not. It is a commonplace that the beauty of things adds nothing to the matter of knowledge. Works of art add nothing to knowledge except themselves. It is their essence that they should be known. The mind which perceives them apprehends them not as new phenomena which are to have their place assigned them, after due consideration, in relation to other objects in the complicated world. The mind apprehends them at once as things which have no other nature than to be apprehended. They are not things which are to be brought into harmony with the mind by having their relations with other things and the universe explained. They are things which have no necessary relation except to the mind; which are from the first akin to the mind and formed for it, so that being seen they are intelligible. They are not any more intelligible in themselves for any trouble that science may take to get beyond them and inside them, to find out the machinery and the secret of them. Science and history may discover a great deal about them, but they remain intelligible in their own way, indifferent to science and history. Their way of being intelligible is not altered by science; science may, indeed, modify the individual's appreciation of works of art or of art effect, but it does not put its explanation in place of the works of art. The student of the science of art hears his lecture (from the Pythagoreans or others), and does not forget his lecture when listening to music; but however the lecture may improve or interfere with his individual appreciation of the music, it does not alter the *mode* in which the music is apprehended by him. The value of the music to the hearer, be it great or small, is a different thing from its value to the student of physics. And its being heard—its being apprehended in this way—is the whole history, the whole life of the piece of music. The things of the object world, the things with which science is busied, have histories of their own, and make a demand upon science that their histories shall be discovered and made clear to the understanding ; that something shall be predicated of them. The work of art makes no such demand. It declares of itself what it is, and refuses to be compared with other things; refuses to have anything predicated of it which can imply that it is different from what it appears. It is above the world of movement. The one relation which is necessary to it is the relation to the mind that apprehends it.

The relations of objective things can never be summed up. The progress of science is an endless progress. Works of art as things of the objective world are not exempt from this law; it is impossible to know everything about them, as it is impossible to know everything about anything. But considered in themselves they are exempt from this law, because at the first view of them they are apprehended, not as appearances with an unknown reality behind them, but as appearances whose reality is in their appearance; not as problematic things, but as the solution of a problem; not as the starting-points of an inquiry, but as unities whose freedom is unimpaired by external or accidental relations.

From one point of view they are unreal and dead, because they have no share in the give and take of the universe. They are removed from all possibility of change, except the change of material decay and the passing into oblivion. This is one aspect of works of art. In another aspect this apparent deadness becomes a life higher than any life of natural things. The changelessness of the works of art is not death. They are unchanging because they are worlds in themselves, their various parts correspond to the various stages of existence in the object world, and the parts of the work of art are apprehended at once in the apprehension of the completed work, as the various stages of existence would be apprehended if the endless progress of science were to come to an end, and the universe be grasped in one intuition. The work of art is *formally* a solution of this contradiction between the abstract unity of science and the endless process towards it—it does not really do anything to make this contradiction less of a contradiction in the objective world, but it gives an example to show that it is not a contradiction in which the mind is in all cases forced to lose itself. The work of art is a proof that completed knowledge —knowledge which does not imply an endless process—is possible to the mind. The freedom gained by art is an earnest of freedom; a proof that freedom is not a mere ideal.

In all knowledge of the objective world there is a contradiction between the two elements of knowledge, the particular and the universal. The particular thing, with its differences, is known only in relation to that which is permanent and unchangeable, and one. At first neither of the sides has much meaning, but with the progress of knowledge both sides increase in meaning; the manifold is seen to be an ordered world, the unity is not an abstraction but the regulating principle in the manifold. The progress of science is, however, subject to this contradiction, which for science is insuperable, that as it is impossible to exhaust the manifold of the object world, it is impossible ever to attain complete knowledge of the unity as it is shown in the manifold. Science has to go on accomplishing its impossibilities, increasing the sum of knowledge, without drawing any nearer the end of the unknown. Art is the first attempt to find a cure for this. It is a mode in which the mind can make part of the objective world intelligible to itself without being troubled by continual reference to other parts of the objective world beyond the limits it has chosen. It is a return of the mind to itself from seeking fact after fact and law after law in the objective world; a recognition that the mind itself is an end to itself, and its own law.

A moral act is analogous to a creation of art in this way, that it is a denial of the necessity which belongs to the objective world and its laws. It differs from the creation of art in this way, that it has to lose itself apparently in the objective world again. It is an act done to carry out principles that are universally true, but as a *matter of fact* its importance is limited. It is a phenomenon whose true nature is not wholly apparent. The freedom asserted is the freedom of the individual, and that freedom is inward. The freedom gained in the work of art is apparent and universal, it remains to be beheld by all men. The moral act, like the work of art, is individual; nothing else can be put in its place, and in that particular phenomenon the universal reason expresses itself. But not, as in the work of art, for the sake of the expression, for the sake of contemplation, not in order to raise the particular phenomenon, the particular matter, above the complication of the outward necessity, but in obedience to an inner law which does not outwardly contradict the necessity. A moral act, like any other event, is subject to the laws of objective relation, to the necessities of time, of cause and effect. It is outwardly finite and passes away disregarded. Only in the character of the man who does the act is it that the act acquires its freedom, only he knows the value of it. Morality progresses, like science, not by withdrawing itself from the necessity of the objective world, but by accepting that necessity in order to conquer it point by point. The man who is working out his moral freedom has to accept all the shocks of events that come upon him in the form of necessity, in order to give them their moral meaning; and the acts by which he asserts his moral freedom have the appearance of natural events. Hence his progress is endless, because the objective world with which he connects himself is an endless series; hence he has to be content to be free without appearing free. His acts are not done for the sake of appearance but for the sake of reality. They differ from the ordinary events of the objective world in that they are not to be understood by reference to the external events with which they are connected. Their true meaning is in themselves, and in this they resemble works of art. They differ from works of art in that their appearance is not their reality. They appear to be nothing but events in a necessary sequence of causes and effects, but their true meaning is not to be exhausted by exhausting all external influences inside or outside the body of the man who has done the acts. Their true meaning can be gained only by knowledge of the character which is the author of them. The moral character cannot express itself otherwise than in particular acts, as the artist's ideal beauty cannot appear except in particular creations. But the particular acts that express the moral character do not fully express it; no moral act is wholly free; whereas the particular beautiful creations which exist only for the sake of appearance do fully express what they are.

The world of morality is the same world as that of science—the world of finite things and particular events—and morality like science is in opposition to it. The opinion with which science begins is that truth is not apparent; that things as perceived are known only partially, that the relations of things to one another and to the universe are secret, and have to be discovered. Science is in opposition to the apparent universe—the disconnected world of particular things—and its progress is to bring to light more and more the real connection of things. But it can never accomplish its progress. It goes on in faith that nowhere will anything be found to contradict its conception of the unity of the universe, but it can never succeed in proving this in detail, in showing the place of each thing in the universe. Morality also begins in a contradiction between reality and appearance, but the progress of morality is not, like that of science, to start from the appearance and reach the hidden reality. It starts from reality, from the self which is reality to itself, but which at first has no connection with the objective world except the pure negative consciousness of freedom from subjection to the objective world. The progress of morality is to make that apparent which is real, to live in the objective world a life whose law is not discoverable among the laws of the objective world, but only in the self which is a law to itself. Morality begins in pure theory. It is pure self-consciousness and nothing more, the negation of all that is outward—the pure negative 'I am not subject to necessity.' But this inward unity which is proof against all the shocks of time, which is not subject to the objective necessity of particular finite events, is so far in contradiction with itself that it is merely inward and therefore finite, limited by those very finite events whose value it theoretically denies. The self-consciousness would believe itself to be absolute in itself, but it finds that it is absolute only so long as it does nothing. Its freedom is not freedom to do anything, it is mere negation. Then begins the endless progress of morality; it is forced outward into the objective world to make that freedom *apparent* which to the self-conscious subject is the reality of realities. The presupposition of morality is that there is a freedom superior to the incomprehensible necessity of events, and that that freedom must make itself the law of outward things, taking up into itself the necessity of outward things, and becoming the only true explanation of actions which apparently are subject to the ordinary necessities of the objective world. Like science morality conquers point by point, and like science its progress is endless. The nature of its conquest is this, that the particular acts which are called moral are not to be explained simply by reference to other particular events in an objective world, which is *one* world *ex hypothesi*, but must be explained by reference to a unity which is not hypothetical, namely the free individual whose conscious self is not an event nor a particular link in the chain of causation.

There is this resemblance between science and morality, that in both cases reality remains reality, behind the appearance, and appearance remains appearance, hiding the reality. The ordinary perception of things remains one thing, and the scientific explanation of things another. The moral act does not outwardly show its real nature, it appears simply as an event. The moral value of an act cannot be proved to a man who is content with discovering an apparent motive of self-interest.

Art resembles both science and morality in that it is a conquest of nature. It differs from them both, first, because it is not an endless process; secondly, because its product is the unity of reality and appearance. The freedom that it gains is complete because it has not to refer to anything beyond itself, to any horizon beyond which all is unknown, or any ought-to-be which is not yet realised. In art the opposition between the one and the many, between the law and its manifestation, between the subject and the object, is overcome. It is overcome not by simple abolition of the distinction between them, but by so uniting them that each receives the meaning of the other. In art the subject does not express itself in its limitation, in its abstraction, asserting abstractly its superiority to nature and to natural conditions. This assertion of freedom is pure emptiness, a beginning of movement, a point, not a universe. In art the subject goes out into the objective world, and redeems part of that world from bondage to natural laws, makes it the revelation of freedom. The subject is no longer a self-conscious atom separated from the world, anxiously craving for increase in its knowledge of an inexhaustible manifold universe; it has learned from morality that the unity of the universe is not to be sought in the objective world and its laws, because the self is higher than those laws. Neither is it bound by the prejudices of morality which would place the

completion of freedom in an unapproachable future. Art is
the vindication of present freedom. Moral freedom may be
always limited on its phenomenal side by particular contingencies ; there is always an apparent contradiction between
what a man appears and what he ought to be ; his best actions
'are not done without a motive,' or 'are not unmixed good,'
or 'are exceedingly well intended.' But the works of art
are perfect, they express what they are intended to express.
They are not simply the acts of an individual, which may be
interpreted as good or bad according to the intention of the
individual. They are not particular things with an unknown essence behind them. They are particular things
which are to be interpreted or apprehended for what they
are. They are particular things whose meaning is universal,
yet whose meaning is nothing apart from the particularity.
Existing in the world of finitude they have nothing to do
with it. They exist only for the mind. They are things
which are not things, because in them particularity does not
mean separation of reality and appearance, as it does with
all other things.

Art is not to be explained by the categories which are
applicable to finite things. Art is not to be explained, *e.g.*,
by any physiological or psychological inquiries about the
physical conditions of æsthetic perception. All such inquiries,
however successful, can only result in what, as far as art is
concerned, is meaningless abstraction, because they explain
something which is totally different from the work of art,
namely its conditions—things which have to be *before* the
work of art can be apprehended. But they can tell nothing
about the work of art as apprehended, because of this self-
sufficingness of art which will not allow any analysis to explain its works without making them something different
from what they really are.

Art is not to be explained by including it in the subject
matter of ethics, by treating it as a stage in the education of
the individual, or as the storehouse of the ideals of virtue,
because the moral worth of art is accidental to it, it is not
the servant of practical life, no pedagogue to show men the
way to a better life ; it stands beyond morality, has overcome the contradiction which morality is overcoming.

Then is art not to be explained in any way? to be left
untroubled in its own kingdom? Perhaps not if there be

N

other methods of explanation than the methods of natural history or physical science. The works of art are to be left to be appreciated one by one, simply to fulfil their own end without question, only if the unity and the freedom which belong to art are the highest attainable by the mind. But there is a finitude in the works of art which is a challenge to the reason, though not the same finitude as that of the natural things which science explains. Its finitude is not that it is an unexplained thing, but that it is an insufficient explanation, a partial revelation. It is infinite because it is raised above the flux of things, free from the darkness and incomprehensibility which is the curse of finite things considered in themselves; free from the infinite multiplicity of reference to all other atoms in the universe which is characteristic of the particular things of the outward world. It is finite because the mind goes beyond it, because it is not the highest mode in which thought reveals itself to itself. Art is subject not to the criticisms of science, but to the thought which has thought itself for an object, which criticises the methods of science as it criticises sensation and perception, and morality, and all the ways in which mind exerts itself.

Art is higher than science in this way, that it is not limited by an objective world which is superior to it, which defies all efforts to exhaust it. Art can boast of conquests which are absolute, can point to finished work which it is impossible to mend, which contains *in itself* no seed of decay.

It conquers by taking that very particularity which forms the limitation of science and making it universal, making it a thing of infinite value, a thing which the mind accepts as in itself intelligible. Any account of the world which rests satisfied with the mechanical categories of science thus shatters itself against the creations of art and is condemned by them as inadequate. But this conquest of art over the limitations of science is purchased at some cost: the particularity of the work of art, which is quite different from the particularity of natural things, still remains as a limitation. It is a limit beyond which lies, not the objective world, but the intellectual world to which the work of art belongs. The science of that world is not an endless process, but the activity of thought which has come to know that the unity

which is the presupposition of science is thought, that the
moral ideal of freedom is thought, and that it is thought
which in the work of art finds its own image.

The philosophy of art must necessarily be less abstract
than pure metaphysics or ethics, because it is not like
them a criticism or a statement of universal conditions;
it does not simply state what is true of all art, as metaphysics or ethics state what is true of all experience and
of all morality. The philosophy of art cannot speak, or
not for long, of the sublime and the beautiful in the abstract. It must recognise what is particular and apparently contingent and inexplicable in the creations of art.
It must recognise that they are necessarily connected each
with its own particular time. Metaphysics and ethics
may look on experience and morality abstractly, apart
from any reference to the history of man, considering the
elements in them that are one and the same in all minds.
The philosophy of art must be a philosophy of history as well.
Its end is not to state abstractly what the elements in art-
creation or æsthetic apprehension are, which are the same in
all cases. It recognises that what is important in creations of
art is not their identity but their difference, their individuality, not their conformity to any type or standard. Part of
their individuality is their relation to particular times and
seasons in the actual history of the world. The problem of
the philosophy of art is to make the history of art intelligible
—not simply a series of biographies or catalogues, of artists
or their works, but a history showing the place of art in the
development of the human reason. It is not a light task,
but it is not an impossibility. It is simply a working out of
the problem which finds many occasions to present itself
nowadays. ' What is meant by saying that the art of a
people or a century enables us to understand the people or
the century?' What is there in art which makes it a kind
of explanation of things apparently so different from itself?
Is it anything but an amiable illusion to suppose that Greek
art has more than an external relation to Greek history? or
that anything can be inferred from the history of art about
the progress of humanity as a whole? The philosophy of
art will have to show whether the creations of art are to
be regarded as fortuitous appearances, inexplicable—as they

certainly are—by any of the ordinary methods of science, or
whether they are to find their place in the history, not of
events, but of the achievements of reason in this actual
world. If it is possible to show that all the changes in man's
ways of regarding the universe are not accidental, but necessities of thought, then there will be a philosophy of art.
All the various kinds of art, and all the artists, and all the
works of art will then become intelligible—not as phenomena in relation to other phenomena (in which case they
are unintelligible), but as comprehended in a system of
knowledge, which is not the science of an objective world,
but the science of all that the mind knows about itself. This
science would include not only abstract metaphysics and ethics,
as sciences of what is necessary in knowledge and morality,
but also a philosophy of the progress of thought in time.
Part of this philosophy will be the philosophy of art, for art
has made good its right to be considered as belonging to the
world of thought, not to the natural world, and yet its connection with particular periods in history is something
which cannot be abstracted from. If the science of thought
is to be purely abstract, then there is no place for the
philosophy of art. But neither will there be room for the
consideration of religion, or of the history of philosophy or
of political science, because all these things imply reference
to the concrete facts of time. This science of the development
of thought will not be empirical, but *à priori* (if there be any
meaning in *à priori*) because it begins not like ordinary
science with a suspicion that there is unity somewhere, an
unexplained presupposition that the universe which it explains is one universe, but with the clear knowledge that
thought is the unity of the universe, and that the apparent
going out of thought to an object apparently external to
thought is only appearance.

Such a philosophy of art will get rid of some annoying
questions. It will get rid of the question about the relation
of art to morality. It will show that art has not to do either
with the furthering or the hindering of the individual's moral
progress. There are at least three possible cases in which
art may appear to have an immoral influence. Two of
these are clearly cases where it is ignorance of art that
really is the misleading power. Art brings with it the
possibility of bad art: but this can hardly be made a

ground of accusation against it; in any case, ignorance or contempt of art will not make bad art less harmful. Or works of art which are pure and great in themselves may be turned to evil, because art as an image of human life includes the element of evil in it—it represents evil on the stage, or in poems. But any bad influence it may exert in this way is plainly accidental—not to be considered except by the pathologist of human nature. Or, thirdly, art though served with unselfishness and sincerity may be unfitted to be the sole end of any one man's life. It may be that the practical life is not sacrificed to the theoretic or the artistic life without retribution. This is not a simple question, but whatever ethics, or casuistry, or any other science may say to it, it is certain that art itself, and the philosophy of art, will make no claim on anyone to become less than other men before he can become an artist. What is it that makes a man moral? Not his actions, but his habitual view of things and events, and men, and himself— his living memory which makes him true to himself and to all his neighbours. The selfish man's memory is one to which the artistic or imaginative representation of things is utterly repugnant. He remembers only what has served or what has baffled him, and values the particulars of his experience only in reference to his own selfish ends. The unselfish memory remembers things and men as the artist remembers them. It values the things of experience according as they are good or bad; that is, according as they fulfil their proper end or not—not using any abstract standard of good or bad, but Plato's science of inexact things, which enables a man to find his way home, using imagination, for which each particular thing has an interest of its own, apart from any question of its use, apart from all abstract preconceptions of what ought to be. Art is the wide world's memory of things, and any man may make his own memory a sharer in its wisdom on one condition—that he shall not hate or love anything that is revealed to him there according as it thwarts or furthers his selfish purposes, but according to its own virtues or vices. The artistic imagination is part of the highest morality, because it gets rid of the last selfishness of all—the Stoic selfishness which is proud of its superiority to external things.

The philosophy of art has no other aim than to bring

together as far as possible into one view all that there is
in the world's memory—to make a history in which the
characters shall speak for themselves, become themselves
the interpreters of the history.   It will regard the artists
as helping to create the mind of the ages in which they
live- (the mind is only what it knows and worships) and the
artists are the means by which the different nations and
ages come to have characters of their own.

The philosophy of art finds periods of ambition, of
achievement, of criticism and barrenness, just as the biographer of any one artist distinguishes the periods in his
life—the periods of youth and imitation, of manhood and
originality, or the period of inspiration and the period of
faultlessness, or otherwise.   Only to the biographer the
succession of phases in the life of his hero is more or less a
matter of contingency—the philosophy of art finds the
periods succeeding one another according to the necessity
of thought.   It does this because it has room enough to
work in.   The biographer finds his labour ended by the
death of the man he is writing about, or perhaps the decay
of his powers; but where it is the art of the world which
is studied there is less of such interruption to inquiry.
Decay of art can be explained because it is seen what succeeds it—what new form of intelligence takes the place
of art, as Greek philosophy grew strong when Greek art
began to decline from its supremacy.   It can compare Greek
art and Christian art, not as two independent phenomena,
but as two different forms of judgment, where the first form
is necessarily first and progress toward the second is inevitable.

To do this it has to consider not only art but religion
and the history of philosophy, and show how the art of an
age is related to the other forms of intellectual activity in
that age, and how all even in their opposition are expressions
of one spirit.   The history of Greek philosophy notes, as
the characteristic of Greek philosophy, that it does not
centre on the conception of the self with his consciousness
and knowledge, opposed to an external real world, that it
accepts at first the unity of thought and being and confuses
clear conception with science.   Greek art and Greek religion
are found to be also on this level of thought.   The gods
are to be worshipped; there is no disputing about the

evidences of their existence: they are accepted because they
are beautiful, more beautiful than any actual thing : the
thought of the worshipper is satisfied with the mere idea of
the god : he does not ask for any proofs of the being of
Apollo or Athena. Greek art is the most perfect of all art,
because it appeals least of all to the understanding which
looks for the meaning of things. Greek sculpture is not
symbolic of anything. It sets up the god before the
worshipper—for his contemplation, not to excite his
curiosity. The Greek gods in sculpture are beautiful as
they are: they do not show their power in any matter-of-
fact way. That they are benefactors of mankind in any
way is kept in the background, and is in no case a necessary
part of their character. They are revered not as helpers,
but as impersonations of what is most admirable in man.
They are most strong and most beautiful, but they take
little part in the earthly contests of men. Greek art is a
progress from this high ideal of pure beauty to less pure,
more complicated forms. The tragedy is an effort to solve
the contradiction implicit in sculpture—namely the contradiction between the Olympian *power* and the Olympian
weakness, between the freedom of the ideal and its incapacity
to influence action. The drama shows the gods and heroes
retaining their worshipfulness, their divinity, and their
heroism even in the entanglement of circumstances. The
end of tragedy comes when it is no longer the spectacle of
the action as a whole that claims the attention, but the
feelings or the inner life of the hero. Then the passions
are not purified as they were by the tragic pity and terror
that had no weakness in them. The pathetic tragedy
against which Plato wrote is part of the same movement of
thought with the rise of the sophistic teaching. It is the
return of mind into itself, making a universe for itself out
of its own accidents. The true remedy for this is comedy,
which is a revolt against pathos, and also a reaction against
the elder tragedy because it finds that anything may be
true of the gods and heroes to a mind robust enough of
imagination. Comedy is not the private fantasy of a mind
which would like to upset the universe. It is unsparing
laughter at everything, even at itself. It confesses that
it is not its business to preserve the heroic aspect of heroes
or the divine aspect of the gods. It cannot keep anything

in order. But it will waken up the sleepers who were too
fond of their own dreams; it will show them all the baseness
and meanness they had shut their eyes to, and at the same
time the beauty of a new heaven, with the clouds in it, and
the deathless race of birds, and of a new earth with cool
green places in it, and the voice of frogs to reprove the
faint-hearted. Aristophanes is not the destroyer : he is the
maker of a new world of art. Sculpture had made gods
who were beautiful but motionless, ineffectual. Tragedy
made the gods and heroes act in their proper characters,
and gradually came to forget the unity of the drama and to
make interesting the sorrows—not the misfortunes, but the
lamentations—of the hero. Then comedy found work to do.
The pathetic tragedy had destroyed the old world of tragedy.
Comedy could not bring back the old simple manner of
regarding things, but it could show at least that there were
other things in the world than weeping heroes. It showed
that there were all sorts of things in the world and pointed
them out, pretending not to know anything about the way
they should be arranged, and finding nothing surprising in
the co-existence of beauty and infamy. The progress of
Greek art is a progress from contemplation, like that of
Xenophanes when he found the secret of the universe by
looking into the open heaven, to dramatic interest. It is a
progress from simplicity to complication, from rest to movement, from the sameness of the statue to the contradiction
of comedy. In one sense it was a decline of art. The
statue is a pure work of art ; the drama cannot avoid raising
more questions than it can answer. But in another way
it was progress. It was the invention of new beauty : the
beauty of movement, of action. Thought could not rest
without trying to include all things in art. The progress
was from the pure beauty of the ideal, in sculpture, to the
perplexed beauty of the actual world as it appears, all in
confusion, in Aristophanes. It is the movement from
abstract to positive thought in the sphere of art.

There is an analogous progress in all art : a progress
from the art which is akin to religion to the art which is
akin to science. Icelandic poetry begins with cosmogonies
and theogonies. When the character of the gods is becoming settled they are represented in action and adventure.
Worship of the gods is not in itself a full satisfaction of the

mind : it must see characters in movement : circumstance
and chance must try their utmost against the hero. Then
the god and the hero are found to be not very different from
ordinary men : to have no different kind of courage from
ordinary men. Then it is the actual life of men that is
interesting, and with an interest far exceeding that of the
stories of the gods. In this kind of art all things are
interesting that are true—the horses and the ships and the
hay-fields, and the children that play at being men, as well
as the wisdom of Njal or the high courage of Gunnar.

In the Christian art of Europe there is the same progress, only there is this difference, that the religious art
which comes first is not like that of Greece or Scandinavia.
The Greek poets and sculptors made the gods they worshipped, because what was clearly seen was reckoned true.
Christianity belongs to a new age which has learned some
things from Stoics and Sceptics—the difference between
reality and appearance, and the opposition of the thinking
subject to the objective world. The distinguishing mark of
Christianity is that it is true in the strict historic sense. It
is not a matter of imagination but of evidence. Hegel
says that there could be no battle between Christ and the
old gods, because they belonged to quite different spheres
of thought. The Greek gods were nowhere but in the
imagination. This makes a difference between Christian
and Greek art from the outset. Art was all-important to
Greek religion, for the god who was not clearly imagined
was nothing. In the art of Christianity there is no need,
no possibility that the image should accurately represent the
reality. They are incommensurate from the first. The
Byzantine image is not the god to be worshipped, but a
symbol. Religion goes beyond art and remains beyond it, a
different kind of life for ever. The progress of Christian
art is as in Greek art towards a complete conquest of the
universe—to find beauty not in gods and heroes only, but
in all levels of existence. It does this, however, always
with the consciousness that its effort is doomed to fail, that
it is less than the reality, that it is in the unseen and the
spiritual that the chief beauty dwells, inexpressible by art.
This very sense of deficiency, however, leads it to be per-
severing beyond all Greek art in presentation of reality, and
of any atom of reality that can be made to have any artistic

interest at all. And the 'soothfastness' of a story comes
to be part of its charm and its claim to immortality, as the
Scottish poet thought.[1] So Giotto painted fewer pictures
for devotion and more for the intelligence, setting down
things in their reality. So Dante portrayed each man he
met in Hell, Purgatory, or Paradise without regard to anything but the nature of the man before him: not being
interested in anything more than in the true nature of the
man, to whom the doom passed on him is an external thing.
There was a separation imminent between religion and art
when it was possible to treat calmly of low human things
unblinded by the light of theology. There was no dis-
appearance of religion. The Norse religion grew weak in
proportion as Norse culture and art and knowledge of
humanity grew. But the Christian religion was stronger
than this: it could not pass away into art. There was a
separation for a time of spiritual religion from art, as there
was a separation of philosophy from both. Art was left
to go its own way. It ceaséd, as philosophy ceased, to be
merely the interpreter of Christian tradition. It expressed
in its own way, as philosophy expressed in its own way, the
idea of Christianity, that it is the individual subject which
is of infinite value. The music which is the creation of the
modern world expresses that which is inexpressible in all
other arts—the mind's freedom from the contingency of the
outward world and obedience to its own law.

W. P. KER.

[1] Barbour, *Bruce*, at the beginning.

VII.

THE SOCIAL ORGANISM.

ENGLISH ethical philosophy is no longer purely individual-istic. Hume pursued the principles of individualism to their logical conclusion, and refuted it as a theory of knowledge by revealing the absolute scepticism which it involves. The question which lies at the basis of the ' Critique of Pure Reason ' shows that Kant considered Hume's work final, and individualism an exhausted vein of thought. History also corroborated the destructive teachings of Hume when indi-vidualism received its practical refutation in the French Revolution. Both theoretically and practically the disinte-grating movement of thought completed its work and ex-hausted itself at the close of the last century. It isolated the individual from his physical and spiritual surroundings, and then found that he was only the shadow of a false philo-sophy. The present age is abandoning the philosophy which regarded mind as a thinking thing acting *in vacuo*, it has lost faith in moral Melchisedecs, and it demands from all the genealogy of their habits of thought and action. The pro-blems of individualism are losing their interest, and fresh problems, which lay beyond the horizon of the past age, have by the silent progress of thought come into the fore-front of our own. The educated attention of the present is directed to the relations of individuals rather than to indi-viduals themselves : and these relations are regarded, in a more or less uncertain sense, as essential to, if not con-stitutive of, individuals. Modern speculation is, in a word, reconstructive in its tendency. It endeavours to free itself of its inherited atomism, and fit the individual into his sur-roundings. Theories of society are supplanting theories of the individual ; and when the individual is made the subject of investigation he is found, at the worst, to be altruistic as well as egoistic.

But although English philosophy is moving away from the problems and practical issues of individualism, it is still, in a great degree, ruled by its presuppositions. Such writers as Mr. Spencer still speculate on its principles, although the thoughts which give them power are alien to it. Like the servants of the wounded Ahab, they stay their master in his chariot till the eve. The interest and worth of the ethical speculations of Mr. Spencer arise from the use which he makes of the conceptions of evolution and organism; but no torture of individualism can cause it to yield these conceptions. They have been adopted out of the current thought of the age on scientific subjects, and then superimposed on an alien philosophy. Having proved themselves useful in the field of biology to a degree which it is difficult to overestimate, they have been immediately applied to that of ethics. Nor do these ideas receive a new meaning from their new application, but they retain in the new context the significance that they had in the old. Now the ideas that are true and relevant in one sphere can be applied to another and different sphere only in the way of analogy and metaphor; and we believe that Mr. Spencer's ethical teachings as a whole consist on the one hand of an inherited Hedonism, and on the other of elaborate analogies drawn between the physical structures and habits of animals and the mental structure and ethical habits of men.

Such at all events is his doctrine of the organic structure of society. The living body is regarded as the type of an organic existence, and society is regarded as organic in so far, and in so far only, as it is like a living body. A quotation from his answer to the question, 'What is a society?' will establish our assertion. 'But now, regarding a society as a thing, what kind of thing must we call it? . . . There are two great classes of aggregates with which the social aggregate may be compared—the inorganic and the organic. Are the attributes of a society, considered apart from its living units, in any way like those of a not-living body? or are they in any way like those of a living body? or are they entirely unlike those of both?

'The first of these questions needs only to be asked to be answered in the negative. A whole of which the parts are alive, cannot, in its general characters, be like lifeless whole. The second question, not to be thus promptly answered, is to be answered in the affirmative. The reasons for asserting that the permanent relations among the parts of a society are analogous to the permanent relations among the parts of a living body, we have now to consider.' [1]

In his next chapter accordingly, Mr. Spencer finds these analogies in great abundance and displays them with great ingenuity. Society grows like a living body; it goes through processes of differentiation and integration like a living body; it adapts itself to its environment like a living body; it has alimentary, distributive, and regulative structures like a living body; it is now starved and now overfed like a living body; it has up-line and down-line railways like the double set of tubes in a living body. In this strain he has proceeded far, but there is no reason in the nature of *things* why he should not have proceeded further; for ingenuity has a greater hand than truth in the production of analogies, and there are no two objects in the universe absolutely different from each other.

' Do you see that cloud, that's almost in shape like a camel?' 'By the mass, and 'tis like a camel, indeed.' 'Methinks, it is like a weasel.' 'It is backed like a weasel.' 'Or, like a whale?' 'Very like a whale.'

In his 'Qualifications and Summary' (Vol. I. p. 614), however, Mr. Spencer says that he has 'used the analogies elaborated but as a scaffolding to help in building up a coherent body of sociological inductions.' 'Let us,' he continues, 'take away the scaffolding; the inductions will stand by themselves.' But an examination will show that the scaffolding has been built into his edifice, and that the structure tumbles down with its removal. Or, dropping metaphor, the moment that society ceases to be like a 'living body' it ceases to be organic. Abandoned by the 'living body' which guides him, Mr. Spencer stumbles into individualism. Failing to detect a social sensorium by the method which revealed the social stomach and nervous system, Mr. Spencer acknowledges that there is an 'extreme unlikeness,' a 'fundamental difference,' between the social organism and the individual organism. 'The parts of an animal form a concrete whole; but the parts of a society form a whole that is

[1] *Sociology*, Vol. I. p. 466.

discrete.'[1] Now, no one can deny the discrete character of
society; and it will always remain true 'that the living
units composing it are not in contact, but more or less
widely dispersed.' But if society is an organic whole this
discreteness must be overcome, and unity must assert itself
through and amidst the differences. In other words, the
notions that society is 'discrete' and that it is a 'whole'
cannot be immediately combined in this way; and discreteness cannot be the permanent characteristic of that which
is organic. But waiving this objection for the present, it is
at least evident that the notion of discreteness is fatal to the
organism of a living body. Hence society is inorganic because discrete; or, the living body is inorganic because concrete; or the living body is not the type and test of that
which is organic.

Mr. Spencer silently admits the first of these suppositions,
and treats society in this particular as if it were inorganic.
'In the one' (the individual organism) he says, 'consciousness is concentrated in a small part of the aggregate. In
the other it is diffused throughout the aggregate. . . . As,
then, there is no social sensorium, it results that the welfare
of the aggregate, considered apart from that of the units, is
not an end to be sought. The society exists for the benefit
of its members; not its members for the benefit of society.'[2]

Before attempting to show that Mr. Spencer in this passage treats society as if it were nothing more than an
aggregate, and from an individualistic point of view, it will
be well to note that 'the welfare of the aggregate considered
apart from that of the units' is a welfare which no one can
contend for or conceive. Verily, 'the claims of the body
politic are nothing *in themselves*, and become something only
in so far as they embody the claims of its component individuals.' No one can deny that society apart from individuals is nothing; but this does not mean that the individual, as an individual, is everything. It is true that
society is nothing apart from individuals; but, if society is
organic, it is equally true that *individuals apart from society*
are nothing. Society must exist for the benefit of its component parts, and the component parts must also exist for
the benefit of society. Nay, more, if society is an organism,
then it is impossible to separate the welfare of the whole

[1] *Sociology.* I. 475.　　　　　[2] *Sociology,* I. 479.

from the welfare of the members, or the welfare of the members from the welfare of the whole. To separate the one from the other is to give independent existence to unreal abstractions and to empty the notion of organic unity of its distinctive content.

Mr. Spencer denies society as an end and makes it a means by which the welfare of individuals is secured; the last and the only end is the welfare of the individuals composing it. But means and end, first of all, exist apart from each other —the former has an existence and a meaning in itself, and the latter has also an existence and meaning in itself and for itself; and, secondly, the meaning of the former is cancelled in that of the latter. The means, say, of the ethical elevation of the life of the nineteenth century is the teaching of Mr. Spencer; that teaching then must first of all *be*, independently of the attainment of its end. If, on the other hand, it attains the end for which it exists, then it is dispensed with, lost in the end, and will be thrown aside as a husk when it has been absorbed into the characters of nineteenth-century Englishmen. Society, if it is a means for individuals, must in the first place exist outside and independently of its individuals, just as this pen exists apart from the ink which flows through it. But society, as Mr. Spencer admits, does not, and never has existed apart from the individuals composing it, and was, therefore, never mere means, but always means + something more. Again, if it is mere means, then, like all other means, it must perish in the attainment of its end; every society, therefore, that secures the welfare of its members perishes in the very act. But, as a matter of fact, it is the society which fails to secure the welfare of its members that is disintegrated, and not that which succeeds in doing so. The ideal of a progressive society which is mere means is the absolute disintegration of itself and the production of isolated, mutually independent individuals; and Mr. Spencer's chapter on 'Society is an Organism' should, consistently with this view, show how, as the world moves, the unity of society becomes more and more disintegrated and dissipated. Moreover, an individual who regards society as mere means, regards the individuals constituting society as mere means— unless society be something apart from them, which neither Mr. Spencer nor anyone else admits; and, if every individual regards his neighbours as means, then the rank and destructive individualism which, in the French Revolution, rent asunder every political and social bond, is the theoretic ideal; and the world is making for the state of nature in which its wise men will be running wild in the woods, and, as Voltaire suggests, 'running on all fours.'

The conception of means and end is, however, not applicable to an organism. It is because that conception breaks down into difference, and, instead of expressing the intimacy and complexity of the relations of whole and members, holds them apart at arm's length, that the conception of organic unity becomes necessary. In the presence of even the lowest life, the scientific point of view must be abandoned for the philosophic.

The perfection of organic well-being is that the collective activities seem to be one. The physical organism into which no alien ingredient, material, chemical, electric, or nervous, has penetrated, 'has no system'; its life is 'a beam of perfect white light, itself unseen, because it is of that perfect whiteness, and no irregular obstruction has yet broken it into colours.' Its energy is one and indivisible; at no time can we say 'here is the activity of the member, there that of the whole'; for the activity of the member *is* that of the whole, and that of the whole *is* the activity of the members. The unity, because it is an organic unity, must not only persist under the differences, but it must differentiate itself, flow out into the parts, and again integrate the differences and flow back through the parts into unity. Here there is none of the self-seeking of means and end. No member secures its welfare at the expense of the whole: indeed it has no welfare except that which is also the welfare of the concrete organism.

If society therefore is an organism, it exists not only as end but also as means. The life that animates the individual is that of the social whole as much as it is his own. His purpose is not his own particular welfare, nor is it the particular welfare of his neighbours; but it is the welfare of the social whole to which they all belong and which lives in them. The notion of organic unity involves that the individual, cut away from society, becomes a severed limb, a lifeless, meaningless mass; that without the purposes of society he has no purposes at all, and cannot even be egoistic: and that the life which he perverts to selfish ends is not merely his own but that of the moral organism which lives in him.

The light that led astray
Was light from heaven,

and heaven holds him responsible; for, although he went astray, 'twas light *from heaven.*

The real meaning of the doctrine that society is an organism is, that an individual has no life except that which is social, and that he cannot realise his own purposes except in realising the larger purposes of society. No concatenation of parts, no contiguity in space, no joints and ligatures, can bind members into an organism. The bond must be inward, not outward; it must be essential, not accidental; it must be such, in a word, that the parts fall asunder into meaningless abstractions when the bond is broken. Whatever the difficulties may be in finding the unity of the social organism, if we hold by the doctrine and make it more than a metaphor, we must recognise that society and individuals actually form such a whole, and that apart from each other they are both nothing but names; and we must cease to speak of individuals as if they ever could exist apart from society, or could attain their purposes except by becoming its organs and carrying out its purposes. It seems to me that the first and last duty of man is to know and to do those things which the social community of which he is a member calls upon him to do. His mission is prescribed to him by the position in society into which he is born and educated, and his welfare depends upon its performance. Hamlet did not create his duties: the time was already out of joint, and he was born to set it right. The demand was not made by himself nor by any other individual, but by the ethical organism of which he was a member, by the spirit of the age whose instrument he was. Nor is this the case with princes alone. Everyone, however humble, finds his duties in the social organism. Let society be dumb, let it cease to prescribe duties and have purposes of its own, and every individual component must hold his hands idle. The interests which men have differ widely in extent, but the interests of all are the interests of the station or circle which constitutes their society, and all do their duties to themselves if they give themselves up to these interests and constitute themselves consciously into organs of their 'universal.' We have very different views

about the extent of the ethical horizon, and our sky is often
so low that we strike it with our sublime heads, but still the
large heavens shelter us all. The humblest breast rises and
falls with the breath of the universal, and our ethical salvation consists in being its willing organs. The heart beats,
the brain operates, the hand works, through the power and
for the sake of the whole; and the highest moral ambition
consists in sacrificing particular ends and realising those
of the social organism. The social ends comprise the highest
ends of all men, for the ends of all are but the product of
the organic life which differentiates itself in the individuals
and returns through them enriched. But Mr. Spencer's
social organism is not this; it is rather a resultant, a
mechanical and temporal equipoise produced by the opposition and collision of individuals, each of whom seeks his own
welfare and not that of society. If society has no purposes,
if there are nothing but ends of individuals, it is difficult to
see how the organism is, after all, anything better than an
aggregate. The social whole is unable to gather itself
back out of its discreteness, and it is inorganic because it is
'fundamentally' unlike a 'living body.'

Must we then give up the doctrine of the organic nature
of society? Does the organic idea as well as the organic
metaphor break down before the discreteness of society?
Or may it not be proved that society is more concrete as
well as more discrete than any physical type of organism;
that it is more concrete *because* it is more discrete; and
that its self-integration is more intense because its self-
differentiation is more complete? In a word, may not
society be unlike a living body because it is *more* organic,
and not because it is less so? I think it may, and must
endeavour to prove it. We cannot here attempt to trace
the organic idea in its successive manifestations from the
vegetable and animal organism up to humanity. It may be
at present sufficient to *assert* that it is first manifested in a
living body, and not in a dead body: and that it is the life—
whether that be, as Mr. Spencer teaches, a power to adapt
itself to its environment or not—and not the tissues and
nervous currents, which bind the parts into a unity. Tissues
and currents can only consist of contiguous atoms: their
parts, however thinned and etherealised, lie outside of each
other. Tissues and currents are only parts of an organism,

but by means of sensation they are retracted out of their outwardness and become organs. I know that my hand is a part of my physical organism, not primarily because I know that it is connected to it by nervous currents, but because it is a source of pain or pleasure to *me*. Sensation abolishes difference. As long as it lasts organ and organism are not distinguishable, but the whole organism in its concrete existence is present in all its sensations. It is not the palate that feels pleasure or the ear that feels pain, but it is the organism as a unit that feels the pleasure and the pain. Although sensation, however, gathers up the parts into an intense unity, it does not gather them into a *permanent* unity. Sensation is itself fleeting; and when it vanishes, the organism falls back into difference and its parts are indifferent to it. Sensations may appear in quick succession, like the atoms of a fluid, but nevertheless they can but repeat the same tale, assert the unity of the organism and then deny it in disappearing. Sensations overcome the outwardness of space, and are themselves overcome by the discreteness of time. But when sensations are related to the ego, when they are known as *in me*, or as *mine*, then they attain fixity and permanence. They are no longer a mere manifold *capable* of being arranged by the intelligence; they are not merely expressed by inarticulate cries; but can be spoken of and described as pleasant or painful, sweet or bitter. In a word, they are thoughts, integral parts of my intellectual possessions that will to some degree modify my future. The unity of the organism, which was not present in the physical structure, and which was only temporarily manifest in sensation, becomes in consciousness a permanent fact. In a more accurate way, and by entirely repudiating this dualism of sense and thought, it might be said that the thought which exists as sensation does not come to itself in sensation, does not overcome its own difference by knowing itself, as it does in self-conscious existence. The life of an animal is not a complete unity because it is not a **unity for** the animal itself. The animal, or at any rate the being which is only sensitive, is not a permanent object to itself; it cannot return upon its sensations and weld them into a single, united experience. It cannot overcome the difference of time. It lives in the moment, and it cannot constitute the past into the possibility of its future, or the future into the motive of the

o 2

present. In truth it has no past, present, or future, but an
undistinguished, ever-recurring *now*. To an observer the
life of an animal may present a rude outline of the complex
organism of his own life, for consistent processes are carried
on through long periods of time by the animal. Means are
subordinated to ends, proximate ends to further ends, and
the whole to an ultimate and all-embracing end. Nor are
such concatenations as we find in the actions of a bird in
building its nest and in producing and protecting its young
accidental or meaningless. They suggest a life ruled by an
end. But it is difficult to believe that the animal itself
grasps this end. The unerring and direct character of its
actions precludes such a notion. The end is nature's and
not the animal's. The animal's function is to obey laws
which it cannot disobey, to realise purposes which it has
not understood, to be an instrument in the hand of a power
which *has* purposes and which attains these purposes through
the actions of the animal. It is, however, a matter for
science, and not for philosophy, to determine what animal
first realises the meaning of its own life; where the line
between consciousness and self-consciousness is drawn is
perfectly indifferent, at least to idealism; and all that we
need insist upon here is that the animal which is incapable of
grasping its own end is an instrument, and not an organism
in the true sense of the word. The necessity of the actions
of such a living body lies outside of itself. But the necessity
of a thing is its deepest meaning, and the instrument can
only be adequately explained in the end for which it exists.
Hence the significance, the meaning, of the animal's life not
only lies beyond its own grasp, but can only be found in the
whole of which the animal is a part. The naturalist knows
the animal when he recognises it as a manifestation of some
of the laws of nature, and looks at it from the point of view
of the species. In other words, it is the wisdom *of nature*
that he detects maintaining itself as an unbroken unity
amidst all the differences of the sensitive and atomic life
of the animal; and it is by no means the wisdom of the
animal itself. The meaning of the life of the animal, the
thought, which it is, and on account of which it is intelligible, does not come back to itself; and hence it is not
completely organic.

But in the intellectual and practical life of man thought
is at home with itself. The meaning of a man's life is within

his own grasp. He can stand above his environment, look before and after, recognise the forces which play around him, and by recognising them overcome them. Like every other animal, he has to assert himself against the complex powers of his environment, which tend to dissipate his life into the self-external atomism of inorganic existence. But, unlike other animals, he can detach himself from his environment—*i.e.* know himself as existing apart from it. He can *understand* his environment, and by understanding it he can take its necessity into himself; or, in other words, he can impress the environment with the stamp of his own intelligence and elevate the natural into the spiritual. The struggle between man and his surroundings is unequal, and must end in the victory of spirit. For the conditions imposed upon a man by his environment are nothing to him until they have penetrated into his consciousness, and when they have done that they have subjected themselves to a power which has transmuted them. They are no longer mere conditions but *thoughts*—parts of the possession of the power which understands them. Into the 'crystal sphere' of the intelligence nothing can enter except by giving up its opposition and submitting to become a part of that sphere. In fact, the struggle between the self-conscious being and his environment must not be compared to the collision of two balls, or the clash of two forces in the same plane. Man is not a particular amongst particulars. Thought does not cease to be where the physical world begins, but it overlaps it and brings it back interpreted into itself. Man, as a rational being, is his own limit. Whatever the necessity may be which encircles his life, it cannot affect his character until he has put his signature to it, adopted it, and made it his motive. But if it is his motive it is *in* him, not around him or above: it is his own necessity and not an alien one. It is not our intention to minimise the significance of that necessity the voice of which we hear, if we are considerate, long before time has furrowed our faces, saying with omnipotent authority, 'This way shalt thou go, not that.' But yet the necessity has no ethical character until I have given it meaning. The humblest can use the words of Cæsar and say—

> We were two lions litter'd in one day,
> And I the elder and more terrible.

My poverty, my wealth, my health, my sickness, seem

almost everything to me; but they are not everything; that which is greatest, after all, is that power which I have of constituting my poverty, my wealth, my health, and my sickness, into my bane or my blessing, my good or my evil. It is I, in the end, who give my surroundings significance.

This doctrine, old as the record of the choice of the forbidden fruit, is the Alpha and Omega of ethics. Man is self-conscious, man is free, man is his own limit, his own necessity, his own fate; this is the last foundation of every theory of ethics which has any meaning. For if this is not true, if man serves purposes which he can neither reject nor accept, if he is the slave of his conditions, then ethics will be a science which treats of the conditions of actions and not the science of human life. Ethics should then be laid aside with astrology, as a science of that which is not; a plaything of the world's infancy, unworthy of the attention of a scientific age. Science should turn away from man, and endeavour only to understand the huge mechanism with which the human cog or crank moves, it should reveal the absurdity of practical hortative ethics, and teach that good and evil are but names of phenomena that appear in man, and emanate out of his conditions. Freedom, self-consciousness, the organic completeness of man, is the fact with which ethics begins and ends; and we cannot begin lower, as Mr. Spencer does, unless we believe that animals, too, are moral and immoral, are ends in themselves, and therefore not to be used as instruments by man. But the necessity to live will be a sufficient practical defence against this side of Mr. Spencer's 'data of ethics;' for we cannot afford to recognise the life of every creeping thing as of infinite value in itself. In the sphere of nature we shall still seek for utility; we shall still recognise that the end for which the life that is not self-conscious exists lies beyond that life, and protect the life by using it with reference to its end.

But on the other hand freedom cannot be disproved, because it is impossible for intelligence to disprove itself by making itself a mere instrument. It is intelligence that guides the disproof as well as the proof; the disproof is only a new manifestation of the existence and energy of intelligence. Reason cannot commit suicide although man can, and absolute scepticism is impossible. 'It is a medicine which removes itself as well as the disease.' Every effort made by theoretical and practical reason is but a reassertion of its own infinitude; it is not the establishment, but the removal, of a limit; it is a process by which something which *was* not for the individual is brought within and made a part of his intellectual or moral being.

In this sense Mr. Spencer's view of society as a 'discrete' whole is true; for every individual is his own limit, a complete organism, with his meaning in himself. The discreteness, however, is far deeper than anything which finds expression in Mr. Spencer's writings. For the social organism is not only 'sensitive' in every part, but it is self-conscious in every part. Individuals are not merely 'not in contact,' but they are ethically isolated in so far as everyone is always his own end. Good and evil are farther from each other than the east and west; and a ruptured society is not so easily put together as a broken pot. The forces that hold men asunder have a stronger repellent power than anything material. Hence, if society is organic, it must conquer difference in its strongest citadel, and conquer it too by ethical means. No theory of the organism of society can avail, if in its ardour to reconstruct society it does violence to the individual's independence and compromises his right to seek his own welfare. Man must be fitted into his surroundings, and made the means of the good of society without compromising his right to realise his own purposes. It is not enough to emphasise his environment, and make him, as Mr. Spencer does, a mere vane which turns round when the wind shifts; for, unless freedom is a myth and ethics a scientific superstition, life is more than a process of self-adaptation. It adapts the environment to itself as well as itself to its environment, and this is a side which Darwinian development, in all its applications, tends to minimise. For the environment which this age is never weary of emphasising, and which individualism of necessity neglects, is after all but the raw material of the life, and only *capable* of being converted into physical or intellectual wealth by the energy of that life. Whatever be the influence of an individual's surroundings, however deeply he is indebted to the past for what he is at present, true as it must be that he is in some sense the heir of the experience of the ages, it is also true that the experience of the ages must receive the stamp of the individual's own character, and thereby assume a meaning and form which could not be inherited.

The doctrine that society is an organism must take up the good that was in individualism into itself. No theory of ethics can afford to cast away the absolute liberty and infinite worth of the individual. Freedom has been bought at too great a price to be bartered away. It is the product of the toil of modern history from the time when Christ taught the equality and brotherhood of mankind, to the time when liberty, equality, and fraternity were abstractly realised in the French Revolution. Before the individual's growing consciousness of freedom, the Roman Empire, the Roman Church, and the terrors of a monotheistic God had to retire. The world at length has been educated into an uncompromising consciousness of its right to freedom, and the individual is now bidden see to himself. This freedom manifested itself in France as a freedom from restraint. It assumed a hostile attitude to the institutions of the time, swept away the accumulated wisdom of the past, and reduced the State into a *carte blanche*. Freedom has the same power in it still; it is omnipotent when opposed to restraint, simply because spirit is stronger than nature. But yet this freedom is itself the only permanent bond of society. In the right of the individual to seek his own welfare lies the possibility of his seeking the welfare of the social organism. Or, to speak from the social point of view, society not only goes out into difference, and invests its component individuals with absolute rights, but gathers itself into a unity through that freedom which is at first repellent, and converts the rights of the individual into duties, and his self-seeking into a means of realising the general good. Out of the dust and powder of individuality it creates a nation which is one because its members are free, and whose members are free because they live its life in their own. The organism of society is only possible because its components are themselves organic. The bond of the social organism, that which is its self-differentiating, self-integrating life, is freedom.

How then is the freedom of the individual consistent with and *constitutive of* the organism of society is the question that now remains. At first there seems to be a contradiction between the individual's right to realise himself, and his duty to realise the purposes of society. When the individual first becomes conscious of his freedom, and recognises that he is to walk in the light of his own spirit, he assumes a negative attitude towards all that seems to limit this freedom. The State with its laws, Society with its habits, the Church with its dogmas, present themselves to him as restraints. It is therefore his highest duty to himself to oppose them; for neither Church, nor Society, nor State can dictate to a free man, and the only categorical imperative to him is that of freedom. Every action is dead unless it is born of freedom, the rights of subjectivity are the highest, and man cannot be compelled to contradict that which is his spiritual life. This, the inviolable character of a free man, was the good which worked amidst the ruins of the French Revolution.

But a deeper consciousness of freedom reveals the abstractness and unreality of subjective liberty. The freedom of indifference has received its quietus from Kant, and it is on all sides theoretically recognised that freedom from limit is freedom *in vacuo*, incapable of movement from the sheer absence of resistance. An individual who is free in this sense repudiates all that comes from without to determine his actions. He can act just as he chooses. He may go here, or there, or nowhere; he may do this, or that, or nothing. He recognises no demands that arise from his environment; they are not *duties*; and the 'ought' is nothing more than inherited habit clad in the terrors of inherited superstition. His actions must flow from the abundance of his own heart, and not be wrung out of him by the pressure of law and duty. His freedom has superannuated him. He finds all his motives in himself. But then comes the question, what motives *can* he find in himself? Is the demand that he find his motives in himself not equivalent to a demand that he should lift himself up by his own waistband? A motive is a reason for action of some sort. This reason or motive is *there*, independent of and outside the individual. It is that which he reaches after, and seeks to bring into himself through his action. Were the end or motive already in him there would be no action. An action arises from a consciousness of limit, and a consciousness of something beyond the limit. Every action seeks after some ideal which is in the future, and the ideal, whether it be true or false, a self or a state of self, is ever outside the present self. Man cannot then find a motive *in himself*. Subjective freedom, freedom from all limit, is therefore nothing more than absolute incapacity to act at all.

Both philosophy and history indicate that the first escape from this bare and motionless freedom is into caprice. As a matter of fact, the individual who repudiates all outward restraint gives himself up to the satisfaction of his own desires, and Hedonism in some of its forms has ever been the prevalent theory of ethics to a people freed from external limit. Hedonism flourished when the paternal Greek States ceased to engross the citizen, when the Roman Empire became indifferent to the individuals that lived within it, and when the terrors of a monarchical God and the restraints of Puritanism lost their hold on English minds. But the escape into the pursuit of pleasure is only an escape into the tyranny and monotony of passion and caprice. To pursue pleasure is to pursue pleasant sensations; and sensations are particular not only in the sense that they are the individual's own, but in the sense that they are fleeting, and have a semblance of permanence only when they are repeated. This pure Hedonism we cannot here criticise, further than to endeavour in a few words to show that because its ideal is particular it has no ethical character. In the first place, the individual is the sole judge of that which gives him pleasure, for his sensations are his own and incommunicable. He can induce his neighbour to read a book or taste a wine which gives pleasure to himself, he can lay before him the conditions of his own pleasure; but he cannot communicate the pleasure to his neighbour, for the pleasure involves the relation of the conditions to the neighbour's feelings. His neighbour can turn upon him and say, 'This wine, or this book, gives me no pleasure;' and there is no room for argument. Each individual is the measure of all things, and he is the measure of all things because he is a sensitive being. Hence Hedonism can afford no universal law. The well-worn 'profligate' has every right, on this view, to prefer the future pain and discontent of self-indulgence and self-degradation to the present pain of self-restraint. He may be pitied in his disappointment, but he has not acted immorally, for he sought his pleasure and endeavoured to realise the ethical ideal.

In the second place, Hedonism can afford no imperative; there is no '*must*' or '*ought*' in the system. This follows immediately from the fact that Hedonism has no universal. The only apparent imperative is, that the individual ought to seek his own pleasure. But this 'ought' is not objective simply because a state of the individual's own feelings is the ideal, and 'state of feelings' is entirely within. The imperative springs from the particular self, and the particular self may at any moment turn round upon the ought, and say, 'I ought not.' But if there is no imperative binding on the individual, then ethics is a mere matter of choice; and no free action is *not* a matter of choice. The drunkard chooses to be drunk rather than sober, the suicide chooses strangling rather than life, and Hedonism turns round and says, 'You are both right, for you choose.'

In the third place, Hedonism can, strictly speaking, afford no ideal. It levels all actions, as already suggested. And, moreover, that which is sought after is a state of feelings, and not a self. The same self is projected into a different and future state; and this state cannot penetrate into the self without escaping out of the sphere of feeling into that of consciousness. Feeling, in other words, cannot attain any fixity; and perhaps the best refutation of Hedonism is the fact that in order to attain this ideal feeling we must forget it, as Mr. Mill admits. But if this be true, if the ideal must not be my conscious ideal, it cannot be an ideal at all. In order to live a life of pleasure, it is better to confine one's self to the moment and forget the future. Pleasure must not be the ideal because we cannot attain it by seeking it; and Hedonism admits of no other ideal. The truth of this contention is attested by the repeated attempts of a 'man of pleasure' to find his ideal in that which has disappointed him. After the satisfaction of that false appetite which comes from the projection of the infinitude of thought into a finite and particular object, comes the consciousness of failure. The ideal was false; he is where he was before. He has not accomplished that progress which an ideal involves. Hence comes the monotonous repetition of the same act and enslavement to a single passion. Life of pleasure is mere tautology; and the ideal is the 'bad infinite' which is both attained and missed in every pleasure-seeking action. The ideal is the same self, and is therefore necessarily attained, but it is a different state of the self, and therefore passes away in the act of attainment. Hence, if Hedonism affords no ideal, the individual must confine himself to the present, and this is what practice teaches as well as theory. But life on these conditions would be disintegrated into a sensitive existence, where everything is well in so far as there is neither past nor future. Well might one say to the Hedonist,—

> 'Still thou art blest, compared wi' me,
> The present only toucheth thee,
> But, oh! I backward cast my ee
> On prospects drear,
> And forward though I canna see,
> I guess and fear.'

Hedonism is an attempt to find the individual's motives in the individual's particular self. Its instruments are external, for pleasure is sought in a relation to objects, but its ideal, if we still call it so, is subjective. Hedonism seeks after no higher and larger self, but for a new state of the present self; whereas the very *nisus* of ethical action comes from the fact that morality is a sphere of comparison, and that the individual, holding his present self in the face of the self that he wishes to be, seeks to be another. Every effort of ethical life is an effort after regeneration. The ideal which the good man seeks to attain is one in which he would merge and forget the present self; and, compared with that, the 'state of feelings' is insignificant.

If, then, the individual cannot find the good in himself, where is he to seek it? The very assertion of the right of subjectivity has given rise to the need of escaping from it. Freedom from the restraint of duty has proved to be self-destructive. He who severs himself from his surroundings, and lives entirely in and for himself, contradicts his freedom. As a matter of fact man cannot absolutely do so. We have never known an intelligent being who has lived entirely apart from society; for an absolutely bad individual is an ethical impossibility. We can no more imagine an individual ' who has not suckled at the breast of the universal ethos,' who has not lived in a spiritual environment and converted (or perverted) that environment into his own nature, than we can conceive an oak tree which has grown where there is neither earth nor water nor air, without light and without darkness. In the environment he finds the raw material of his character; and there, too, he must find the standard of his action.

But what is that standard? Where can he find a *good* that is universal and imperative, and lifts him above the slavery of capricious subjectivity? Are we to find the law of conduct in a universal will which is opposed to the wills of all individuals as such ?

In the first place, it is to be noticed that the good cannot, as Mr. Spencer contends, be evolved out of the struggles of individuals against their natural environment. The only motive that can come into play in such a struggle is that of the preservation of self as a particular existence. It is only in the presence of another self-conscious being, recognised as such and not reduced into a thing, that the individual finds it necessary to regulate his conduct according to a law other than his own caprice. It is in the collision of wills, as Rousseau teaches, that evil arises ; and, we may add, there too does good. It is the collision of wills that first reveals the need and existence of a Universal will ; a Universal will which stands equally above all individuals, and is, so far, the escape of all out of the caprice of subjectivity. But the Good will must be a universal in another sense also. It must be a permanent ideal, one that can always be realised by all without contradiction.

Nor has the individual the choice of obeying or not obeying it. The Good will confronts him with an imperative ; it is armed with an ought from which there is no appeal. For if he is allowed a choice, morality is again subjected to caprice, and the individual lapses into that subjectivity from which he seeks to be free.

Lastly, the Good will is to be realised for its own sake. Obedience to it from desire to attain such a further good as that of the pleasure of virtuous conduct is obedience to pleasure and not to the will : the Universal will is but means that *happen* to be necessary. But the law must be obeyed for its own sake, not from the contemplation of further good, nor from particular impulse, habit, or sentiment. The Good will must alone fill the mind, and the maxim of action will be to obey the law for the sake of the law. Thus escape from subjectivity is apparently found in a Universal, Objective, Imperative will. But is it an escape ?

Our criticism of this law must be shorter even than our statement. This universal law is formal in the sense that it has no content and can suggest none, and yet is indifferent to any content. Nothing can be got out of it, and everything can be put under it. It demands that man should act from contemplation of duty ; but its duty is duty in general,

and man must act in *particular* ways and perform particular
definite duties.

It is objective; but it is objective only because it is not
*sub*jective. It is an eternal *not-self*, and as a pure *not-self*
it is nothing to the individual. It so immediately suggests
despair that it crushes effort. It is a universal which cannot
be either realised in a particular action or by a particular
being. It is universal and objective, but it is also alien. It
is the demand of an alien law, and springs from an alien
authority. But the true ethical ideal is a self as well as a
not-self. It is the individual's future self, it is that which he
conceives himself able to work into his own character, and
what he wishes to *be*. By attaining it he attains his true
self; apart from the attainment he *ought* to *be*, but is not.
And here is the source of the categorical imperative. The
good is my true self; and it is imperative because I must be
real. It is an ethical necessity, deeper than the physical
necessity, which compels me to maintain my existence.
Lastly, the universal *is* not, until it is realised in the individual's life. Prior to that it is only an ' ought,' a mere
conception, a picture flung out by a well-intentioned individual on the canvas of the future. And unless the ' ought '
is, it has no power over and no claim on the individual.
The ethical ideal must not only be itself real, but it must be
that which makes the individual real.

Thus the categorical imperative corrects the errors of
subjectivity, but it falls itself into the opposite errors. The
one ideal is a mere *seyn*, the other is a mere *sollen*; the one
is subjective only, the other is objective only; the one is a
mere particular, the other is a bare universal. Both are
abstract, they each stand in need of the other. The ideal
for the individual must be also real; the objective not-self
must also be the individual's self, realisable though not
realised; the universal must be also particular, and live in
its own details. In a word, the good must be an organism
really existing in the world and yet an ideal for every
individual.

Such an ideal is found in the social organism, or rather
in the moral organism which is embodied in the various
forms of society. In it all the demands of what we may
call subjectivity and objectivity are met. It is on the one
hand not a mere ' ought,' but really exists in the world. It

is that to which the family, the social communities, and the State owe their strength and their stability. They *are*, because their laws are; and their laws are ethical facts. A family that departs from the ethical law of love, a commercial community which violates its law of measured rectitude, and a State which seeks no longer to advance the complex rights of the freedom of its components, already totter to their ruin. They cease to be, when that which 'ought' to be no longer is. But, on the other hand, the ideal is not a mere *seyn*, like subjectivity. It is a law, an ideal, a *sollen* for the individual. The task of his life is to answer the demands of his station and to perform duties which he has not chosen, but finds imposed upon him by his social environment.

Moreover, the moral organism is not a formal universal without content, but is differentiated into laws and institutions which direct the conduct of individuals in the details of daily life. Nor is this ideal indifferent and alien to the individual. He himself gives voice to and interprets his social environment, and in that sense *creates* his ideal. He recognises the tasks which he finds in the sphere into which he has been educated as his duties, and therefore as the law of his action and his ideal self. And by this means he gives force to the social imperative. He knows himself to be moral only when he finds that he has duties, and he knows his duties and has duties only when he knows himself to be free; and he is free because there is a social imperative.

Thus subjective and objective, the self and the not-self, the particular and the universal, the individual and society, interpenetrate and become an organic whole. Society exists only in the individual, and the individual exists only in society. Apart from society the individual cannot realise his freedom; neither his own particular self nor the Universal will could afford him a single motive. The individual is free only because he finds his duties in society, and his duties are his ethical life. And, on the other hand, it is the freedom of the components of a society that gives the society real and permanent existence. It is because the State is a higher realisation of freedom that it has greater permanence than the family. The unity of the family, which is thought in the latent state of feeling, *i.e.* love, is broken against the growth of its components into maturity and independence,

and is always in danger from its property; but the unity of
the State, which is self-conscious, where every individual is
his own master and carries his own responsibilities within
him, this unity, like self-consciousness itself, is a unity that
has overcome its differences and cannot be broken by them.
The freedom of its components is the force of attraction that
binds its members together. A State of slaves, for instance,
is impossible. A slave has no rights, and therefore has no
duties. In the eye of his master he is a *thing*, and a thing
is not consulted and persuaded, but *forced*. The claims that
are made on the slave are such that he will contend against,
and if possible repudiate. And a State of slaves would be
nothing but a sphere where force holds force in check. But
such a State never existed; for no State can be alien to the
individuals that compose it. A constitution which is either
too good or too bad for a people · cannot be held together.
A people must feel *itself* in the constitution, find it to be *its*
law of social life; that is, its necessity, its law of conduct
must not be an alien necessity, but a necessity which the
people has taken into itself and which therefore constitutes
its freedom. The individual then finds his freedom in society,
and society is possible only because its members are free.

It is on these accounts that society is an organism. Not
because it is like an animal, and because the individual components are like joints and limbs; but because the individual
realises himself as an ethical being in society, and society
realises itself in the individual. The individual is free
because he is a member of society, and society realises its
aims in the freedom of the individuals. Freedom is the *life*
which forms the unity of the moral organism. The State,
for instance, endows its individuals with freedom, and thereby
creates an ethical claim on their services. It points out *duties*
by means of its laws, and the duties have moral force because
the laws are recognised by the individuals as their *own* laws,
their own guide of conduct, their own ideal self, and not a
foreign necessity. Freedom, the unity, the life, differentiates
itself; it flows out into the individual in the form of rights,
and returns to itself through its members in the form of
services and duties.

The social organism is thus a concrete, living, self-integrating, self-differentiating whole, apart from which neither
the universal—the abstract society, nor the particular—the

abstract individual, can be. Isolated from each other they are but names; sunder their relations and they cease to exist. They exist in and through each other, and are constituted by their relation.

If this be true, then we can no longer speak of individual aims and individual welfare, apart from social aims and social welfare, any more than we can speak of social aims that are not also aims of individuals. The welfare of the individual is in the performance of his duty (whatever that be) and his duty is nothing other than the demand of his environment, the welfare of his sphere. From this point of view it becomes unnecessary to effect a 'compromise' or to 'conciliate' egoism and altruism—the last effort of inconsistent Hedonism to extend its narrow teachings so as to correspond with the facts of ethical life.[1] We have already endeavoured to show that egoism—pure subjectivity—is an impossible and self-contradictory aim. It remains to show that altruism is as one-sided as egoism; and that a man who, if he could, lived for the sake of others only, is as immoral as who, if he could, lived solely for himself and in himself. Altruism is in fact the opposite abstraction to egoism. It is its logical other, just as the 'enthusiasm of humanity' of the Comtist, which tends to extinguish the individual for the sake of the general good,[2] is the logical counterpart of the teachings of Rousseau, which abolished the general good for the sake of the individual. The latter neglects the fact that the individual's life is universal, the former that the universal is particular, and that the purposes of humanity are those of the individuals composing it. Rousseau would not wash the feet of his neighbour. Comte would wash 'not his feet only but his hands and his head,' and drown himself in addition. Altruism as opposed to egoism is the realisation of the aims of another as opposed to the realisation of one's own aims. But morality from beginning to end is *self*-realisation. He who has made the welfare of the race his aim, has done so, not from a generous choice, but because he regards the pursuit of this welfare as his imperative duty. The welfare of the race is his own ideal; what he must realise in order to be what he *ought* to be. The welfare of the race is his own welfare, which he must seek because he must be *himself*.

---

[1] Spencer's *Data of Ethics*, chapters 13 and 14.

[2] See Comte's *Doctrine of Immortality*.

Cromwell, Luther, Mohammed, were heroes, not because they did something over and above what they *ought* to have done, but because their *ideal self* was co-extensive with the larger self of their world. ' *Ich kann nichts anders,*' was the voice of each. A necessity had been laid on them as on Paul to ' preach their gospel.' They were compelled by their conception of their duty to rise above the pursuits of mere individual or family welfare—to transcend the ordinary limits of the ethical efforts of ordinary individuals. Their large purposes were what they owed to themselves just as much as to their world. They were instruments in the hand of a divine power ; for the good that is in the world called upon them with the stern imperative of duty. This imperative duty had become so truly their *own,* that they were its conscious willing instruments. It was their *enthusiasm*, it had penetrated their whole being, it *was* their whole being for it had absorbed them. The conflict between the particular and the universal self had ended in the victory of the latter, not by crushing the former but by penetrating it, and elevating even feeling into a power which worked for the good that had become their ideal.

Thus the largest altruism is after all but an earnest struggle for one's own ethical life. Altruism and egoism are but abstract theories that can attain meaning only when they are taken up into an organism in which altruism exists through egoism, and egoism through altruism. They are not 'compromised' or 'reconciled,' but lost in that which takes both into itself. The progress of humanity is not from egoism to altruism, but from an egoism which is from the first altruistic to an altruism which must ever remain egoistic. The growth of character is intensive as well as extensive, and intensive because extensive. If I have larger interests, I have a larger and deeper self. The life which seeks the welfare of the community as well as that of the family, of the State as well as of the community, and of humanity as well as the State, is a life that has brought their interests within itself and cannot realise itself except in them. Morality is not a generous knight-errantry which has to seek for wrongs to rectify. It ever finds the wrongs within itself; its earnest and engrossing business is to perform the duties that are its own and obey its own imperative. Morality is not a mere flow from the superabundance

of a generous heart. 'It is a necessity which is not chosen but chooses.' It is not an ill-regulated generosity which is weakness rather than strength, which ruins its agent and pauperises its object; but it is a universal imperative, immovable and stern and eternal.

There is still one point which our limits will allow us to touch upon. The great difficulty of recognising the organic character of society, according to Mr. Spencer, comes from the fact that it has no individual consciousness. Its life, which, if it is an organism, ought to be *one* in the deepest sense, seems to be broken up amongst the individuals which compose it. 'Consciousness is diffused throughout the aggregate. . . . There is no social sensorium.'[1] 'The parts of a society form a whole that is discrete . . . the living units composing it are free, not in contact, and more or less widely dispersed.'[2] We think Mr. Spencer's attempt to re-create the social unity by means of 'emotional language, and by the language, oral and written, of the intellect,' inadequate and superficial, though we cannot here fully discuss it. For what is community of language apart from the deeper community of thought which it expresses? Is there such power in words, and will the universal brotherhood come by the adoption of one language? Even 'patriotic feeling' often asserts itself against a common language, and patriotic feeling roused into national excitement such as broke the strength of Napoleon in Spain is not an adequate bond of society. Language is a bond only where there is a deeper bond of common interests, and these interests are ultimately ethical, if they are permanent. Language is often one of the evidences of the unity of a social life, but it is not the unity itself.

Where, then, is the unity, the individual self-consciousness of the social organism? The directest answer is to say that there exists no such thing as individual self-consciousness. To seek it is to lapse back into that view which regards the individual as existing apart from the universal, and the universal apart from the individual. It is to neglect the fact that the individual is conscious of himself only because he has distinguished himself from his environment. But this distinction is impossible except in so far as he knows both in some degree. The division of the self and

[1] Spencer's *Sociology*, I. p. 479.   [2] *Ibid.* I. p. 475.

not-self is one of the facts I am certain of; the distinction is one of *my* ideas and is within me. Consciousness reaches under both factors; the individual overlaps his other; the notself is *his* not-self.

It is true that we cannot find a social sensorium or social pineal gland, and say of its self-consciousness, Lo here! or Lo there! But still the social organism is self-conscious, for it is conscious of itself in every self-conscious being. To say that I know myself in society is exactly equivalent to saying that society knows itself in me. In knowledge the universal and particular come together. But to illustrate. We have seen that the individual finds his duties confronting him in the social community of which he is a member. He finds them because they are *there*, ready to hand, awaiting his performance. But on the other hand they became duties only through his interpretation of them. They are duties only because he first recognises them and then adopts them. Or, to take another example, an artist finds an idea in a picture because it is *there*: and his neighbour, if he has a cultivated taste, will also find it there. The idea is in the picture for everyone. But, on the other hand, the idea comes into actual existence only when it is interpreted. The picture becomes something more than a mass of colours only when the idea is lifted out of the dead material by the power of an artistic intelligence. We can either say that the artist finds meaning in the picture, or that the picture reveals itself to the artist. We can either say that the scientific man discovers the thoughts of nature, or that the thoughts of nature reveal themselves to the scientific man. The idea of the transmutation of forces is that of the scientific man, but it is his only because it is nature's also. The true attitude of science is to abandon preconceived opinions, submit itself to nature, put itself in its path and on its lines, and wait for the interpretation which it gives of itself. The continued effort of experiment is an effort of the individual to place himself in such an attitude that he can hear nature speak. Experiment, in a word, is the abstraction of foreign elements, the help which the scientific man gives to nature, that its many sounds may be disentangled, and that its voice may be articulate. In science, in art, in ethics and theology, the individual must stoop to conquer; make himself the vehicle of the universal, and thereby both understand the universal and make it articulate.

As a literary half-poetic, half-mystic truth, it has long been recognised that a great man is the voice of his age, the articulate expression of its otherwise inarticulate forces. This we would prove as a hard fact; that every individual, however humble, is, in his own little way, the exponent as well as the product of his time. Apart from the individual the social forces and duties are not actually there: it is he that gives them voice and utterance; it is in him that they attain external and definite existence. The necessity of a time that fails to find voice in the life of an individual or people that understand it is a blind and monstrous force, and not an ethical necessity. As in the French Revolution, it works fortuitously, confounding and crushing together the good and the evil. But the individual who recognises the necessity labouring beneath the contingencies of his time lifts it from a natural into an ethical existence, makes it first an object of thought and then an ideal of conduct. Society, in a word, finds its meaning, comes to self-consciousness in him. It is thus in some degree that society comes to self-consciousness and attains its purposes in the self-consciousness and purposes of *every* individual. The social organism is an organism of organisms. The life of the whole is the life of every part. Nor is it torn amongst them into shreds and patches. The reason that is in the world in all its wealth and greatness is the legitimate inheritance of everyone, and this inheritance is an *ethical* inheritance, where there is no mutual exclusion. It is the kingdom of heaven upon earth where all are kings because all are subjects.

HENRY JONES.

VIII.

THE STRUGGLE FOR EXISTENCE.—HINTS FOR A PHILOSOPHY OF ECONOMICS.

'OF all the quacks that ever quacked, political economists are the loudest. Instead of telling what is meant by one's country, by what causes men are happy, moral, religious, or the contrary, they tell us how flannel jackets are exchanged for pork hams, and speak much about the land last taken into cultivation.'

It is half a century since those words were written; and many things have happened since then. Political economists no longer thank heaven for their superior wisdom. They know their place, and are beginning to discover that the laird of Craigenputtock was right, that the burning questions of their future will be, not the sale of hams and jackets, but the cure of souls, and all the border questions of economics and politics,—that, indeed, their study will not have its perfect work till it leads them even beyond politics into social philosophy. The political effects of an industrial movement may be more important than the economical; but the society in which both are set is more important than either. The charming mottoes of political agitators must not distract our attention from a struggle less lively than theirs, the struggle of the most unhappy members of a moderately happy community for bare life. 'The struggle for existence' is no charming motto. It is a mere memorandum or placard of ill-favoured facts, not well forgotten but not gladly remembered. It points the fancy to a region where fancy seldom goes of her own accord—the abodes of the 30,000 distressed needlewomen and their less apocryphal brothers and sisters in suffering, who are even weaker limbs of the body politic than the wasteful idlers at the other extremity. Whoso, however, would not willingly stop at the Lamentations of Jeremiah, but would continue his reading into the Acts of the Apostles, must look at the social surroundings and political position of the strugglers, as well as their obvious misery and moral helplessness. How far are the noble purposes of the strong hindered by the woes of the weak? Do the efforts of the poor, in the first place to avoid starvation, and in the second place to become rich, form a permanent feature in civilised life, essential to the very idea of the modern State, and therefore indispensable to human progress? This question is common ground to philosophy and economics; and it is one of the questions which a Philosophy of Economics must face and answer.

Its interest for philosophy needs no proof. To the philosopher nothing human is foreign. His chief end is to stand on a sort of Pisgah hill and, viewing all the world at large, to see what is the place of man in it, what his work is, what is the goal of his social progress, and what he means by his civilisation. The political economist, on the other hand, studying the causes of wealth and poverty, finds them in close connection with society and government, and therefore cannot help considering, in some measure, how far the mutual influence of economical and political facts may extend. The philosopher, however, must do more than this; and he has not simply the same work to do more thoroughly, he has a distinct task of his own, beginning sooner and ending later than the work of the ordinary economist. He begins sooner, for he is not content to take the plant as it stands; he examines its soil and climate, air and food. On the other hand, he ends later than the economist, for he takes up the remote bearings of economical facts at the far-off point where they pass into cosmopolitan politics and religion. In short, he needs to furnish at once the prologue and the epilogue to economics—the former perhaps the easier task, for the materials are, in a sense, finished and ready to hand,— the latter perhaps too hard for him till the industrial revolution is fully ripe. In either case, the philosophical student attacks a subject which the ordinary economist judiciously lets alone, as beyond both his time and his purposes.

There are many sages on both sides of the North Sea and Atlantic who would make merry over any attempt to adjust the relations of political economy to philosophy. The one they would say, is not yet a science; the other can never be. Though they have tender scruples about indicting a whole nation for anything whatsoever, they indict a whole universe for unintelligibility; they pronounce philosophy an impossibility; and they tolerate no evolution except of the earth, earthy. Darwin may steal a horse, while Idealists may not look over a hedge. It is not great presumption to disregard such obstructionists, and, taking economists as they are, and philosophers as they might be, to consider how much light they can throw on common sense and on one another.

The questions of political economy, as they have actually been discussed by the most diverse economists for 150 years, are all branches of one common topic, the causes of national wealth and national poverty; and, tacitly if not avowedly, all economists understand by wealth the abundance, and by poverty the scarcity, of the good things of this life, the outward tangible means of satisfying the wants of man. In the third place, the commercial ambition spoken of in the 'Wealth of Nations' as the constant desire of every man to better his own condition, a desire which is with him from the cradle to the grave, may no doubt be considered by economists in various ways. It may be looked on as a blessing, or it may be regarded as a misfortune. It may be considered abstractly by itself as a ruling or over-ruling motive, 'whereby a man's conduct can be predicted with the greatest nicety;' or it may be considered simply as one co-ordinate motive out of many, in a combination that baffles not only prediction but analysis. But, whether set on a throne by itself or herded with a crowd of serving-men, this desire for gain is never, at least, entirely ignored by any treatise that calls itself economical. One other feature all economists have in common—they have always regarded their own study as dealing with a part, not with the whole of human nature. Even the orthodox among them, who regard commercial ambition as the strongest of all the motives of an average modern human being, admit that he has other and weaker ones, though they cancel each other. The acknowledged position, therefore, of political economy among scientific studies is a standing invitation to some larger study to round off its work for it, and bring the whole man into view. Whether this will be done by a Sociology which includes all the moral and anthropological sciences, but goes no further than man—or by a philosophy which does not stop at man, but goes on to the world,—in either case all economical facts will get a new bearing. The 'struggle for existence,' for example, is an economical fact that. reaches far beyond economy, and is a crucial problem for the philosophy of man. What part does it play, not merely in industry, but in civilisation? Is it one of the indispensable features of a modern State? Must all human societies be made perfect through this suffering, and is this suffering to go on after the perfection is secured?

It would not be possible, in a few pages, to do more than draw the outlines of a possible answer to this question. It is well, in the first place, to note that the phrase 'struggle for existence' is by no means free from ambiguity. We must not allow its great biological prestige to win it any uncritical indulgence in a region that is above biology. There is, undoubtedly, a sense in which the 'struggle for existence' is the essential condition of all progress;—there is another sense in which the same statement is entirely false. It is false if 'existence' means bare life. Starvation is no stimulus. The mere struggle for a bare existence, the effort to save oneself from extinction, never leads to progress, either in a society or in an individual. This may seem a paradox. Did not poverty convert Scott into a novelist, and Horace into a poet? Was it not the struggle for room and food that sent the Cimbri and Teutones, Goths and Vandals, to the sunny South? No; penury less often fires than freezes the genial current, and neither 'Waverley' nor the Ode to Pyrrha was written for mere bread. Even the English nation made no progress so long as self-defence absorbed her every energy. Wherever there is progress, there is something more spiritual at work than frantic efforts after self-preservation; and that is ideals, or at least ideas. If we throw a man into deep water and leave him there, his terrified struggling will not teach him to swim, though it may enable him to clutch the bank. The effort to make both ends meet, and the consciousness that even half a day's holiday would defeat the purpose, does not stimulate a man; it enervates a man, whether in Labrador or in Drury Lane. He may become perfect through, that is to say, in the teeth of this suffering, but not by means of it. When people are told not to trust to the Poor Laws or to their neighbours to save them from destitution, this does not mean that if they are once thoroughly destitute they will have the smallest power to save themselves. It is a common saying that those nearest pauperism take least pains to avoid it. The destitute man may never happen to become a pauper, and the habitual pauper may never allow himself to become destitute; but the wings are as effectually clipped by the destitution as by the indolence. Carry depression beyond a certain point, and it kills the power of effort by killing all hope; and the point is reached, if ever anywhere short of death, at the moment when the struggle of the human being becomes an endeavour to gain not an abundance of life but an escape from death.

There are many examples of this at home. Novelists have spoken of England as two nations, but there is a miserable third, and the third is to the first and second as the less civilised nations of the world-without are to the more civilised. If we choose, however, we may detach the truth from ourselves, and make our neighbours' misfortunes rather than our own, picturesque. The noble Red Man is a conspicuous example of a 'struggle for existence' that has led to no progress whatever. There is less and less of him left now, and what is left does not feel any charm in its situation. Its romance exists only for us, though, if we have a heart, its miseries will exist for us also. The Red Man suffers much from famine, war, and disease. His wife and children run the gauntlet of tribal customs, compared with which the Lancashire boot discipline is a holiday pastime. It is small wonder that in his physique he is the very picture of a man; no weak child could ever have survived the woes of his upbringing, and there is no native recording angel to chronicle the pangs of his dead brothers and sisters. He has survived for the novelist, while they have simply added a few thousands to the great unnumbered multitude of out-trodden lives, the unfit that did not survive. Destitution may lead to such happy inventions as cannibalism, which at once increases food and lessens population, and it may account for the proverbial cunning and the cowardly strategy of many savages. But (1) this means no progress so long as the *status quo* is not altered, and so long as the wolf of starvation is still at the door. Progress is 'something more, a bringer of new things,' built on the foundation of the old ; it is not a defence of my bare life, but a clothing of the bareness and a cultivation of the barrenness. Moreover (2) it is not safe to argue as if the same environments had the same effect on all living creatures, even of the same genus. Difficulties which in one case generate talents and provoke a spirited reaction, in another case meet a merely passive resistance, and cause a fading of the old faculties rather than a creation of new. It has even been argued that the new faculties which the difficulties generate are purely fictitious, being useless except to cope with their parent difficulties. They must however be natural or they could not be acquired—'nature' meaning as much the state into which we come as the state in which we are born, and our faculties being all alike developed by objects and obstacles. But it is at least true that the difficulties sometimes fail to generate the faculties. What is physiologically the same vital force meets the same obstacles with very different results in different tribes of men. The difficulties of the European have made him progress; the difficulties of the native American have killed him. We may of course elect for the theory which explains these anomalies by original and inherent differences of race. But this is to fall comfortably back on a pillow for the laziness of thought ; it is to give up the problem of race, and thereby of all progress, for we know no races of men that have not been altered by history, and, if we knew the whole history of a race, we should probably know why it differed from its neighbours. There is no reason to suppose that, where starvation does not stimulate, race blocks the way. It seems better to assume an original identity of race for the whole of humanity, and to suppose it altered by circumstances as the world goes on—among the circumstances being new laws and new ideas. Instead of beginning in the poorest places, where it had not much earth, progress would more probably begin in the favoured places that yielded a moderate abundance of food without excessive labour. Hunger would drive the sons of men Cain-like over the face of the earth, till they found out all the most fertile and convenient spots upon it ; and then being at a measurable distance from famine, they would collect their wits a little and exercise their invention. The 'eternal question of a livelihood' would no longer keep them at 'a level from which no ideal is visible.' Climate and soil do not indeed grow ideas as they grow grass, but they enable men to follow occupations that conduce to the growth of ideas. Once in being, the ideas may be transplanted and made full of growing, like man himself, in any part of the globe.

It is, therefore, the early steps that cost. When a man has once known what comfort is, he will probably work hard to keep it; but if he is like a mere animal, with no idea of abundance, or ideal of any kind to work for, then he will do no work of supererogation, none that does more than keep him alive. The fear of starvation is not merely in its degree, but in its kind, entirely alien to that happy discontent which never 'is' but always 'to be' blest. To be capable of progress is to have gained a purely human idea, the idea of comfort, the idea of a sum total of good things, which can be indefinitely increased to keep up with increasing wants. It is to eat of the tree which gives knowledge of good and evil. Now, whether men get this notion from 'natural impulse,' or from the teachings of other men, it is in any case the creature of leisure rather than of care. Some one has remarked that it was when our first parents had plenty of time to look about them in paradise, that they began to think about the forbidden fruit; it would not have occurred to them if they needed to work all day long for a livelihood. It was not because the French people were more miserable than their neighbours that they accomplished the Great Revolution, but largely because they were less miserable; they were not too oppressed to have time for thinking. It was not because the North American colonies were treated more tyrannically by the mother country than the colonies of other nations by theirs that they lost loyalty and declared themselves independent; history says they were better treated. Political oppression and religious persecution, to be quite successful, must be quite thorough. Half-hearted cruelty is usually unsuccessful, for it allows the victim enough strength to resist; he is too unhappy not to lay greedy hold on any scheme for escaping; he is not so unhappy as to be unable to move at all.

What leads to progress, then, it appears, is ideas; it is some end or aim, to be defined not negatively, as escape from pain, but positively, as the gain of some good thing. Indeed, the history of every civilised nation may, under this aspect, be divided into two stages, the one in which the moving force is self-defence, the other in which it is self-development; and the strata of any civilised society, at any given time, may be divided into two, the lowest stratum, in which the struggle for existence means a struggle for bare life, and all the strata above it, in which the 'struggle for existence' means the struggle for well-being, gain, or glory. The modern notion of a State demands a free course for the second struggle, but not for the first. In other words, *laissez faire* is to prevail high up rather than low down the ranks. There is, perhaps, no full proof of this apart from metaphysics; but the view is involved in the mere description of a modern State, and, if we durst make the slightly hazardous assumption that whatever is modern is right, then it would be as in certain geometrical propositions, where the proof of the problems is the drawing of the figures. To understand the meaning of 'State' is first and chiefly to understand what we mean by 'our country' and 'our nation.'

Clothes do not make a gentleman; and numbers do not make a nation. The name of Nation, says the distinguished author of a recent pamphlet on this subject, is not to be given to a people because of their multitude, or because they are of one race, or of one language, or of one religion; nor even because they have common material interests, or a country plainly marked off from others by geographical boundaries or strategical features. National unity is something more intangible than these: it is a community of feeling, a partnership in past traditions, present privileges, and future hopes. This is true; but if material or commercial interests are not the main bond they have at least some inferior binding force of their own; and it may even be held that, as the struggle for existence is allowed to prevail most in the higher strata of a good State, and least in the lowest, so commerce may safely have greater sway in the most developed, and least in the least developed of modern States. It is no doubt true that material interests, though they can produce a commercial treaty, a customs union, or a joint control, cannot produce a nation. Nations are not joint-stock companies for co-operative trading, and even England is not a nation of shopkeepers. This may be our goal in the twentieth or thirtieth century; it was certainly not our starting-point in the sixth or eleventh. Men did not first desire comforts and then say, Go to, let us form a club to provide them. On the contrary, their social life preceded the very idea of comforts, and gave them their very notions of enjoyment, for all human enjoyment is social. It is hard then to understand how anyone can represent the struggle for good living (to say nothing of the struggle for bare life) as either the first beginning or the chief end of the State. It is, however, the first to Plato, and the second to the Manchester School of Politics.

Extreme partisans of these schools will perhaps think them too incongruous to be contrasted. But they are not utterly alien. According to the airy sketch in the ' Republic,' States come into being because men find it better to divide labour and exchange the things made by it, than to work separately each man for himself. Cobden's nineteenth-century Essays and Speeches tell us that, by that large division of labour which is called Free Trade, all nations will eventually be drawn together into unity of spirit, bonds of peace, and even righteousness of life. To the one, commerce is the origin of cities, States, and nations, to the other it is the origin of an international union of all men that makes the world into one city. The historical context makes these theories the more singular. Plato writes from one of a galaxy of little States, too little to be nations, and at a time when the Roman power, too great to be a nation, was not yet ready to swallow up the little Greek States, but was waiting for Macedon to do its work. There have been few periods in history when commercial considerations could enter less into politics, and kinship was still in theory the only firm tie between two States. Yet Plato, with his propensity to feign incidents for the needs of his Dialogues, makes believe that the body politic is born of the struggle to satisfy physical wants. He cares much less about prosaic accuracy than about the fitness of his narrations to illustrate his philosophy; and accordingly, in his account of the genesis of the State, he means to do little more than show, in parable, the correspondence between the rule of ethics, ' Do that duty which lies nearest to thee,' and the rule of politics, ' Unto everyone his work.' In Plato, however, the struggle for existence among the fortuitously concurring atoms ends almost as soon as it has begun ; in the upper circles of the State it does not go on at all. His selection is not natural but artificial, not worked out by the atoms themselves, but performed for them by the rulers. Of course, in Greece as it then was, the 'struggle' of the lower, so far as they were slaves, had no place in the body politic; it was over before they entered it; and, so far as they were not slaves, it was at least not the struggle of an industrious class against an idle, still less the competition of the industrious among one another; it was rather the struggle of one idle class against a still idler. Single States, like Phœnicia and Carthage, had no doubt owed much to trade and colonisation; but the power of purely commercial considerations to alter the balance of parties, to give a character to public policy, and to deform, reform, and transform legislation, had never been fully known. Greek political philosophers instinctively felt that commerce meant competition, and competition friction, restlessness, and perhaps anarchy. If men ran to and fro to buy and sell, the knowledge of good and evil would be increased at the expense of wisdom and steadiness. In modern times, however, fondness for travel has not in our country produced political unsteadiness; and on the other hand the French, who are not, notoriously, stable in government, are the most home-loving of modern nations. Though all progress is said to be Greek in its origin, the sort of progress that England has made in the last hundred years, every step of it resting on industry, must seek another genealogy. There is in fact one feature in the modern State which was ignored in the ancient, the liberty of the individual. There were, no doubt, theorists then, as now, who wished to dispense with States altogether. Aristippus wished to be a citizen of the whole world by being a citizen of no particular part of it; he wished, Irish fashion, to be at home everywhere by being at home nowhere. But no ancient theorist that was anxious to save his ideal commonwealth from self-destruction would have provided in it an 'open career' for all men of all classes, and complete freedom of trade at home and abroad. He would have thought it an attempt to combine cosmos with chaos.

Nevertheless, in the modern notion of freedom, this chaos plays a great part. We do not regard the State as an accidental collection of individuals; it is no more accidental than the collection of a syllogism from the premisses or

the development of the flower from the leaf. But we have
learned to draw a distinction between things political and
things social. We have acquired 'a horror of losing our
individuality.' Our notion of the State nowadays would
probably include the life of the family and the free enterprise of individuals outside of the family—with something
else over and above, to crown the whole and do for the citizen
what he can neither get done for him at home nor do for
himself out of doors. Our test of political progress will be
like Mr. Ruskin's test of a good picture. The best picture
is that which suggests the greatest number of the greatest
ideas; and the best State is that which developes the
greatest number of the best qualities of its people,—perhaps
both of them particular cases of the general rule that that
theory is truest which explains most difficulties, and that
truest of all which seems to increase in its powers of explanation the more widely it is applied. But, howsoever
known and tested, our ideal State must provide that free
scope for individuality which is the most modern feature of
modern politics. Perhaps it is dearly bought. The price
we pay for popular government is the possibility of occasional disorder. The price we pay for our Protestantism is
the possibility of error and 'variations.' The price we pay
for our Free Trade is the possibility of gluts and panics.
But, still, freedom in our soul's just estimation is prized
above all price.

Some of the eccentric philosophers who expect as much
good sense in human history as in the movements of the
'flies, worms, and snails' so extolled by Dr. Watts and the
entomologists, have described history itself as 'man's progress
in Freedom.' Does this mean that every movement is an
emancipation movement, and every society a Liberation
Society? If this were all, then the meaning of freedom
would be more intelligible than the value of it. But it is
not half the truth. Whether or not there is an unconscious
logic in all human action, there is at least an unconscious
ethics, an unwritten body of morality, in the language
and the actions of a people. It contains their standard of
right and wrong, and their ideal of a good life, sometimes
practised and always respected; and, if we consult this
oracle properly, it will give us the outlines of a definite
theory of freedom, which only the indefinite future can fill

in to the full, but which the present will find a useful chart.

To modern notions, then, society is made for man, not man for society.   The whole exists for the good of all the parts without exception, and not simply, as utilitarians would have it, for the good of the greatest number.   Our communities have grown up in strange ways and fulfilled many alien ends ; but now at least they shall exist for the sake of the individuals in it.   The chief end of society is not production or acquisition, or any other separate act or state of man—but man himself and his most human nature. The most successful and prosperous society, therefore, will be that in which the citizens are making the most of their powers. This does not mean that it will be a large training school for adults, supplying gymnastic exercises for all the mental and bodily faculties of each individual.   A uniform development of all the faculties seems the more impossible the more we understand the largeness of the world.   Alike to idealism, materialism, and common sense, there is no meaning in a 'faculty' out of relation to an 'object'; they were married in heaven, and go mad, or at least make nonsense, when parted on earth.   In the second place, there is no apparent limit to a faculty and its objects ; any road leads to the end of the world, and any study leads to infinity.   If education, therefore, meant the equal improvement of all the faculties, it would make us try to follow all the roads at once ; and ' we cannot, therefore we ought not.'   To attempt to develope all our powers, or even as many of them as possible, would perhaps end in a high average ; but it would bring down the best, as well as raise up the lowest ; and would injure the most human feature of human labour, its originality and independence.   If we are to ' do the duty which lies nearest to us,' we are also to ' know ourselves, and what we can work at.'   The man who devotes himself to those, of the things then needful for his time and country, which he can do best, is not far from the chief end of man.

That he has at least average worldly opportunities, ' as is said in the Ethics,' and is not struggling for bare livelihood, follows from the very terms of the commandment.   The weak and starving are not likely to be able to choose what they can work at, and are still less likely to be able to do the work when chosen.   The struggle for mere being would

Q

from childhood exclude them from the struggle for well-being. Not only would the weakest go to the wall, but many who might have become strong would be kept weak. But in these latter days society knows the value of human life, and wishes, with Christianity, that ' all men should be saved,' and that ' all the Lord's people should be prophets.' Where Darwinism was wont to rule absolutely, it may not now rule at all. Public welfare demands that the border strife should be checked and its victims tended. A modern State need not pass a Poor Law, but it needs to see that the poor are cared for. It will make elementary instruction compulsory, not from any desire to respite the upper classes by educating their masters, but from a belief that a people is not free and united till all of its members are placed in possession of their powers and made equal in opportunity.

Such a view of liberty, however, implies much more than a policy of abstention. The common as distinguished from the common-sense conception of liberty is the right to do as I please; but this kind of autocracy is only good for a man if he at once abdicates in favour of constitutional government, and suits himself to his circumstances, in order to improve both himself and them. Else his liberty will be a cloak of maliciousness, a wayward, unchastened self-will which ' profits no one, not even himself; ' and to give effect to that kind of liberty in the border regions of society will be to make the equilibrium of opposing forces more brutal than it is, to make the ills of the poor more cureless, and to withhold from them the better liberty, the power to use their powers, at the price of the barren privilege of being let alone. Modern society is beginning to recognise the distinction between these two kinds of liberty ; and, instead of letting the struggle for existence rage itself out in the lower strata, takes every possible pains to end it. It recognises the claims of weakness even more than the claims of strength, knowing that old strength can see to itself, while young strength, no less than young weakness, may be powerless without its Greatheart. It honours all men, and its schools and hospitals and charities are designed to raise the lowest of them to the true level of their manhood and give to all alike the open career. Like a wise parent, society will keep a tight hold on its children in their tender years; and it will gradually relax its hold as they grow mature and strong enough to take care of themselves.

Some such idea of liberty is contained in the language and laws of all modern civilisation. Nevertheless there is an impression, too widely-spread to be entirely false, that, even if freedom be not waywardness, it is not without it. There is a feeling that freedom must include the negative element, ' the glorious liberty of being independent,' as well as the positive element of ' doing one's best.' It must include a right as well as a duty, and even a right that is not to be identified with any ascertainable duty. It may be that, *sub specie eternitatis,* or from the point of view of Omniscience, duty and right always coincide ; some philosophers say it is ever so. Still the point of view of Omniscience is not attainable for most mortals ; and they will think a little before they allow that there is no right that is not a duty and no duty that is not a right, and that too, ' in one and the same respect.' If the dogma were sound it would be hard to comprehend the claims of individuality. Why do we give scope to individuality nowadays, not only in freedom of speech and of writing, but in choice of a profession, in wideness of speculation, in defiance of conventionality and fashion, and in all matters where there is any orthodoxy, whether in art, religion, science, education, or dress ? In spite of the refinements of philosophers, this toleration means that society grants to its individual members a number of rights that are not duties, or at least not in one and the same respect. Trade is a good example. Perhaps it is always a man's duty to devote himself to the trade or profession for which he is best suited, always supposing that society has fulfilled her own duty and seen to it that he is in the position to make any choice at all. Here then his duty and his right are on all fours. But is it his duty as well as his right to make new ways where no ways were, or to invent the oil lamp in place of the tallow candle, gaslight in place of oil, and the electric light in place of all ? It is perhaps his duty, because ' it is his nature to ' invent. But, unless from the point of view of Omniscience, we cannot tell that he ' ought ' to have turned his inventiveness into one particular branch of discovery more than another ; his powers seem to his fellows as well capable of serving him and them in one way as in another. Almost every great inventor has been guided to his chief field of invention by what is called chance ; and it is, at any rate, not by any clear

law to his fellows ascertainable or any fixed rule by his
fellows prescribable.   Not even Mr. Wilberforce himself
could have known that the path of duty would lead him
through philanthropy to the oil trade.   He had a ' right' to
take one out of perhaps twenty courses, and even to his
conscientious mind it may have been much clearer what he
ought not to do than what he ought to do.   Popular morality
allows a man to amass a fortune and spend it well, and to
stop short of a fortune and live a simple life.   It cannot
pronounce which of them is his duty, and it grants that
both are within his ' right.'   They are 'within his right'
indeed in two senses ; the law allows them, and the public
conscience does not forbid.   The general rule has come to
be that full-grown men are left to choose their own careers,
and the country gains more from their possible waywardness
than if it interfered with their ' struggles ' and insisted on
choosing their weapons for them.   In all circles except the
lowest the rule must be 'hands off.'   It is a postulate of the
modern notion of liberty.

Here, however, we wake up the Old Quarrel between the
economists and the philanthropists.   A man's legal right, it
is said, can be morally wrong ; an economical good may be
a moral evil.   To do justice to this quarrel we need to
remember that it arose, ran its course, and really became
obsolete, at a time when both economists and philanthropists
were too proud to understand each other.   Whether in the
Palestine of Isaiah, the Rome of the Gracchi, the merry
England of Sir Thomas More, or the modern England of
the younger Pitt, every great economical change has gone
along with suffering, hard dealing, public indignation, and,
as a rule, useless remedial measures.   It is hard to say on
whose side history has declared herself, for if the failure
of the laws be a point against the philanthropists, the invariable public indignation is a point in their favour.
History, as usual, gives us the premisses and leaves us to
draw our own conclusions.   The difficulty is not to be
solved by dates and records ; it is a case of conscience.
The question is, whether the man who dares to add field to
field, or to feed sheep instead of human beings, or to use a
machine instead of a man, can be morally wrong and eco-
nomically right.   The philanthropists have a certain furtive
pleasure in the contradiction; few things would so dis-

concert them as the discovery that political economy is at peace with the ten commandments. The economists are more conciliatory, some even seeming to contend that economical rightness would of itself produce moral rightness, and so prevent the contradiction altogether. Interference by the State or even voluntary refraining on the part of the innovators will not, they think, in the long run benefit the sufferers nearly so much as a courageous perseverance in the straight road to wealth.

It is not too much to say that the average Englishman is a philanthropist in his words and an economist in his deeds. This does not mean that he is generous in theory and selfish in practice, but only that he has a half-understood feeling that all is not generosity, neither is all selfishness that seems so, and he has learned to distinguish State from Society. He understands better than his fathers what are the real limits that fence in the citizen engaging in trade, and in what way society can best lay hold of him and his customers, so as to ensure the maximum of gain and the minimum of loss from the proceedings of both of them. The same considerations apply to a professional, artistic, or any other career. It is only most useful to apply them to trade, because, on the whole, at the present day, trade is the most conspicuous agency in moulding nations and men into new shapes; and it is the best instance of the ambiguity of the word 'selfish' and of the thoroughly social character of the most 'selfish' endeavours.

'The American,' says his best critic, 'throws himself one moment into politics, as if the State was all in all to him; and the next he devotes himself to his private business as if he were alone in the world.' How is the alternation possible? Can a man be quite social and quite selfish by turns? Can he keep opposite qualities in separate pigeon-holes out of contact with each other? Of course there are no spiritual pigeon-holes. To take up business, the generous man does not lay aside his generosity. It is a question, however, whether the apparently unsocial feelings, often associated with the motto 'business is business,' are really so unsocial as they seem, and whether the contents of the mythical pigeon-holes are not inextricably shaken together. There is a *ne plus ultra* of cold-hearted avarice, who is often pilloried in literary sermons as the ideal Wise Man of political economy. The magazine writer would miss him if he were gone; but, if truth is to conquer fiction, his place will know him no more. It is easier to ask whether Macrowdy has 'left off' grinding the faces of the poor than to prove that he ever did so. Cruelty and coldness are often, no doubt, practised by commercial men; but they are not entirely unknown in other walks of life, and the typical man of business has no greater affinity for them than the statesman, the theologian, or the justice of the peace. Ricardo is perhaps the only economist whose works lend colour to the opposite view. The occasional hardness of tone in the 'Wealth of Nations' is largely due to the author's fondness for stating one side at a time, lawyer fashion; and it is not difficult to show that his selfish pedlar principle of turning a penny where a penny is to be got has much in it besides selfishness. He often, it is true, identifies himself with the pedlar. He says that the lifelong human desire of bettering one's own condition usually takes a commercial form, and through commerce benefits society far better than any laws; gain is the chief motive of all improvements, and by pursuing his own interest a man usually does more good to his neighbours than if he deliberately intended their good. 'I have never known much good done by those who affected to trade for the public good,' advertising elixirs of life and sales at enormous sacrifice. If a man makes no such pretensions, but simply seeks his own gain, then he is 'led by an invisible hand' to promote the gain of other people. The moral is, leave trade and traders perfectly free. 'All restraints therefore being taken away, the simple system of natural liberty establishes itself of its own accord;' and both the making of wealth and the sharing of it will be at their best.

It is the penalty of comprehensiveness to give temptation to the eclectic; and Adam Smith does not escape the penalty. Writers have taken hold of his sentences about 'natural liberty' and 'freedom of trade,' and they have founded on them the doctrine of '*laissez faire*,' or 'hands off.' Writers have pointed out that a little anarchy is better for trade than a great deal of interference: the Hanseatic and Italian towns in their palmiest days were not conspicuous for good government, and much good government can go with bad trade. We have theorists accordingly who recommend administrative Nihilism, or anarchy *plus* the constable, by which they mean no more government than is required to keep thieves in order and preserve to every man the fruits of his labour. We ought not to have even a Post Office by law established, but trust to the tender mercies of individual enterprise, disciplined by the fear of competition. We are never to do for a man what he can possibly do for himself; all are to fend for themselves; and division of labour, that great spontaneous organiser of industrial forces, will work out in good time the salvation of society.

There are many cheap and obvious objections to this *laissez faire* theory. Logically, we ought not on these principles even to use the policeman or the judge; it would make us more independent, to trust in our own muscle and brain against our neighbour's force and fraud. This would be a kind of Darwinism in politics; and the issue, whatever it was, would not be a State. Individualists, as a rule, do not go so far. They do not yet believe with the eighteenth century that the fulness of time will dispense with all government, all offences disappearing of their own accord on the advent of human perfection. But Adam Smith does not even go so far as our present individualists. Every scientific doctrine of *laissez faire* must trace its genealogy to him; and yet he claimed no small field for the action of the State. The State, to his mind, was profitable for defence, justice, and public works. He was so far from believing in the infallible power of individualism to cure its own wounds, that he advocated an Education Act expressly to save the working man from being degraded by the division of labour. In other words he did not regard the 'struggle for existence' as a panacea when we are at the bottom of the scale, but only when we are in the upper parts of it, where it becomes the hopeful desire of bettering one's own condition. A totally uneducated man is very unlikely to conceive the idea of bettering his own condition; and yet otherwise he has not entered on the full heritage of his manhood. Therefore it is that for one man to die ignorant who is capable of learning is the most tragic of all facts, and therefore it is that a man's education is not the private interest of his parents, but the public concern of all citizens. 'Natural liberty,' in short, as it is conceived by the father of political economy, is rather the positive

power to use powers than the negative absence of restraint;
it is not without law, still less without society. Rousseau's
famous exordium, 'Man is born free, and he is everywhere
in chains,' might in this light be interpreted quite literally,
to signify that the citizen of a civilised State is not free
from society but free in society, not free from the laws, but
free because of them, for they enable him to work out the
aims and interests of a reasonable being. So understood,
the laws of the State are not the limits of the citizen so
much as his opportunities, not his enemies but his friends;
and the State itself possesses a positive function towards
him, fulfilling his ends, not a mere overruling or repres-
sive function, reining in his aberrations. The general life
of the body politic would then be no mystical fiction, but the
most substantial and vital of secular realities; and it would
be as true now as it was twenty centuries ago, that the
greatest service a father can do to his son is to make him
citizen of a good State.

The *laissez faire* of the Manchester School of Politics
is, on the whole, in harmony with this view of the State. It
proceeds always on a basis of law. Its unlimited competition is the competition of law-obeying citizens. The Manchester politicians believe that society has now developed so
completely out of status to contract, or in plain English out
of custom to bargain, that bargain is now the only proper
régime for Englishmen. But it is not bargain *in vacuo*; it
is bargain under the conditions of English law; it is the
acquisition, use, and transfer of property under the conditions of English law. Even if the whole Manchester pro-
gramme were passed and all special interference with trade
were abolished, there would still be the restriction of the
laws. Open competition does not mean a game without
rules, but a game in which all may take part if they submit
to the conditions of it, the conditions being in this case
the etiquette of trade and the law of the land. The etiquette
of trade may leave much room for private interpretation,
but it sensibly tones down the roughness of competition.
It is better to be defeated by an army than by a mob; it
is better to be knocked about by a good fencer than by a
bad; and it is better to struggle for existence with chivalrous opponents who observe the rules of the game and secure
their end with the least possible suffering to all parties,

than with those who have no ties and recognise no limit but their own self-will. In the second place, to strive lawfully means to obey the law of the land, the entire digested and undigested mass of statute and case law which Englishmen believe to be, in some mysterious way, essential to their security and bound in the bundle of their civilisation. These facts, however, are as easily turned against the one side as against the other in the old quarrel. The philanthropist may see in them a precedent for interference; trade has never been free. The economist may see a presumption against any interference; trade has never been lawless. He might add that, besides the gross and palpable fetters of law, there are other less tangible bonds whose subtle grip is never eluded, and which may be called the social sentiments.

It is a significant fact that the book called the 'Moral Sentiments' was written many years before the 'Wealth of Nations.' There is no doubt that the author meant the two books to be part first and part second of a complete system of sociology. In printing them so far away (in all senses of the word) from one another he was simply following his favourite plan of stating one side at a time. He wished us therefore to supplement the one book by the other; and, so doing, we shall find that he understands commercial competition, from the very nature of the political society where it takes place, to rest first on positive law, and in the second place on social sentiment. This makes it easier to understand how 'the invisible hand' is able to lead the selfish action of men to the best results. The competitors are fellow-citizens; they have not only the laws but the feelings of citizenship to diminish the friction of their competition. We have long passed the period when a belief in actual kinship was needed to hold men together under one government; but States have not yet become matters of mere bargain, or convenient arrangements concluded purely for material interests between people careless of each other's welfare. Such a State would have no stronger bond than a European concert; and it is not simply the absence of a controlling force that exposes such a concert to possibility of discord; it is the want, among its members, of that common understanding which enables the members of the same nation (as distinguished from the parties to the same bargain) to enter into one another's feelings, and really desire one another's welfare, or at least to feel ashamed of not seeming to do so. It is the want of the feeling which makes a man say he feels at home with his countrymen and not with foreigners. Countrymen have had the same upbringing; they have shared the same traditions, history, and customs; they have had a common literature; they have loved and hated the same men, or, if not, they have agreed to bury schismatic passions, that there might be no schism in the body politic. All true Frenchmen have forgotten Saint Bartholomew, and all true Britons Flodden. Patriotism is simply comradeship on a large scale; it is the feeling that usually exists between old boys of a good school, or old members of a good college. As patriotism must precede cosmopolitanism, patriotism itself must be preceded by provinciality, and that by home sickness or the attachment of a man to his little platoon or subdivision. The same series, stated in terms of history, becomes the aphorism, 'Society developes from the family to the tribe—from the tribe to the State.' Expressed in terms of 'the Revolution,' it becomes the paradox, or the axiom, 'Before liberty, fraternity, and before equality, both of them.' From either it follows that the union of men in a State is the effect, not the cause, of their union in a nation or society, from which in turn it follows that the most thorough reform must begin from below with society, not from above with the State, however well the two may help each other. At the same time, every building is something more than its materials; public opinion, defined by laws, has something more in it than public opinion left undefined. A nation's customs, its long-established use and wont, regulating the distribution of property, whether in land or in goods, lose their mere vegetable nature when definitely set forth in the form of laws. Somebody has said that human laws are to human customs as these are to the instincts of animals. Perhaps they are to each other as word is to feeling. State a custom as a law, and it becomes a general principle, applicable to all cases—not a vague particular feeling, which people obey without reason and may occasionally violate without reproach. Now here it is that the negative functions of the State which relate to Order are connected with the positive that relate to Progress. If in its police or soldiery the State may be regarded simply as a committee of public safety, in its legislation it enters on a path that does not simply return on itself but goes indefinitely forward. Society is never so truly State as when it is converting customs into laws; and in popular governments legislation and progress generally go together. When a usage becomes the law of the land, it invites criticism of the reason or unreason of it; and, the more accessible the laws, the oftener it will be asked if there is no fault or flaw anywhere to be found in them. In other words, the laws, that seemed to be intended only to preserve order and define rules that were already in force *de facto*, lead to progress and the making of new rules. Science may even supersede custom, and may cause legislation to anticipate public opinion instead of following it. It may be that 'the great organiser of modern States is scientific knowledge;' it may be that the philosopher must be king. But in most cases, at least in the present era, the beginning will be from beneath. It will be the ripe growth of ideas that are first local, then general, and lastly universal. All government, we are told, was at first local government, and, if the English parish is a miniature of the English State, it is not because the parish has learned of the State, but because the State has learned of the parish. The mercantile law of England has grown out of the customs of merchants gradually recognised by tribunals and formulated in decisions and laws, the law even now refusing to override an invariable custom. The most important matter is in every case not the law itself, but the popular feeling to which it points, the national idea or ideal of which it is an expression. It is this that gives to all antiquated statutes, whether they relate to game, paupers, or primogeniture, such a melancholy interest.

The moral is, that a social training in the family and its expansions precedes selfish action in the market and the world. The life of a well-governed family supplies at least half of the whole moral training; it teaches reverence for what is above, below, and around; it gives a capacity of deference and co-operation; and even an ill-governed family may have good traditions of a past generation, giving the ingenuous youth something to aspire after. It is quite true that, to have the whole nature drawn out, and all the powers tested, a man must go out into the world and face its competitive examinations; he cannot escape the 'struggle for existence.' But, at the very first beginnings of his life, the citizen will see more of the union than of the division in society, and these early lessons will not be lost upon him. Here again the argument has a double edge. The philanthropist may say, 'Behold how justified is government in interfering with free competition; fraternity always came before liberty.' The economist may reply, ' See how little need there is for any interference; liberty was always qualified by fraternity.'

Psychology, too, may have a word to say on the subject. It may be shown that the desire to better one's condition is not Selfish in the most invidious sense of the word. The feelings of patriotism and love of kindred are usually characterised as social feelings, in contrast to commercial ambition which is selfish. No one denies nowadays that honest trading means mutual gain to the traders; it is neither beggaring my neighbour nor beggaring myself, but serving both. But, though the result is public benefit, the motive was personal or selfish. To the trader 'business is business,' and he is always pictured as refusing to bate a stiver unless it is so nominated in the bond. He is assumed to be as much devoted to his small hungry shivering self, and regardless of others, as Robinson Crusoe alone on the island. But even Crusoe could not be ' himself alone.' He lived in the world of memory; and all his acts and thoughts had reference to the society of which he was an absent member, and for which he wrote his 'Life and Adventures.' Society refuses to be pitched out with a fork; Crusoe was quite as selfish in his English home as on the island. Indeed everyone feels, at the very mention of the change of scene, that it was only among his fellow-men that he could have had any opportunity for being either selfish or unselfish, or for having any character at all. There is a sense in which no one, and a sense in which everyone is selfish, and there is a companion paradox—that society does not kill character, it creates it; if we rub each other's angles down, we draw each other's talents out. But let us ride over the 'first wave' first. How are we to show that in one sense there is no such thing as selfishness when clever philosophers resolve all sin into it, and have seemed therein to be much better understood of the people than their tribe usually are? The answer is that their arguments may prove that all sin is selfishness, but not that all selfish-

ness is sin. The extreme of selfishness is certainly the extreme
of sin. The separation of part of the world from the whole
is what they mean by metaphysical evil, chaos, or ' objective
selfishness ; ' the attempt of any individuals to separate
themselves from the whole body of human beings is the
essence of moral evil or ' subjective selfishness.' But the
perfect isolation of an individual is as impossible as chaos.
Either of them would put us to ' permanent intellectual
confusion.' The highest degree of moral and metaphysical
evil would be reached if every atom, human or otherwise,
were to set up for itself, and try to be ' itself alone.' Goodness, on the other hand, combines freedom and law ; to be a
law unto oneself does not mean to defy the rest of the universe. The wicked (according to Plato), try the defiance and
find it impossible ; and the righteous will not try it at all.
The very worst kind of selfishness recognises the impossibility of isolation by making others the means of its ends,
and feeding on the spoils of its rivals. It may not be right to
derive all a man's moral sentiments solely from his power
of putting himself in another man's place ; that may be
only one special example of a general power to convert a
particular into a genus. But, whatever its origin, its efficacy
in this region is undoubted. In the first place ambition
courts opposition in order to have the pleasure of overcoming it ; and victory itself is tasteless without the spectator's applause and the foe's submission. In the second place,
ambition seeks spoils for its friends, relations, or family,
who are a great part of its own life. Even when the heart
is set on science, travel, art, invention, and all the large
interests which our latter-day civilisation has done so much
to multiply and make popular, there is always a latent
thought of others in the mind of the most single-hearted
enthusiast. The savant, if there be such, whose labours
are so purely ' objective ' that he carries their achievements unrecorded into the grave with him, is chiefly sustained by the Pharisaic consciousness of originality. Men
may often be destitute of any deliberate intention either to
benefit or to injure their fellows ; but do what they please
they cannot be neutral. They cannot unspin or unweave
themselves, they are threads either of warp or woof. They
cannot be singular and separate, either in their ends or in
their means. ' No man liveth to himself, and no man dieth

to himself.' ' A man ' in fact ' is an abstraction, and there is nothing real but humanity.' A man owes his character to his action upon others and their action upon him. The industrial counterpart of these psychological facts, the division of labour, is a commonplace of work-a-day life, and perhaps the only one which gives a show of reason to the anti-jesuitical saying, ' means are more important than ends.' There is no end in life which can be fulfilled by one man without the work of other men past and present, dead and living, practical and intellectual. No man can be a protectionist in his own country or among his own kindred; division of labour made perfect by co-operation is the key to the greatest movements of industrial civilisation. There is a famous passage in the ' Wealth of Nations ' where Adam Smith, perhaps thinking of Rousseau, contrasts the unaccommodated noble savage with the civilised agricultural labourer, and finds that there is a wider distance between humble Hodge and the King of Dahomey, than between King George and humble Hodge. The savage king has perhaps made all his wardrobe himself, down to the very primitive stitchings, if they have any, of his very primitive garments, if they are plural. The English peasant does not let his neighbours off so easily. If we take account of all the materials of his jacket alone, and their treatment from first to last, it will take a long time to exhaust the list of trades and traders who have worked for him, from the sailor to the bricklayer, from the chemist to the ironfounder. He has not so much majesty as an African chief; but he has more of the comforts of life which are owing to civilisation. If civilisation gives us only the elements of happiness, and not the happiness itself, still it is something to have the elements; the happiness may come hereafter.

Industrial union, therefore, fastens another fetter on the competition of selfish atoms, or at least tones down the effects of their selfishness. When Hegel, who knew little economics beyond the ' Wealth of Nations,' rejoiced in Adam Smith's extension of the reign of law to matters of trade, he was thinking chiefly of the 'simple system of natural liberty' and the mutual dependence due to division of labour. Mutual dependence is no doubt not the same thing as the consciousness of it, and the latter can only keep pace with the former through the constant reiteration of proofs as well

as truths. But both of them bear out the same conclusion;
—it is simply impossible for a man to be so selfish as completely to separate himself from others. On the other hand
it is impossible for a man to be so unselfish as to give himself up completely into the hands of others. It is as in
the old dispute of private judgment against authority.
Even the Catholic exercises the right of private judgment
at the moment when he decides that as for him and his
house he will serve the Church. It is he and not another
who wills the act by which he gives up his will to another.
The only person who would have no private judgment would
be the man who never sufficiently awoke out of the sleep of
custom to have any judgment at all, but lived on as his
fathers did before him. So the man who wills to be unselfish
does not get rid of self; on that point we are all utilitarians
of the old school; we believe that every action has the self in
it. But, as the old school delighted to confound pleasure
with good pleasure, an intellectual element with an
emotional, so ' common sense ' confounds regenerate with un-
regenerate selfishness; she shakes her head and says they
are all the same, though there are really good and bad sorts,
and, whether a man's selfishness is of the one or the other
depends on the aims on which his heart is set, and which
really give him his character. To a man whose self includes
other selves the reproach of selfishness has no sting; its
bite is for the man who has a narrow notion of self, and would
like not only gravitation but reform to cease when he goes
by. Even the worst men have something social in their
notion of self; and the good men have more than a little—
they have all the social interests that make life valuable.
But, if selfishness is so ambiguous, and if moral character
depends on the nature of the interests which almost constitute the self, it is useless for moralists to erect self-
denial into a cardinal virtue. It is a duty turned inside
out; and their exhortations are only useful when they are
immediately followed by a positive description of the end to
be sought. We must not quote ' if a man would be my
disciple, let him take up his cross,' without adding ' and
follow me.' To cast aside every weight becomes a matter of
course as soon as we are convinced that we have something
to run for. Self-sacrifice is often as canting a phrase in
moral lectures as Evolution in scientific, though for very

different reasons. Abstinence and self-denial mean suffering
and evil; and to defend any practice of them at all we must
look at their motives. The great elevating force in the world
has been not any abstract idea of self-denial, which might
easily become a glorification of suicide, but the expulsive
power of a new affection which would have expelled no evil
if it had not impelled to some good. It is positive well-doing
and the enthusiasm of humanity that are the first and great
commandment of Christians. It is not a resolve to avoid
sin, but a strong attraction for good persons and causes that
makes any sin impossible. It is a positive ideal, not a de-
terrent fear, that will elevate humanity; and a good spirit
will not try so much to cast out the devils, as to make the
very devils subject unto him.

This principle may be applied, amongst other passions,
to the love of money. How does it happen that modern
economists have, on the whole, been so nearly unanimous in
regarding commercial ambition as a good thing for humanity,
while ancient morality frowned on it and ancient economists
thought it a vice, though a vice that might occasionally
become a public benefit? Simply because the phrase 'love
of money' meant the love of what money brings, and what
it brought was even more often evil long ago than it is
now. It was never, even to the miser, the childish liking
for a glittering metal; still less can it be so now, when hard
coin has been lowered from the absolute into the constitutional monarch of the money market. It means the desire
of wealth; wealth means what satisfies wants; and wants
vary with the civilisation of men. The desire to make
money may perhaps most commonly be the desire to make
others feel our power over them. But it may be the
chivalrous desire to have the first place in one's own trade,
to build the best ships, to have the best farm. It may be
something still further away from actual trade; a man may
only desire a fortune in order to get into Parliament, or to be
a great philanthropist, or to promote a religious mission, or
to have leisure for writing books. In other words, commercial ambition is not itself the universal motor force of modern
society, but rather the necessary machinery by which the
forces work; it is not the steam or the work done; it is only
the engine. Strictly speaking, wealth means the abundance
of good things, not the tools for exchanging them or the

means of getting them ; and men's notions of good things
vary with their wants, and their wants vary with their
country, climate, and history. This is not an accidental
variation. No doubt there is a variation of fashions, which
means simply the momentary revival of past and dropping
of present, without regard to any requirements of new knowledge or improved taste. But over and· above the mere
changes of fashion there is a progressive expansion of wants
which takes place in all but the very lowest strata of civilised society. The luxuries of one age become the necessaries
of the next. The general cheapening of the comforts of life,
under a *régime* of free trade, bring the good things of the
rich within reach of the poor. The poor become loth to lose
them ; they desire to have a permanently higher rate of
wages rather than to multiply their numbers down to the
rate at which those worked who had not tasted the new
comforts. The physical or animal minimum of wages, which
is the object of the struggle for bare existence, is almost a
fixed quantity; its variations are not progressive. But the
social minimum, the necessaries of good existence, is in its
normal state when it is ever adding to itself. It is good to
think that the British workman's savings and spendings
alike imply a margin beyond bare necessaries. The ' struggle
for existence,' when it means this struggle to retain acquired
or social necessaries, is so far from evil that it is perhaps
the chief redeeming feature of our civilisation; and the
greatest enemies of the modern State are those of either
extreme of political party who would persuade men that
such a progress is not contemplated or even admitted by the
organisation of our present State.

A modern writer, who is too wise to be either optimist or
pessimist, has made an eloquent protest against the common
glorification of industrial progress. He declares that not the
progressive but the stationary state of wealth is the best for
the spiritual interests and true happiness of humanity. It
is not good, he thinks, that luxurious wants should multiply,
and that the making of material good things should absorb
the best energies of humanity. In this revolt against economical tradition he was probably guided by the true
philosophical instinct which refuses to confound the spiritual
infinity of the shoeblack with the boundless greediness of
the shoeblack's finite appetites. At the same time it is difficult

R

to believe the arrest of material progress to be compatible with the continuation of spiritual. A man's knowledge of himself and his knowledge of nature go hand in hand. Moreover, great wealth differs from small wealth far less in the quantity than in the quality of its good things. Material progress does not mean merely an indefinite multiplication of useless enjoyments, but an improvement in the character of the enjoyments themselves, together with such a cheapening of them as brings them within reach of a large circle of people instead of a small. Progress here, as elsewhere, comes from ideas. Ideas of well-being have far more influence in industry than any other cause whatever.

These are a few of the social prolegomena, without which economical science is abstract and unreal. They have a double bearing. They point to the entire impossibility of the Ricardian *régime* of rigorous competition ; and, granting the possibility, they would qualify the conclusions of orthodox economics. In the *first* place it was seen that the 'struggle for existence' in the lower strata of society is not a political good but a political evil. Starvation is no stimulus, except to wrongdoing; the true stimulus is ideas, and therefore, in the *second* place, in all strata except the lowest, and in the middle strata most of all, the 'struggle for existence' means ambition. In the *third* place, in our time this ambition, whatever its end, depends largely for its means on material wealth. Commercial ambition is therefore the most common variety of the species, and it is the most influential in its social consequences. At the same time, just because the immediate is not the real end of it, it has an infinite variety of social complexion and moral character, depending as these do rather on its real than on its apparent end. In the *fourth* place, the 'struggle for existence,' in the sense of the unlimited competition of ambitious men of business, is neither so unfeeling nor so unlimited as it seems. Political molecules must have political characteristics; and commercial competitors are not dots on a slate or atoms in free space, but very concrete and sensitive human beings beset on all sides with limitations. They are limited (*a*) by the written laws which provide for the safety of the country and the security and freedom of its citizens, (*b*) by the laws which define into a clear general rule the old usage of their nation concerning the holding and transferring of property,

(c) by the old usage itself, by the unwritten laws of etiquette and custom, and by the common feelings, religious and otherwise, of their nationality, (d) by the fact that even the selfish actions of a human being have the stamp of society upon them, and are always less selfish than he intends. The self of a man means the interest he follows : and he cannot pursue even the narrower interests of himself or his smallest circle without unintentionally serving the public. (e) Economical progress by division of labour and union of labourers confirms this necessity. But (f), if a man would be a good citizen in his own person, if he would strengthen the bonds of the society which has made him what he is, he must have the good will as well as the good deed ; he must know the doctrine as well as do the will. It is not enough to be, he must know, for the life of a people depends far more on its ideas and sentiments than on its social machinery.

The same positions may be stated in more formal philosophical language. The objective idealism of Germany, if it has done nothing else, has loosened the old English belief in the separateness of things distinguishable, a belief which invented many insoluble problems and created many doubts out of certainties. Political economists used to speak as if their method of study must be either inductive or deductive but not both, and as if production and distribution moved on two different lines because they could be treated in two separate chapters. But, here as elsewhere, and especially on the borders of the social sciences, while we cannot be too careful to distinguish, we cannot be too careful not to separate. The higher the scale of life in the world, the more numerous will be the elements that enter into it, and the more truly they will become at once distinguishable and inseparable. The greater therefore will be the felt impossibility of describing the living thing by any category which does not share in the living thing's complexity. It follows in the *first* place, then, that to describe men as ' animals struggling for food ' is no more satisfactory than to describe the United Kingdom as two pieces of land surrounded by water. When men are no more than struggling animals, they are depressed below their humanity and hardly worthy of a description by greater categories. The civil society in which they first become truly human owes some of its materials but none of its distinctive attributes to the merely

animal instincts of struggling men ; a statue does not owe
its beauty to the plaster or the marble.   In the *second*
place, man's life in civil society cannot be adequately
described in terms of his mere repulsion from his fellows
or his struggles with them.   He is not an atom falling
against others in a chance passage through space.   He is
an individual member of a union of men which was formed
by no accident; he is distinct from the rest but not
separable from them, having a character of his own but
owing its development to them.   In the *third* place, civil
society, which is the sum total of competing individuals,
their families, and their associations, is quite distinct from
the State, and yet inseparable from it.   The State represents
not the particular aims of the several parts, but the chief
ends of the whole.   If the parts depend on society for their
character, they depend on the State for their career; and on
the other hand the general life which culminates in the
State as its chief organ would be a mere abstraction if it
were not consciously present to the thoughts and sentiments
of the citizens.   It is not enough then to say that the one is
universal and the other particular.   These categories are
nearly as meagre as the one and the many.   Even life and
animal life fall short of the truth, and we dare not use
human life, for it is the thing to be defined.   Organism
will best serve the purpose, if it be clearly understood not
to mean the animal union of members in one body but
the type of an ideal union of members in one life, of
which the best known example is not the body but the body
politic.   For, in the body politic, the general life is from first
to last the foundation of all individual energy ; and yet the
individual members pay back the debt by a felt sympathy
and conscious union with the commonwealth, to which the
commonwealth in turn owes all its perennial health and
vigour.   The citizen owes much to his country ; the country
is nothing without its citizens.   To make the State all in
all with Bismarck, or the individual all in all with Spencer,
is to fall into equally false speculation and equally dangerous
policy.

These prolegomena may perhaps point to a partial
solution of some social problems, and few problems can
hope for more.   The philosopher has happily no powers of
prediction.   He cannot tell what will become of States and

nations in the moral and economical millennium, or even sixty years hence, when the earth's inhabitants know each other better and the enthusiasm of humanity has a fairer chance. He only knows that it is the peculiarity of human development to incorporate its conquests, and that nothing good will be lost. The most violent reformations, revolutions, and reactions have never done more than seem to break the continuity of progress; and philosophers best anticipate the future when they understand the present. It may be thought that their reach should always exceed their grasp; but is it not written, in the book of the Fables of Æsop, that in reaching after the future a certain too sanguine aspirant lost his hold of the present, of which alas! in the end he found it only the reflection?

JAMES BONAR.

IX.

PESSIMISM AND THE RELIGIOUS CONSCIOUSNESS.

THE presupposition of thought and life in the eighteenth century was the supremacy of the individual. Applied to the prevailing absolutism of the day, this principle proved itself mighty for destruction, and secured the overthrow of the *ancien régime* in all its forms, in politics, religion, and philosophy. When, however, it came to be employed as an instrument of reconstruction its powerlessness speedily became manifest. In the philosophy of Hume the current individualism was gathered up in its full significance, and wrought out to conclusions in which its inability to afford a rational theory of experience or a practical force for life stands well-nigh confessed. In the fate of the French Revolution, the inherent weakness of the system, thus speculatively expressed, became manifest to the world's perception. The individualism of the last century is bequeathed, accordingly, to the present, as at once an axiom and a problem. On the one hand it is impossible to return to the system which it overthrew; and on the other it is impossible to abide in it, for it has itself been overthrown. That the individual has in himself, apart from all non-essential circumstances, an infinite value—a man's a man for a' that—and has therefore a rightful claim upon the universe for satisfaction, has been wrought into the public opinion of our day. No theory of reform which ignores this element in the social problem can be of any practical worth. Every scheme for the future must give ample scope to the principle which has won for itself inalienable right to recognition. At the same time, the mere assertion of this doctrine is fatal to the interests, and even to the existence of society. When the individual makes his claim to infinite satisfaction, he is immediately confronted by another with the same demand, and there ensues an infinite opposition. Each makes an exclusive claim to a central position in the universe; the very presence of the one to the other involves the necessity of a combat, whose antagonism is as incalculable as the greatness of the prize contended for, and which with all its anguish, felt as keenly by the victor as by the vanquished, must endure till both vanish from the scene of conflict. The state of war to which a society conceived as an aggregate of such elements is reduced, is, however, no more than a realisation in outward fact of a conflict which takes place within the individual consciousness. The self claims infinite satisfaction; but, by the very terms of its claim, it shows itself to be merely finite, and therefore incapable of the satisfaction which it demands. The claim is a mere claim, the formal ascription of absoluteness, infinitude, freedom, to the subject, without filling these terms with any positive meaning. As infinite and free the self claims the world as its own; but, since its conception of infinitude and freedom involves no positive relation to the world, it sets itself against the world, is accordingly limited by it, and is therefore not infinite, not free. Nor can any progressive series of victories over the world get rid of the defect of its first start on its career. With a merely abstract claim, every object of desire as it presents itself is external, and therefore a limit. The acquisition of such objects, even in an endless manner, is no nearer approach to the satisfaction craved for than the first most trifling gain. The limit is still there, and the self, whose demand was that nothing should limit it, is no more free than when first it asserted its right to freedom, while it has to suffer the added pain of weariness.

This doctrine of the infinitude of the finite self, with all its rightfulness, and self-contradiction, and suffering, has been wrought out during the present century with every variety of practical consequence. Literature has been filled with it. If men do not now retire like Obermann to mourn amid Alpine solitudes, it is chiefly because grief can find no loneliness in a world where conflict and sorrow are absolutely universal. Byron might exhibit 'the pageant of his bleeding heart through Europe to the Ætolian shore,' without attracting the slightest attention from a world too well

aware that every heart is bleeding to need any demonstration
of the fact. In the sphere of politics there is abundant
ground for the very greatest alarm. There is no State in
Europe which has not before it a problem that may at any
moment find for itself tragic utterance, a problem constituted
by the presence of an element which force can never crush,
which must continue to assert itself till, by justice done to
it, it be lifted beyond the possibility of harmful activity.
It is in the domain of mercantile life, however, which now in
England is practically co-extensive with the social sphere,
that individualism has had its most disintegrating effect.
With the magic formula of *laissez faire* for its motto, it has
occupied the whole field of political economy. Even by those
who would acknowledge its inadequacy in other departments
of life, it has been held to be the sole possibly regnant
principle of the 'market, till the commercial world, isolated
from a realm where higher principles are allowed to prevail,
has become practically destitute of them, and conducts its
affairs without any reference to them, and too often in direct
defiance of them. Markets are becoming daily more crowded,
practice more sharp; amid large sections of the community,
embracing multitudes who could not be classed among the
poor, the aim of business is being ever more nearly narrowed
to the problem of bare existence ; while on every hand there is
manifest a dissatisfaction that is abundantly justified by the
repeated occurrence of commercial crises.

When such an experience is seen in its unity and receives a reflective expression, there results pessimism as a
philosophical system, which, whatever be the speculative
affiliation of its various forms, is no more than a description
of existing facts, and the assertion that these constitute
the whole inevitable truth of life. The interest and
the strength of pessimistic systems lie, accordingly, in that
individualism which is their unquestioned presupposition, and
which, if it be granted to them, constitutes a quite impreg-
nable position. They make, indeed, the profession which
every system that pretends to be philosophical must make,
of starting from experience and aiming at nothing more
than a comprehension of its meaning, a grasp of its reality,
in the unity of some intelligible principle. But the experience from which they start has already been conceived in
an individualistic fashion. The facts with which they deal

are the facts of a world so long dominated by individualism
that the latter seems to be part of its original constitution,
presenting not theories to be discussed but data to be
accepted. Their investigations therefore are predetermined
towards individualistic conclusions. Whatever be the line
of argument adopted, whatever be the metaphysical school
to which allegiance is professed, the result is still the same,
and ultimately consists in the explicit statement of the
individualism which constituted the starting-point.

Schopenhauer, for instance, in his elevation of the thing-
in-itself, which to Kant had been the unrealisable ideal of pure
reason, the unverifiable reality of the practical reason, into
the principle of the universe, was simply following the lines
upon which the whole movement of thought subsequent to
Kant proceeded. His *pessimism* emerges when he identifies
the last manifestation of will with the individual self, and
abides by this position, refusing to leave it save by a movement which is not a transcendence of the individuality of
the self, but an extinction of the self altogether. We may
admit with him that every assertion of the individual in his
exclusive individuality only increases his misery, that hope
lies only in the stoppage of all such assertion, in the prompt
cessation of this 'luckless episode in the blissful repose of
nothing.' But that the individual can exist only in exclusive individuality, that there is no possibility of a life for
him in which, through devotion to an end beyond himself,
he may achieve the fulness of his own being, is for Schopenhauer a foregone conclusion, an axiom which he never
dreams of proving; and it is precisely this that is the point
at issue.

Hartmann, in like manner, does no more than participate
in the spirit of all post-Kantian development, when he seeks
a principle whose unity shall underlie and account for all
the differences of the universe. His pessimism, however,
arises from his identification of consciousness with exclusiveness. The knowledge to which a man awakes in consciousness is certainly of himself as confronted by the world,
forced to maintain himself against it, to win his satisfaction
from it by contest with it. But this, which is undeniably a
stage in the history of self-consciousness, is given by Hartmann as the whole account of it. The final manifestation
of the unconscious is, accordingly, a world of mutually ex-

clusive beings, each to be judged from the standpoint of his mere individuality. Hartmann's proof of pessimism is thus simple and conclusive; take the happiness of each individual as a test, and forthwith the world stands utterly condemned. Whatever be the sphere in which happiness is sought, whether the present life, the life beyond the grave, or the future of humanity, in all alike it is unattainable, the effort after it fraught with nothing but misery. A pessimistic philosophy is exhibited by Hartmann to be the necessary consequence of an individualistic ethic. Conceive of happiness as the satisfaction of the individual in his isolation, and at once the world is seen to be incapable of affording it. The inevitableness of the conclusion may be fully conceded; the question that remains is the rightfulness of the presupposition.

The horrors of pessimism accordingly cannot be used as an argument against it. In its gloomiest statements pessimism is simply developing the consequences of a view of the world that is common to' it with many theories which have refrained from drawing pessimistic conclusions. If human nature be so limited that any passage across its barriers into a wider life beyond, any real identity with interests more than individual, is impossible; if, being what he is, a man can have no other end than the satisfaction of his exclusive self, and if the whole movement of the world be towards the endless repetition of such isolated points of humanity, no conclusion is possible but misery, the agony of a thinly-disguised anarchic war, the anguish of an infinite disappointment. It is the last and fullest account of the world as it is presented to us by individualism. This is, however, from the other side, the criticism of individualism upon itself; and pessimism is doing for our age what Hume did for his, wrenching the presuppositions of the day from their position of unquestioned acceptance, giving explicit statement to their full significance, and setting them in the light of their legitimate and necessary consequences. Pessimism involves and promulgates, as the only hope for the world, the destruction of every form of life, the cessation of the present development, and the exhaustion of the possibility of any other; but this is just the paradoxical statement of the impossibility of any intelligible or rational experience on the principles by means of which it has reached these results.

If this view of the significance of pessimism be correct,

it evidently admits of no direct reply, and our interest in it does not lie in its confutation. It is not a one-sided statement of some of the facts of life, which may be sufficiently disposed of by calling attention to others. It is a conception of life as a whole, and can be met by nothing less comprehensive than itself. The presence of pessimism in modern thought is the demand for the reconstruction of modern life. Its function is to set forth the manifold elements of which the modern world is composed, in all the isolation which individualistic principles have conferred upon them, and by a truthful statement of the consequent conflict, in all its misery and hopelessness, to give utterance to the ultimate need of the age, the need of a principle which shall deliver these elements from the discord of their isolation, and bring them into a harmony of working which shall secure a triumphant issue. The world which pessimism describes to us is a world in fragments; its evil is its fragmentary character. Its first necessity therefore is a principle of synthesis, the extent of whose application shall be as wide as the criticism of pessimism, which shall be able to penetrate throughout the whole sphere which individualism has disintegrated, and reconstitute it as an organic unity. With the vindication of such a principle the function of pessimism would be over, for its demand would have been answered; its truth would cease, for the world would no longer answer to its description.

It is through the power of some such principle of synthesis that the best ethical results have hitherto been secured. History proves that men have laboured most effectively when they have realised their identity with a principle supreme throughout their world, leaving no element in it in isolation, but leading all to the unity of one result. The family has formed the centre of a fair and harmonious existence, with attractive force sufficient to issue in tragic deeds of loyalty; the State has afforded the sphere of an intense and brilliant life, and has claimed and received the passionate service of its citizens; the Church has its treasury of heroic memories, in which even its exiles find a grateful heritage. In this new world, accordingly, where new elements have arisen to give the problem of life a deeper form, deliverance from despair and inspiration of hope can come only through the realisation of a life which shall be the harmony of all its varied elements, so that each shall manifest the whole, and in the whole find its place and justification, a life therefore open to man as the source and strength of his activity, the starting-point of his career, and its victorious achievement.

In the pages that follow we endeavour to gain some outline of the conditions under which such a synthesis is possible, and of the nature of the response which it makes to the problem of pessimism. It will be helpful, however, in our quest for the needed synthesis to begin by a brief study of the synthesis proposed by Positivism. In this way we may have the better hope of being borne through criticism to our conclusion.

The importance of Positivism lies in the fact that it has faced the problem of the day, and in full consciousness of the need of men, has offered itself to them as its complete response. Its founder is emphatically a product of this century, with its strict affiliation to the last and its earnest effort to effect a transition from it. Comte accepts the speculative principles of the individualism of which Hume gave the complete exposition. He holds its theory of knowledge, and has made its rejection of theology and metaphysics peculiarly his own. He does not, however, belong to the era in which individualism was preached as a gospel. There has intervened the terrible criticism of the French Revolution, and modern thought has begun its onward movement with a strong reaction. In this reaction Comte so far participates as to see clearly the negative character of individualism, its incapacity to afford a basis of moral experience or to inaugurate a process of social organisation. At the same time he well understands the futility of a mere reaction, the impossibility of blotting out an eloquent page of history, and returning to a life that had been left behind for ever. In full accord with the best thought of his day, he points out the priority of society to the individual, who, indeed, apart from his social relations, would be neither self-conscious nor moral. Moral life depends on the attainment of a unity, which has been defined for us by an English positivist ' as that state of man's moral, intellectual, and physical functions which allows the greatest sum of resultant energy; in which there is the greatest vigour of each part consistent with the vigour of the whole; in which all human forces converge freely toward a common end, as few of them as possible being wasted by mutual antagonism or by misdirection.'[1] He recognises accordingly, as the first necessity of the age, a principle of synthesis whereby elements constantly tending to disintegration may be wrought into the unity of one all-pervasive life. It must confront the individual as a power to which he must submit, bringing into subjection to it every wandering impulse, every selfish aim; it must come close to him as a personality whom he may love, in communion with whom he may find the satisfaction of his purest and tenderest emotions; while finally, he must stand free in the presence of it, only, however, that with the more perfect moral effect he may devote himself to it, finding for the first time in its service perfect freedom.

In reaching such a principle of synthesis, Comte is guided not simply by his desire to transcend the standpoint of an individualistic ethic, but also by his determination to avoid, in obedience to speculative principles which he never questioned, the absolute position of theology or metaphysics. Synthesis is necessary, but it must content itself with the limits of subjectivity. To the required position we are brought by the development of science, which presents, as its culmination, the idea of humanity as ' an organic and self-developing unity.' Although such a position refrains from making the extravagant and unreal claims of theology, it is only that it may substantiate others more practical. It allows that there is much which man can never know, to which he can never relate himself; but it claims to afford within the boundlessness of the universe a sphere within which man may dwell, and find himself perfectly at home, living a life of perfect harmony in all loveliness and hope. Here all divergent faculties and impulses are disciplined and organised in reference to one supreme end; here men are delivered from isolation and are brought into unity with the power to which they owe everything; here they are redeemed from self-seeking, and their lives become the expression of their gratitude. It is true that beyond the walls of this holy city there lies an alien world, into perfect harmony with which man can never be brought. But this evil is reduced to a minimum by the beneficent action of humanity, and need cast no shadow on the brightness of man's reconciled life. With the surrounding unfriendly element

---

[1] Bridges' *Letter to J. S. Mill*, p. 32.

the individual is never brought into direct conflict; between him and it there ever intervenes as his substitute and deliverer the gracious presence of humanity. The hard pressure of external fate, as it is transmitted through this medium, becomes ever more modified and transformed till, when at length it does reach the individual, it is scarcely distinguishable from the tender touch of love. True it is, when all is done, the Divine Redeemer is not omnipotent; but this, so far from diminishing our reverence, only adds to it the beauty of a compassion that knows nothing of contempt. Thus drawing us to itself, this holy and beautiful object of worship fills our whole horizon, constitutes our whole world, affords our complete satisfaction.

Thus Positivism solves the problem of pessimism by a synthesis which, disclaiming all absolute pretensions, maintains that it relates organically to one another all elements within its limits, so that within these limits each can find itself secure and live in confidence. To the extent of the domain won by this principle, good is certainly victorious; for those who live wholly within these bounds, whose lives are completely determined by this principle, evil is no invincible foe, and their world is the sphere of their triumph. Before the beauty of the positivist ideal, criticism is silent; it can concern itself only with the competency of Positivism to vindicate for its ideal the character of possibility. In the first place, therefore, there meets us the notion of humanity as an organic unity, at once the sphere and the principle of moral life; while in the second place, inasmuch as humanity is confessedly not an ultimate standpoint, there remains the question of the validity of a method which, discerning a goal that is unattainable, can bring us on our way to it precisely thus far and no further.

I. In the first place, then, it is as an organism, that humanity is proposed as competent to give a synthetic and satisfactory view of life. This position is not reached by any study of the conditions under which experience is possible; it is simply accepted from science, without any attempt to give a deduction of it, without even the slightest consciousness that such a thing is necessary. Humanity is held to be an organism in the same sense as any physical frame, and is treated, according to this analogy, as though, without any further question, this amounted to a complete explanation. Positivism has seized a category which throughout this century has been rising into favour; and disdaining, as metaphysics, any account of its validity and limits, has treated it as completely independent and self-sufficient. The defects of the positivist synthesis are due to this inability to see the need of justifying the forms of thought which are used, and the consequent confusion between figure of speech and matter of fact, between metaphor and category. When, accordingly, we consider humanity as an organism, we find it regarded in aspects which may have a certain truth in reference to single physical organisms, but which are quite inadequate in reference to experience as a whole.

(1) Thus we find that humanity stands in the midst of an environment not organically connected with itself. The standpoint of humanity is certainly higher than that of the individual, yet even from this loftier position the world is not seen in its truth, and knowledge still remains at best phenomenal. Between nature and humanity, accordingly, there is still a great gulf fixed. On the one hand, humanity constitutes the sole sphere of human life, and affords within its limits security and scope for self-realisation. On the other, there exists beyond humanity a domain where a power bears sway of which men know nothing, save that its ends are not identical with those of humanity, its actions not always and never necessarily tending to the good of the human race. Thus absolutely beyond their ken, even its hostility incapable of being reduced to some consistent scheme, this power for ever confronts men, unconquered and unconquerable. Optimism prevails throughout the extent of the organism; the world beyond is left to the condemnation of pessimism. Such a modified optimism, however, cannot be a valid answer to pessimism. The strength of pessimism, the presupposition from which its conclusions are inevitable, is that the individual stands in no necessary relations to his surroundings, is independent of them, and maintains himself in conflict with them. It matters not how wide a sphere we include within our conception of the individual, nor how much we encroach upon the surrounding space, so long as we admit an absolute division anywhere, we have failed to deliver life from the ceaselessness of war, the certainty of defeat. Whether we define the individual as isolated human being or isolated humanity, we have still

left a world beyond, unincluded in the life of the individual, definable only by negatives. The distinction which we make between ourselves and it is the enduring token that it is still external to us. The synthesis of humanity, therefore, places the whole domain of nature beyond the sphere of its influence. In this outer world the prevailing principle is one which, compared with the standard that prevails within humanity, can be conceived only as evil, and it is surely not too much to say that the shadow of this condemnation must lie even upon the life which has escaped it. But beyond this, the existence of a sphere where alien principles bear sway is a constant menace to the peace of humanity. The walls of the positivist Zion may be strong and high, yet the life that is spent behind them gains its whole character from the foe against whom they have been reared. Thus to bear up for ever against the pressure of an unknown and unknowable force, with no guarantee of victory, in the constant consciousness of the possibility of ruin, would fill life with a doubt and misgiving that would take away all gladness of labour and destroy every germ of hope. No synthesis which is not universal can be an adequate answer to pessimism. Experience is still given up to anarchy and misery, if every element in it be not grasped and comprehended by one all-determining principle.

Some vague conviction of this inspires the efforts made by Comte to evade the consequences of the dualism with which he started, or even to surmount it altogether.

It is a commonplace with him to insist on the fact that the fate which confronts human life is, even in its externality, a benefit to man. If it were not for this external and hostile force, man would never learn the lesson of that subjugation of egoistic instincts which constitutes the triumph of humanity, and which issues in the highest possible results of self-realisation. That development proceeds by way of conflict, is indeed a truth which admits of no question, but it makes impossible the dualistic position from which Comte has started. That by which an organism developes cannot be merely external to it. There is always a point of view from which the environment is seen to be so related to the organism as to be delivered from any merely alien character. Comte's merit is that he has thus related the individual to humanity; but the speculative individualism from which he never freed himself hinders him from extending this view to the relations of nature and humanity, and allows him to say of humanity what he has denied of the individual, that it can have life and being in the midst of a world to which it stands in no organic relation. It is therefore only in the metaphors of poetry that his synthetic instinct finds satisfaction, and accomplishes what his metaphysic had forbidden. The antagonism which nothing can overcome we may wreathe in clouds till it vanishes from our sight. Casting the beauty of humanity's holiness round the outer world, we may join space and the earth to humanity in one threefold object of worship. This certainly is the dream of a synthesis which is completely universal, constitutive of a world the complete reconciliation of whose elements leaves no room for pessimism. It is a dream, however, of which Comte has no right to be the dreamer. He who in the outset condemned the world as alien to humanity, and placed his ban on any study of it which had no bearing on human welfare, has no right in the end to confer upon it divine honours and claim for it our worship, sanctifying the remotest, most minute investigations as religious duties. And at best it is but a dream, which, however beautifully it represent the response to our age's need, is powerless to withstand the attack, or overcome the opposition, of a pessimistic criticism, stout-hearted enough to endure the terror of its own despair.

(2) Thus also humanity is held to furnish a sufficient principle of life within the organism, while it is admitted that beyond the organism other principles may prevail. The theological synthesis which maintained that God is the end in reference to which human life is to be determined, is unverifiable and unreal. In its stead the relative synthesis of humanity provides an end which, without dogmatising upon problems insoluble by human intellect, is practically sufficient to concentrate upon itself every activity of man, and so to convey to life the unity which is needed to deliver it from despair.

This is a function, however, to which no principle that is merely relative is adequate. A relative principle is one that, by its own confession, leaves, pressing upon the life which it professes to determine, a world beyond its control. In its relations to this external world, therefore, the life is not determined by this principle, but by others independent of it. Its claim to govern the whole of life is thus reduced to dominion over one of its departments. But a principle which is capable of conveying unity to one set of relations, while confessedly abandoning another to other influences, is, even in the sphere to which it confines itself, without warrant for its authority. This difficulty is not obviated by enlarging the extent of the sphere over which supremacy is claimed for the principle. It may be admitted that humanity is an end far higher than the State, capable of constituting a far wider realm of interest and duties. But so long as it is not absolutely supreme, subduing to itself the whole of life, the dominion to which it does lay claim is baseless. It is but one end, at best supreme in a certain limited sphere. It is thus external to the principles which bear sway where its authority is not acknowledged, and therefore stands with them on a footing of mere equality. By the very conception of humanity as a relative synthesis, we are presented, not with one principle constituting experience into one harmonious whole, but with a group of principles dividing among themselves the territory of human life. There immediately therefore arises the need of a principle superior to them all, in virtue of which this division may be made, which may assign to each its appropriate value and give harmony to their mutual relations. Apart from this, devotion to one would imply antagonism to the others, and would fill life with distraction and weakness rather than peace and strength, while devotion to one rather than to another would lack any rational vindication. It matters not how wide an application is claimed for the principle which is to determine life; if it be not universal, it is as little worthy of devotion as a religion whose authority is 'relative' to the Sundays, while the week days are abandoned to other influences, is as little capable of inspiring every energy and bending all to the unity of one result.

The synthesis of humanity, therefore, brings no solution of that conflict of elements in experience which constitutes the problem of pessimism. By the emphasis which it has laid upon one of these elements, by the claim which it has so ably urged for its recognition, it has rather given a deeper form to that problem. It is not likely that any higher end of action will be discovered than humanity, any fairer ideal depicted than that which is summarised in the command *Vivre pour autrui*. They are the utmost that science can suggest, that a relative synthesis can effect. If, therefore, they have failed to secure to human life immunity from terror and inspiration of certain hope, the pessimism which returns is the deeper for the heights that have been reached. That 'struggle with the certainty of being beaten,' to which pessimism reduces life, becomes more fearful when on the one side of the conflict there is ranged the whole race of man, in the unity of a single personality. The doom is the more terrible the more concretely it is realised.[1] The synthesis which is to meet the necessity of the case must now be more than relative.

II. In the second place, accordingly, we have to inquire into the feasibility of a method which, claiming to be synthetic, arrests itself at precisely this point short of completeness. The position of Positivism is confessedly a compromise between individualism on the one hand and universalism on the other. In opposition to the extreme doctrines of both these philosophies, it maintains, with respect to the general question of experience, that in knowledge a synthesis is at work, which is, however, only subjective, and that in thought we occupy the standpoint neither of individual nor of absolute mind, but of the human mind ; with respect to the problem of morality, that our lives may be determined not by merely selfish ends nor yet by an all-comprehensive, all-victorious principle, but by a principle valid in its own sphere, although not beyond it, viz., the well-being of man. The question therefore which emerges, concerns not now the sufficiency of humanity as solvent of the moral problem, but the soundness of any compromise, the possibility of moving beyond the standpoint of the individual, while modestly declining that of the universal. The answer to this question can come only in the effort to ascertain under what conditions the transcendence of the individual is in any sense possible. The settlement of how far we may go in this movement is given when we see how the first step in it is taken.

In the outset it is evident that the quest will be vain unless the starting point be definitely conceived. If the aim be to reach a position above that of the individualism which

[1] The pessimism of Hartmann recognises the answer of Positivism, but denies its competency.

disintegrates experience and makes pessimism inevitable, hope of attaining it can be based only on a thorough conception of what individuality is, a complete realisation of it in its utmost extremity. Apart from this any conclusion would be merely arbitrary, incapable of rational vindication, helpless in presence of a consistent criticism. The field of nature does not provide the requisite starting-point. No object in nature is yet completely individual. In no case, from the inorganic mass to the most highly developed organism, is the connection with the physical surroundings broken, or the isolation of complete self-containedness achieved. It is in the sphere of self-consciousness that for the first time we discover that extreme of individuality which is to raise the problem of its transcendence and to make possible the solution. The complete realisation of individuality is to be found in the self, with its infinite concentration upon one centre, its infinite exclusion of the whole surrounding universe. It is the assertion that I am I, that the self has its whole being within itself. It is, therefore, at the same time the correspondent negation, that I am not not-I, that the self has no mingling of elements in its constitution, that it is no compounded essence, no constructed fabric. It is the self against the world; the whole universe, in its utmost nearness as well as in its furthest distance, is excluded from the self; the self is to itself sufficient. Self-consciousness therefore involves a consciousness of that which is beyond the self, between which and the self there is a great gulf fixed. There are no degrees in this antagonism. It matters not how familiar an object may be; as beyond the self it is infinitely apart from it, and raises the problem of the possibility of knowledge in a form as complete as though it had been the strangest, most distant object that could come within the range of the widest experience. The problem is not how transition can be made from the seclusion of the self to knowledge of this or that object, but how such transition is possible at all; and the principle which has effected this in the simplest case has effected it finally. The statement of the problem in this infinite form, however, at once involves the impossibility of individualism as a theory of experience. If the self were a bare identity, which was not conscious of itself as permanent amid a flux of differences, a mere individuality which did not withdraw itself from an alien world, consciousness of self would be impossible and the problem of experience could not be raised. If the self were really confined within the limits of its own exclusiveness, there would be no world for it to know, and that assertion of itself in infinite differentiation from the world, which is the essence of its self-consciousness, would be rendered impossible. It is only because in self-consciousness the self is not confined to its mere individuality that it can be aware of anything confronting it; only, therefore, for the same reason, can it be aware of itself as individual. The consciousness which is aware of the self and the object cannot be identical merely with the individual self, but is dependent on and identical with a principle of synthesis which comprehends both in one grasp, and bestows upon both organic relations to one another. Consciousness of individuality, therefore, in its extreme distinction from the external world, is grounded in, and is only possible to, a self-consciousness which is universal, and includes as an element in itself what is beyond the individual. In knowledge of any object, by the conditions of its possibility we are raised completely from the individual point of view, are placed in a position which is truly central in reference to the universe, are brought into unity with the principle through which we ourselves and the world which confronts us are alike intelligible.

It is, accordingly, no adequate description of thought to speak of it as a faculty or force, whether of the individual or of the race, whereby objects presented to it are recognised and reduced to some sort of order. An analysis of the conditions of experience which discerns that, if thought and things were really external to one another, knowledge would be impossible, and even the formal activity of thought would cease, conceives of thought as the synthetic principle which constitutes for the individual his consciousness of self, and at the same time gives him a world to know, through an ever-growing acquaintance with which his own self may be enriched. In knowledge, therefore, the individual is not entering upon an endless task, dependent on limited resources. He is in his first recognition of an object lifted finally out of all such isolation and weakness, and brought into unity with the principle which is constitutive of the intelligible world. His chief intellectual virtue is thus submission, the surrender of his private subjectivity to the principle through which the world is possible as an object of knowledge, and which also constitutes his true self. By this principle the process of his knowledge is conducted, so that its results are not new masses of facts rescued from a chaos of ignorance, but the growing consciousness and realisation of the riches of a realm in which he finds himself at home.

Such a view of knowledge and the condition of its possibility takes up into itself and justifies all the definitions which are usually framed with a view to avoiding the claim of absolute validity. That knowledge is relative, for instance, is a truth capable of being vindicated only from a point of view which refuses to leave any object unrelated to thought; to say that knowledge is related to mind, and at the same time to define mind as a sphere which, however extended, is still limited, beyond which objects are known to exist, is a contradiction in terms. In one sense of the word all objects are external to thought, and it shows an inadequate grasp of the problem to affirm that some are not. In another no object is thus external. The externality of an object is, indeed, the abstraction of its first presentation to thought, and of this abstraction the process of knowledge is the gradual correction. Every achievement of science is simply the fuller recognition of the thought which is in things, the further determination of matter as not alien to mind, but organically connected with it in the unity of experience. Thought, or self-consciousness, therefore, is the ultimate explanation of the world. No object, even the remotest and most material, is seen in its truth, save in the light of this universally determining principle. Even if thought be regarded as the conclusion of a process of evolution, it is such a conclusion as rises out of the time development, and is the re-interpretation of all that preceded it. It is the full realisation of that which is involved in all the sciences, of which the sciences are the growingly explicit statement. It therefore includes them and reacts upon them, assigning to them their limits, vindicating for them their truth. In the same way knowledge may be described as subjective; but this can imply no reference to an ideal of knowledge which, by contrast with our own, might be characterised as objective. The subjectivity is not that which a spectator might attribute to one object distinct from others.

It is that of an individuality completely realised, pressed to its utmost extremity, and therefore grounded in and made possible by a universal consciousness. It is a subjectivity therefore which belongs not to the knowledge possessed by the individual or the race, but to knowledge as such, and is accordingly objective. The sense in which subjectivity attaches to thought as a defect is as much an abstraction as the externality of the object, and receives in the same process a precisely similar correction. The advance of knowledge is the deliverance of thought from the subjectivity and formality of its first contrast with the world, the exposition of it as it relates itself to, and manifests itself in, the manifold forms of the world's life. The problem of the transition from thought to things thus falls away, for the dualism which gave it significance is seen to rest upon a principle which includes and determines towards one another both its elements, and has transformed itself into the task of exhibiting this principle in the completeness of its synthetic activity, penetrating to every department of knowledge, correcting all partial results by reference to itself. A point of view, therefore, which is universal and objective, is no more than the completion of the effort to do justice to individuality and subjectivity, the necessary condition of the simplest consciousness of self and the simplest knowledge of an object.

It is the error of Comte that he has not fully realised the extreme of individuality, and has thus missed the universal consciousness which it involves. Instead of this, by a kind of scientific metaphor, he has seized a position midway between these two points, which has all the defects of the one and none of the advantages of the other. He does not see the subjectivity which is involved in all knowledge, and is therefore universal and objective. His synthesis accordingly remains subjective in the bad sense of a subjectivity imposed on knowledge, and so casting upon it the shadow of a merely phenomenal character. In like manner, in the moral sphere, he has not gone down into the depths of the individualism which he wished to overcome, and thus his emergence from it is still incomplete. His error may be described, not unjustly, as that of socialism, which sees truly that man realises himself only in society, but takes away all significance from this truth by giving him no self to realise. Deliverance from individualism is impossible if it be not thoroughgoing. Pessimism will return inevitably, and in more fearful shapes the fairer have been our fancies, unless there be found a principle of synthesis which shall bind not simply man to man, but man to the world and to God, in the closeness of completed reconciliation, in the unity of a life and hope which become fuller and surer through pain and sorrow and death. This century, as well in its historical events as in the teaching of those who, like Comte, have endeavoured to express the principles which have been at work throughout its course, has taught us the lesson that the consequences of individualism can only be avoided by drawing them to their last results by a stricter logic and a more destructive criticism. Only so can hope arise of reaching a principle capable of delivering experience both in its intellectual and moral aspects from the ban of mere subjectivity, and exhibiting it as at once possible and objectively valid.

In endeavouring, therefore, to do justice to the problem of pessimism, as the only legitimate method of rising above its conclusions, it is necessary in the first place fully to realise that element of the individual which is the presupposition of all pessimistic philosophising. The individual in ethics, accordingly, even as in the problem of experience in general, can be found only in the sphere of self-consciousness. It cannot be found in the sensuous consciousness, which is capable of pursuing only the ends presented to it by its instinctive tendencies, and is fully satisfied with the gratification which they afford. This is the consciousness of the animal, which has never broken with the natural surroundings of its life, has never thought of them as beyond itself, constituting a sphere in which it may find satisfaction and from which it may be repelled. It knows no self apart from nature, finds the perfection of its being in nature, and has never experienced any separation from nature which could give to this union the character of a reconciliation. The light, and the beauty, and the gladness of nature pass into it, and become in it glancing eye, and graceful frame, and exulting motion. For it, therefore, since its whole life lies within nature, there is no standpoint attainable from which nature could be criticised. For it, there has emerged no problem in connection with the environment of its life. It has never withdrawn itself from the world in which it lives, so as to estimate its character or pronounce its sentence. When in nature it fails to find satisfaction, when the summer herbage has vanished and the summer sun has gone, it never dreams of rebellion, never withdraws into any proud isolation, but in many a 'tragedy of copse and hedge-row' creeps back into the bosom of the mother that cast it forth, to die in a dumbness of pain unbroken by reproach.

It is the essential characteristic of self-consciousness, on the other hand, that for it this immediate union with nature is impossible. Man, even in the lowest forms of humanity, has made that distinction of himself from the world in which he lives which constitutes the uniqueness of his character. He approaches the world as a domain external to him, which must furnish him with means for the maintenance of his existence and the gratification of his desires. In his first attitude towards the world, accordingly, he is critical of it, and estimates it according to its capacity to meet the demand which he makes upon it. It is a demand, however, to which the world is never adequate. Upon the basis of every satisfaction the demand is made for the same source to supply another, greater still. By the very satisfaction which man gains from the world, he is raised above it, and with the world whose distinction from himself becomes the keener the higher is the gratification which it affords, he can never be content. When full consciousness of this inadequacy of the world awakes, man realises and enters upon the might of his individuality. There can be for him no tame submission, no painful dragging of wounded limbs to some dark covert. He occupies a standing-ground aloof from the world; from this he can judge the world, and in the exclusiveness and security of his own domain proclaim himself supreme. Here, then, for the first time is there reached the utmost extreme of individuality; here, for the first time, is there made possible that judgment upon the world which finds in pessimism its fullest emphasis. There is here an infinite antagonism, with the possibility of infinite evil, and a consciousness of it which amounts to infinite despair. The self, inviolable and immutable, confronts the world, between them an impassable chasm. No 'relative' synthesis will suffice to overcome this antagonism. To define the world of human life as Family, or State, or Humanity, and to show that, as a matter of fact, man does realise himself in it, is to make a mere assertion and to ignore the real problem. The question is not how a man can so far surpass the limits of his individuality as to identify himself with *this* or *that* end beyond himself, and find in devotion to it the highest satisfaction of his nature; but how is it possible *in any degree* to cross these limits, to rise out of the exclusiveness of self, and to make that the determining principle of life which does not lie within the sphere of the individual subject. It matters not how close the interest may lie, how little it may involve reference to other persons; as beyond the individual, it is infinitely apart from him, and raises the question of the possibility of his pursuit of it as completely as the loftiest and most disinterested end of action. The problem of morality is identical in its simplest and in its most complex forms, and is in all susceptible of but one solution. The principle which is able to effect in one instance the transition beyond the limits of the individual self is adequate to every form of the same difficulty. The antagonism, overcome once, has been vanquished finally. The realisation of this antagonism in its infinitude, however, makes impossible any consistently individualistic theory of ethics. A consciousness which was strictly confined to the limits of individual subjectivity could never conceive of the world as external to itself, a sphere beyond itself in which to act and find satisfaction. It could never make a universal claim upon that world, and consequently could never recognise that inadequacy of the world from which it might learn its own independence and self-sufficiency. The recognition of self and of ends to be pursued is impossible for a consciousness which is merely of the individual self. A consistent individualism makes impossible any consciousness of the world, whether as object of knowledge or sphere of action; and in the same way, any consciousness of self, whether as intelligent being or moral agent. Such a twofold consciousness is constituted only by a principle of synthesis which comprehends both elements, and transforms their apparent antagonism into an organic relationship. The utmost extravagance of self-assertion is possible only for a self-consciousness which includes as an element in itself that which is beyond the individual self. In action, therefore, so far are we from being confined to the merely individual point of view, that it is possible only because we are not thus limited, but are raised to a position from which all ends, whether personal or disinterested, are seen to be given through the same principle that is constitutive of our separate individuality. In the moment when first we rise out of the life of instinct to pursue an end conceived as external to us, we are united to a principle of universal application, which presents to us the world as the sphere of our self-realisation, and which constitutes in us the self which is to be realised. It is not true that we can follow only the objects presented to us by our own desire, for such pursuit is possible only through the same principle which makes possible for us the most complete self-surrender; and our judgment of a man as selfish is valid, because the principle in virtue of which he seeks the satisfaction of his private self is adequate to set before him ends the most unselfish, and to secure for him in their pursuit the completeness of his moral being. As moral, the individual does not stand alone in a world that is foreign to him, possessed of a 'faculty' by which he may, or may not, maintain himself. He is delivered, on the contrary, from the weakness and inevitable failure of such a position, and has entered upon a realm which is the manifestation of the principle through which he is self-conscious and moral, so that his action in it is not the haphazard achievement of isolated results, but the growing realisation of a life which is in truth his own. It is therefore only from the point of view of this principle that the world is ethically significant. Only through occupation of this position can any estimate of the world be taken or any conclusions expressed concerning it. There is no standing-ground for criticism of the world, save that of the principle through which the world exists as a sphere of action. No element in the world can be accurately defined save through its place in this moral organism; only when set in this light does it become available as the basis for a valid inference. The sphere of the principle which makes morality possible is universal; beyond it no problem can arise. The darkest pessimism, as well as the brightest optimism, can legitimately reach its conclusions only through the recognition of the facts before it as they are determined by this universal principle.

In the light of it, accordingly, evil for the first time becomes a significant conception. An analysis of the conditions of morality which discerns that the world and the

individual are organically related to one another, so that
the realisation of the individual in the world is possible only
through his surrender to, and identification of himself with,
the principle which is constitutive of it, gives a deeper meaning to the antagonism of the individual to the world, and
his consequent denunciation of it as evil.   That antagonism
becomes now the opposition of the self, which asserts itself
in its individuality, to the principle which is the ground and
the truth of its being.   The evil, to the experience of which
the individual awakes, becomes now the assertion of himself
against the principle which, even in the moment of such
assertion, he knows to be his true self.   Evil is transferred
from a supposed external somewhat which he had regarded
as hostile to him, and becomes the consequence of a division
of his own nature against itself which is his own doing.
The conflict which fills life with misery is not that of two
separate entities, but of elements related organically to one
another in the unity of one self-consciousness.   The antagonism is recognisable by the self, its conquest is felt to
be the first necessity of life, only because in it the self is
divided against itself.   Evil that was merely external could
not be felt as such, and could raise no longing for its removal.
Evil is accordingly essentially subjective, and can attach
only to consciousness of self.   The subjectivity, however,
is not that of an individual, but of a universal consciousness.
It is only a universal consciousness which can concentrate
itself upon the extreme point of individuality, and act in
defiance of the principle which is the condition of its
possibility ; and this, which to it is evil, is, because of its
universality, the secret of all evil, the gathering of all evil
into this first iniquity.   In like manner, therefore, the
synthesis in which the elements of this conflict are to be
reconciled must be in the fullest sense of the word ' subjective.'   No synthesis effected beyond the subject can be
available for it.   It must be accomplished within the sphere
to which the antagonism belongs.   Since, however, this
sphere comprehends the whole moral world, this ' subjective
synthesis' is at the same time objective and universal.   The
opposition and its pain lie wholly within the self ; but
since the self is not individual merely, but constitutive and
explanatory of the world, the conquest of its self-contradiction is the solution of the problem of evil in all its

forms; its reconciliation with itself involves the harmony of the world.

It is impossible to do more than indicate the comprehension of all evil in our consciousness of it. In the first place, there is no evil of which the individual is conscious in his own life which is not due to his own act. The problems in connection with personal responsibility are many, and their difficulty cannot be overrated. There is an unspeakable sadness in the sight of a human being stained with vices and enduring the penalty of crimes which seem to be the necessary consequences of tendencies which he has inherited by birth, or of circumstances in which he was placed by no will of his. A consistent individualism will maintain that to such an one guilt cannot attach, and the conclusions of pessimism follow at once. Such a view is possible, however, only by regarding the individual as a point·in the series of the world's development. Such a being will indeed be free of guilt, as free as any death-working object in nature, but also as destitute of moral character. The difficulty of attributing responsibility to the individual in face of these external influences can be surmounted only by considering that their externality is not their truth. They can be presented to consciousness and can influence the will, only because they are not external, because the individual in recognising them is lifted out of his individuality, and is united to the principle through which the world is for him, by which therefore his action in it may be determined. In action the individual is raised to the position of the principle which is constitutive of the world, and is thus endowed with mastery over it. The evil of his action, therefore, cannot be attributed to any pressure of circumstances; it is his alone. There is thus also made possible for him that experience of compunction or repentance which constitutes the first condition of his conquest of evil and attainment of a higher life.

In like manner, in the second place, since the self-consciousness of the individual involves his organic relationship to his environment, it is impossible to make an absolute distinction between the evil which belongs to it and that which he acknowledges as his. That humanity is an organism apart from which the individual has no existence, is a truth implied in the conditions of the individual's self-consciousness. It is impossible to make any exceptions in the completeness of this organic relationship. The part lives in the whole, and in this case, which is an organic unity more perfect than the physical organism, lives the life of the whole. The achievements of humanity are one. In all labour the individual is participating in a common energy, is entering upon and adding to a universal inheritance. It would be quite arbitrary, however, to confine this conception of organism to the advantages which are held to accrue without extending it to the disadvantages which are equally involved. The progress of humanity is open to the individual : his function in it is the spur of his endeavour. On the same principles, therefore, he must acknowledge the evil of humanity as his own, must admit that his own enters into it in a more than quantitative sense. On the one hand, his evil is not an attribute of his individual self. His wrongdoing, as it passes from him, becomes an element in a life that is not his merely, but that of the world in which he lives. There is no wrong of which a man may repent in the privacy of his individual reflections, mitigating its enormity by the consideration that it was confined wholly to himself. His membership in humanity cannot be thus evaded. His wrong is his, but, since he is no isolated individual, it extends to all with whom his life is bound up. So also, on the other hand, the evil of humanity centres itself in the individual, so that his realisation of it amounts in a very true sense to a consciousness of personal responsibility. His participation in the life of the organism cannot stop short of the evil that attaches to it. To say that he bears the burden of an iniquity in which he had no part, and pays in his own loss the penalty of another's transgression, is no mere metaphor ; it is the expression of an organic relationship which, as in another connection it is admitted and maintained, remains true here also. The bonds which connect him with his fellows cannot be relaxed in favour of his relief from their evil-doing. The shame and misery which they bring to him cannot be alleviated by the conviction of his innocence ; rather must these be deepened with a real sense of his blameworthiness. He cannot descend so far into the evil of humanity as to escape his own. His horror in presence of the foulest wrong is but a deeper realisation of his own guilt. Out of these depths alone can there rise for him a ray of hope. Finally, the principle which connects the individual's consciousness of self with his consciousness of that which is external to him, extends also to nature, and includes its evil in the moral judgment. In reference to the connection of man with his natural, as with his social environment, it is impossible at any point to surrender the organic relationship which is shown, by an analysis of the conditions of experience, to subsist between them. The view which finds in thought or self-consciousness the culmination and explanation of nature, so that of an object unrelated to thought we can have no experience, must be inclusive of all the facts of nature. It is impossible to give a complete explanation of any natural object, apart altogether from the principle through which it is for us as an object of knowledge. Even where, to all appearance, this is most completely the case, it is but a convenience of scientific method, and is justified by the fact that the sciences necessarily make an abstraction, each of its special department, which must be corrected in the light of the principle that determines their mutual relations. In like manner the evil which we recognise to be in nature gains its character from the principle in virtue of which it is recognisable by us. We can have no experience of an evil in nature wholly external to the principle which, as it constitutes our consciousness of self, so also gives us a world to know. It would not be for us : regarding it we could say nothing, not even in condemnation. It is impossible for us to abandon our position as reflective beings, and occupy that of the merely sensuous consciousness. It is impossible therefore for us to know what pain or evil can mean for such a consciousness. Our knowledge of evil is knowledge, and not feeling ; is, therefore, even in its nearest approach to feeling, already determined by our self-consciousness. Our conception of nature's evil is filled with the consciousness of our own, and on this account alone is for us a unity, a comprehensive whole, a world-pain. Evil in us is therefore the key to evil in nature. The self-consciousness which is the explanation of nature is divided against itself, and out of this primeval discord emerges all other pain. Thus also our evil finds in the evil of nature its 'illustrated catalogue.' The sombreness of autumn, the gloom of winter, the tearful gladness of spring, the ebbing of bright and graceful life amid moss and fern, the anguish of death, the yet keener anguish of birth—these, and all the infinite sadness of creation, could find no answer in our sympathy if they stood in no living relation to us, if they were, not the projection into space and time of an iniquity whose completeness is to be found in self-consciousness, which is therefore aloof from all spacial and temporal conditions. The principle in virtue of which we know the world and live in it, charges all its evil upon us, lays upon us the judgment of this gigantic wrong. It is neither sentiment nor paradox to say that our sympathy with the pain of nature and our condemnation of it as evil must partake of the nature of repentance.

The principle which makes evil thus significant, and comprehends every form of it in one consciousness, is, accordingly, the only quarter to which we can look for the triumph of good; and a consideration of the significance which it attaches to evil contains the guarantee of this victory. The only evil which is recognisable as a problem, in which is summarised and interpreted all conceivable evil, is the division which takes place within the sphere of self-consciousness. It is the assertion of the self in its individuality against the principle through which alone, even in such assertion, it has being. Its individuality however, is not its truth. So far, indeed, is this from being the case, that the extreme consciousness of individuality, which withdraws into itself from everything which is apart from it, is possible only as grounded in a universal consciousness which includes, as an element in itself, this apparently external world. There is thus possible a surrender of this false independence, and a return of the self out of the individuality which is its evil, and the denial of its true being, into unity with the principle which constitutes for it its truth and life. It is because in its individuality the self contradicts the conditions of its own-possibility, that it is aware of evil in itself and in the world. For the same reason, therefore, there is possible for it such an abandonment of its false antagonism, and such an identification of itself with the truth of its own being, as constitute the conquest of evil and the final accomplishment of good. The intense realisation of individuality, and its consequent evil, depends for its possibility on a consciousness of good which is triumphant over them.

The despair of the individual who finds himself at this extremity of isolation and evil, is rendered possible by, and is indeed the moment of transition to, a good which is for him and for the world already and finally victorious. This consciousness of good, known to religion as 'righteousness,' is not an emotion or virtue of the individual. It is consciousness of, and identity with, the principle which is constitutive at once of the true self of the individual, and of the world which confronts him as the sphere of his action. To be determined by this principle is therefore to be brought into harmony with that world, to find in it no element hostile to self-realisation. In one word, from the point of view of this identity, the world becomes in its completeness that 'kingdom of ends' which a just estimate of morality shows to be the condition of its possibility, but which, for any ethic that is not wholly delivered from individualism, is an unrealisable ideal.[1] A synthesis this which is 'subjective;' but inasmuch as the subjectivity is that of a universal self-consciousness, it is at the same time objective, and overcomes in its activity every form of discord. When all forms of evil are comprehended in that evil of self-consciousness, its conquest is seen to be at the same time theirs. When, accordingly, we occupy the standpoint of this accomplished good, which is the basis of our moral experience and the standard of our moral judgments, all conflict with evil gains a transformed significance. It is no longer a meaningless and interminable warfare with an unknown antagonist, but the progressive realisation of a victory which is achieved already. It is thus delivered, even in its most terrible forms, from all possibility of despair, the intensest realisation of it being in fact but the necessary correlate of perfect confidence.

Any view of evil which regards it as the ultimate fact of the universe involves a contradiction; and a consistent pessimism must be 'speechless.' Evil is either relative to consciousness, or it is not. If the latter, it constitutes no

---

[1] It is interesting to note the form which this Kantian conception takes in a philosophy which claims to be the development and vindication of Kantian principles: 'Die neue Religion sprich sich aus als ein neues Bewusstseyn— Bewusstseyn der Versöhnung des Men- schen mit Gott; diese Versöhnung als *Zustand* ausgesprochen ist das *Reich Gottes*, das Ewige als die Heimath für den Geist, eine Wirklichkeit, in der Gottherrscht.'—Hegel, *Werke*,12.Band, S. 288.

problem ; it is unrecognisable and inconceivable. If the
former, the principle which makes it a significant conception is superior to it, and involves its conquest. No criticism of the world is sound which is not made from the
point of view of that by which it is constituted as an object
of knowledge, which is therefore its interpretation. Apart
from this, any verdict upon the world can be no more than
the expression of individual subjectivity, and as such is
meaningless. That judgment of the world, on the contrary,
which is based on the principle of which the world is the
manifestation, can be none other than the statement of a
good already accomplished, the prophecy of a good which,
through all conflict, is becoming ever more perfectly
achieved.

It is impossible, in conclusion, to do more than, in a
single paragraph, illustrate this victory of good, complete in
self-consciousness and progressively realised in time. It is
this accomplished good which, in the individual life, is the
strength of moral endeavour. Good would be impossible as
the result of isolated effort. It can be attained by labour in
the world only when the individual has abandoned the
unreality of his independence, and submitted himself to the
principle which is his true self, through which the world is
open to him, which therefore is victorious in it. From the
standpoint of this reconciliation with himself and with the law
of the universe, evil has for him no more existence ; as a power
determining his life, it has been finally vanquished. The
conflict with it, therefore, which is conducted amid the temporal conditions of experience is no longer a ' struggle with
the certainty of being beaten,' but the growing revelation of
good, and its growing realisation. It is from this point of
view alone that the authority of the moral law can be vindicated. It can be recognised as imperative only because it
is the expression of the principle which makes obedience to
it possible. Morality is thus confessedly not the final rest-
ing-place of spirit, but points beyond itself for its justification. It involves progress—for that which made it possible
is not, but is to be realised—and effort, from the humble,
glad recognition of ends nobler than those already attained,
to the unspeakable agony with which a man tears himself
from objects, which had been his whole life and love, to
cling, faint but desperate, to the cross that raises him ; but

these, so far from being disproof of the existence or all-con-
quering might of the principle implied, are the very tokens
of its presence, the guarantee of its final victory.

The victory of good in the individual is, however, not the
experience merely of an individual. It is indeed possible for
him only through the surrender of his individuality, and consists in his identity with the principle of synthesis to which is
due the world in which he lives and acts. In his consciousness of good, accordingly, the individual finds himself, no
longer one amid a multitude of warring atoms, but member
of an infinite organic whole, by the principle constitutive of
which the mutual relations of its parts are determined. The
good of which the individual is conscious accordingly involves,
as the condition of his permanent possession of it, that it be
the law of his life in relation to those with whom it brings
him into organic connection. As, however, the synthesis
of which this law is the expression, is effected not beyond
him but in the sphere of self-consciousness, it does not
stand over him with an abstract assertion of authority. It
awakes within him as a power of love, devoting him to the
service of that humanity for whom the good with which he
is united is also available. He can labour for his fellow-men
only because his deliverance from evil is his union with a
principle which makes him a member of the social organism,
and of this union that labour is the necessary manifestation.
The ' enthusiasm of humanity ' is thus not an ' unselfish ' as
opposed to a ' self-regarding ' instinct. It is rather the
practical expression of the principle which constitutes the
true self of the individual, in determination by which the
harmony and completeness of his nature is attained. The
same principle by which the actions of the individual become the realisation of a wider than individual end, en-
lightens also his suffering with a transfigured nobleness.
It is no longer merely significant of the evil which caused
it, and which in it comes to clearer consciousness. It becomes part of the revelation of the corresponding good, part,
therefore, of its achievement for the individual, and for that
wider life with which his is inextricably connected. Thus
have men in all ages attributed to suffering a certain purify-
ing and redemptive efficacy. Deep beneath their complain-
ing has lain the conviction that the fullest experience of
suffering is explicable by a principle which, as it gives to

suffering its utmost keenness of anguish, so also raises it to the rank of a moment in the being of perfection, the one adequate means to its peace and blessedness. Finally, this consciousness of good extends its victory to the evil of nature. The evil of self-consciousness concentrates in itself every form of evil, even that which is visible in the externality of nature. The conquest of this evil, therefore, includes every evil which is in it explained. The principle which overcomes the division of self-consciousness, and restores it to unity with itself, effects at the same time the reconciliation of all things, ' whether they be things on earth or things in heaven.' From this point of view the evil which fills the history of creation with sadness gains a transformed significance. The pain, of which natural development is the growing experience, deepens in its anguish, till in the evil of man it is closed and interpreted. When, accordingly, this intensest realisation of evil issues in union with accomplished good, the process of pain which led up to it becomes the expectancy of this result, a waiting of creation ' for the manifestation of the sons of God.' All recognisable instances of evil in nature find their explanation in the evil of self-consciousness. Conceived thus as part of the evil of man they deepen his repentance, and so hasten the moment of transition from the extremity of individuality, and of evil, to union with the principle which makes possible the realisation of such a position, and in the very act effects the deliverance from it. Thus also in the relations of nature to human life in which man is often a sufferer, it is impossible to pronounce upon nature any judgment of condemnation. That evil, too, is part of the discord which lies wholly within self-consciousness, and therefore in the light of the reconciliation effected there, the realisation of it may become a means towards the attainment of higher good. Nature is not a hostile power confronting man, harassing and repressing him in many ways, and often inflicting grievous injury upon him. It is part of the manifestation of that principle which constitutes the self-consciousness of man. In his relations to it, accordingly, man is not bearing up against an external fatality, but is coming evermore completely to realise the truth of his own being. The opposition, therefore, which in many cases nature presents to his efforts, with the evil consequences which this often involves, is due not to nature but to himself. His conflict with nature is thus the means whereby he is able to realise, and to transcend, the individuality which made it inevitable. Dwelling in the midst of nature he is not placed in an alien sphere, but in a realm constituted by the principle which in him is consciousness of self, and so in truth the home of his spirit. In all action in and towards nature, he may be inspired by the confidence that all that nature manifests itself to be, constitutes a stage towards the completeness of his well-being.

In a word, on a true estimate of the conditions of the possibility of experience, any judgment of the world must be such as may be termed optimistic. It is an optimism, however, which includes, and is based upon, that fact of evil on which pessimism lays so great an emphasis. Pessimism is always strong against any view of the world which, proceeding on the same presuppositions, seeks to draw opposite conclusions. Any empirical view of the universe, any bare enumeration of its phenomena, necessarily leads to pessimism. If the evil of the world be set over against its good, as a fact co-ordinate with it, a glance is sufficient to show that the evil immeasurably predominates. Deliverance can come only in the effort to do justice to the facts by seeking the explanation of their possibility; and, from the point of view thus attained, the conclusions of pessimism are seen to be impossible.

Pessimism has in this century spoken its last word. From it we have learned the anarchy of the world; but this is, from the other side, the problem of its reconstruction. Positivism has failed as a solution. It remains therefore to descend still further into the depths of the problem, and inquire into the conditions of its possibility. By such a method alone can we reach the response to that ultimate need of man which in this age has found its fullest expression.

T. B. KILPATRICK.

LIBRARY OF THE UNIVERSITY CALIFORNIA

LONDON : PRINTED BY
SPOTTISWOODE AND CO., NEW-STREET SQUARE
AND PARLIAMENT STREET

· A CATALOGUE OF

WORKS IN GENERAL LITERATURE & SCIENCE

PUBLISHED BY

MESSRS. LONGMANS, GREEN, & CO.

39 PATERNOSTER ROW, LONDON, E.C.

Classified Index.

A CATALOGUE

OF

WORKS IN GENERAL LITERATURE & SCIENCE

PUBLISHED BY

MESSRS. LONGMANS, GREEN & CO.

39 PATERNOSTER ROW, LONDON, E.C.

ABBEY and OVERTON.—*THE ENGLISH CHURCH IN THE EIGHTEENTH CENTURY.* By the Rev. C. J. ABBEY and the Rev. J. H. OVERTON. 2 vols. 8vo. 36s.

ABBOTT. — *THE ELEMENTS OF LOGIC.* By T. K. ABBOTT, B.D. 12mo. 2s. 6d. sewed, or 3s. cloth.

ACTON. — *MODERN COOKERY FOR PRIVATE FAMILIES*, reduced to a System of Easy Practice in a Series of carefully tested Receipts. By ELIZA ACTON. With upwards of 150 Woodcuts. Fcp. 8vo. 4s. 6d.

A. K. H. B.—*THE ESSAYS AND CONTRIBUTIONS OF A. K. H. B.*—Uniform Cabinet Editions in crown 8vo.

Autumn Holidays, 3s. 6d.
Changed Aspects of Unchanged Truths, 3s. 6d.
Commonplace Philosopher, 3s. 6d.
Counsel and Comfort, 3s. 6d.
Critical Essays, 3s. 6d.
Graver Thoughts of a Country Parson. Three Series, 3s. 6d. each.
Landscapes, Churches, and Moralities, 3s. 6d.
Leisure Hours in Town, 3s. 6d.
Lessons of Middle Age, 3s. 6d.
Our Little Life. Two Series, 3s. 6d. each.
Present Day Thoughts, 3s. 6d.
Recreations of a Country Parson. Three Series, 3s. 6d. each.
Seaside Musings, 3s. 6d.
Sunday Afternoons, 3s. 6d.

ALDRIDGE. — *RANCH NOTES IN KANSAS, COLORADO, THE INDIAN TERRITORY AND NORTHERN TEXAS.* By REGINALD ALDRIDGE. Crown 8vo. with 4 Illustrations engraved on Wood by G. Pearson, 5s.

ALLEN.—*FLOWERS AND THEIR PEDIGREES.* By GRANT ALLEN. With 50 Illustrations engraved on Wood. Crown 8vo. 7s. 6d.

ALPINE CLUB (The).—*GUIDES AND MAPS.*

THE ALPINE GUIDE. By JOHN BALL, M.R.I.A. Post 8vo. with Maps and other Illustrations :—

THE EASTERN ALPS, 10s. 6d.

CENTRAL ALPS, including all the Oberland District, 7s. 6d.

WESTERN ALPS, including Mont Blanc, Monte Rosa, Zermatt, &c. 6s. 6d.

THE ALPINE CLUB MAP OF SWITZERLAND, on the Scale of Four Miles to an Inch. Edited by R. C. NICHOLS, F.R.G.S. 4 Sheets in Portfolio, 42s. coloured, or 34s. uncoloured.

ENLARGED ALPINE CLUB MAP OF THE SWISS AND ITALIAN ALPS, on the Scale of Three English Statute Miles to One Inch, in 8 Sheets, price 1s. 6d. each.

ON ALPINE TRAVELLING AND THE GEOLOGY OF THE ALPS. Price 1s. Either of the Three Volumes or Parts of the 'Alpine Guide' may be had with this Introduction prefixed, 1s. extra.

AMOS.—*WORKS BY SHELDON AMOS, M.A.*

A PRIMER OF THE ENGLISH CONSTITUTION AND GOVERNMENT. Crown 8vo. 6s.

A SYSTEMATIC VIEW OF THE SCIENCE OF JURISPRUDENCE. 8vo. 18s.

FIFTY YEARS OF THE ENGLISH CONSTITUTION, 1830–1880. Crown 8vo. 10s. 6d.

ANSTEY.—*THE BLACK POODLE*, and other Stories. By F. ANSTEY, Author of 'Vice-Versâ.' With Frontispiece by G. Du Maurier and Initial Letters by the Author. Crown 8vo. 6s.

ANTINOUS.—An Historical Romance of the Roman Empire. By GEORGE TAYLOR (Professor HAUSRATH). Translated from the German by J. D. M. Crown 8vo. 6s.

ARISTOPHANES. — *THE ACHAR-NIANS OF ARISTOPHANES.* Translated into English Verse by ROBERT YELVERTON TYRRELL, M.A. Dublin. Crown 8vo. 2s. 6d.

ARISTOTLE.—*THE WORKS OF.*

THE POLITICS, G. Bekker's Greek Text of Books I. III. IV. (VII.) with an English Translation by W. E. BOLLAND, M.A. ; and short Introductory Essays by A. LANG, M.A. Crown 8vo. 7s. 6d.

THE ETHICS ; Greek Text, illustrated with Essays and Notes. By Sir ALEXANDER GRANT, Bart. M.A. LL.D. 2 vols. 8vo. 32s.

THE NICOMACHEAN ETHICS, Newly Translated into English. By ROBERT WILLIAMS, Barrister-at-Law. Crown 8vo. 7s. 6d.

ARNOLD. — *WORKS BY THOMAS ARNOLD, D.D. Late Head-master of Rugby School.*

INTRODUCTORY LECTURES ON MODERN HISTORY, delivered in 1841 and 1842. 8vo. 7s. 6d.

SERMONS PREACHED MOSTLY IN THE CHAPEL OF RUGBY SCHOOL. 6 vols. crown 8vo. 30s. or separately, 5s. each.

MISCELLANEOUS WORKS. 8vo. 7s. 6d.

ARNOLD. — *WORKS BY THOMAS ARNOLD, M.A.*

A MANUAL OF ENGLISH LITERATURE, Historical and Critical. By THOMAS ARNOLD, M.A. Crown 8vo. 7s. 6d.

ENGLISH POETRY AND PROSE : a Collection of Illustrative Passages from the Writings of English Authors, from the Anglo-Saxon Period to the Present Time. Crown 8vo. 6s.

ARNOTT.—*THE ELEMENTS OF PHYSICS OR NATURAL PHILOSOPHY.* By NEIL ARNOTT, M.D. Edited by A. BAIN, LL.D. and A. S. TAYLOR, M.D. F.R.S. Woodcuts. Crown 8vo. 12s. 6d.

ASHBY. — *NOTES ON PHYSIOLOGY FOR THE USE OF STUDENTS PREPARING FOR EXAMINATION.* With 120 Woodcuts. By HENRY ASHBY, M.D. Lond., Physician to the General Hospital for Sick Children, Manchester. Fcp. 8vo. 5s.

AYRE. —*THE TREASURY OF BIBLE KNOWLEDGE ;* being a Dictionary of the Books, Persons, Places, Events, and other matters of which mention is made in Holy Scripture. By the Rev. J. AYRE, M.A. With 5 Maps, 15 Plates, and 300 Woodcuts. Fcp. 8vo. 6s.

BACON.—*THE WORKS AND LIFE OF.*

COMPLETE WORKS. Collected and Edited by R. L. ELLIS, M.A. J. SPEDDING, M.A. and D. D. HEATH. 7 vols. 8vo. £3. 13s. 6d.

LETTERS AND LIFE, INCLUDING ALL HIS OCCASIONAL WORKS. Collected and Edited, with a Commentary, by J. SPEDDING. 7 vols. 8vo. £4. 4s.

THE ESSAYS ; with Annotations. By RICHARD WHATELY, D.D., sometime Archbishop of Dublin. 8vo. 10s. 6d.

THE ESSAYS ; with Introduction, Notes, and Index. By E. A. ABBOTT, D.D. 2 vols. fcp. 8vo. price 6s. The Text and Index only, without Introduction and Notes, in 1 vol. fcp. 8vo. price 2s. 6d.

THE ESSAYS ; with Critical and Illustrative Notes, and other Aids for Students. By the Rev. JOHN HUNTER, M.A. Crown 8vo. 3s. 6d.

THE PROMUS OF FORMULARIES AND ELEGANCIES, illustrated by Passages from SHAKESPEARE. By Mrs. H. POTT. Preface by E. A. ABBOTT, D.D. 8vo 16s.

BAGEHOT. — *WORKS BY WALTER BAGEHOT, M.A.*

BIOGRAPHICAL STUDIES. 8vo. 12s.

ECONOMIC STUDIES. 8vo. 10s. 6d.

LITERARY STUDIES. 2 vols. 8vo. Portrait. 28s.

BAILEY. — *FESTUS, A POEM.* By PHILIP JAMES BAILEY. Crown 8vo. 12s. 6d.

BAKER.—*WORKS BY SIR SAMUEL W. BAKER, M.A.*

EIGHT YEARS IN CEYLON. Crown 8vo. Woodcuts. 5s.

THE RIFLE AND THE HOUND IN CEYLON. Crown 8vo. Woodcuts. 5s.

BAIN. — *WORKS BY ALEXANDER BAIN, LL.D.*

MENTAL AND MORAL SCIENCE; a Compendium of Psychology and Ethics. Crown 8vo. 10s. 6d.

THE SENSES AND THE INTELLECT. 8vo. 15s.

THE EMOTIONS AND THE WILL. 8vo. 15s.

PRACTICAL ESSAYS. Crown 8vo. 4s. 6d.

LOGIC, DEDUCTIVE AND INDUCTIVE. PART I. *Deduction*, 4s. PART II. *Induction*, 6s. 6d.

JAMES MILL; a Biography. Crown 8vo. 5s.

JOHN STUART MILL; a Criticism, with Personal Recollections. Crown 8vo. 2s. 6d.

BARRY & BRAMWELL. — *RAILWAYS AND LOCOMOTIVES:* a Series of Lectures delivered at the School of Military Engineering, Chatham. *Railways*, by J. W. BARRY, M. Inst. C.E. *Locomotives*, by Sir F. J. BRAMWELL, F.R.S., M. Inst. C.E. With 228 Wood Engravings. 8vo. 21s.

BEACONSFIELD. — *WORKS BY THE EARL OF BEACONSFIELD, K.G.*

NOVELS AND TALES. The Cabinet Edition. 11 vols. Crown 8vo. 6s. each.

Endymion.	
Lothair.	Henrietta Temple.
Coningsby.	Contarini Fleming, &c.
Sybil.	Alroy, Ixion, &c.
Tancred.	The Young Duke, &c.
Venetia.	Vivian Grey, &c.

NOVELS AND TALES. The Hughenden Edition. With 2 Portraits and 11 Vignettes. 11 vols. Crown 8vo. 42s.

NOVELS AND TALES. Modern Novelist's Library Edition, complete in 11 vols. Crown 8vo. 22s. boards, or 27s. 6d. cloth.

SELECTED SPEECHES. With Introduction and Notes, by T. E. KEBBEL, M.A. 2 vols. 8vo. Portrait, 32s.

THE WIT AND WISDOM OF BENJAMIN DISRAELI, EARL OF BEACONSFIELD. Crown 8vo. 3s. 6d.

THE BEACONSFIELD BIRTHDAY-BOOK: Selected from the Writings and Speeches of the Right Hon. the Earl of Beaconsfield, K.G. With 2 Portraits and 11 Views of Hughenden Manor and its Surroundings. 18mo. 2s. 6d. cloth, gilt; 4s. 6d. bound.

BECKER. — *WORKS BY PROFESSOR BECKER, translated from the German by the Rev. F. METCALF.*

GALLUS; or, Roman Scenes in the Time of Augustus. Post 8vo. 7s. 6d.

CHARICLES; or, Illustrations of the Private Life of the Ancient Greeks. Post 8vo. 7s. 6d.

BLACK. — *PRACTICAL TREATISE ON BREWING;* with Formulæ for Public Brewers and Instructions for Private Families. By W. Black. 8vo. 10s. 6d.

BLACKLEY & FRIEDLÄNDER. — *A PRACTICAL DICTIONARY OF THE GERMAN AND ENGLISH LANGUAGES:* containing New Words in General Use not found in other Dictionaries. By the Rev. W. L. BLACKLEY, M.A. and C. M. FRIEDLÄNDER, Ph.D. Post 8vo. 7s. 6d.

BOULTBEE. — *WORKS BY THE REV. T. P. BOULTBEE, LL.D.*

A COMMENTARY ON THE 39 ARTICLES, forming an introduction to the Theology of the Church of England. Crown 8vo. 6s.

A HISTORY OF THE CHURCH OF ENGLAND; Pre-Reformation Period. 8vo. 15s.

BOURNE. — *WORKS BY JOHN BOURNE, C.E.*

A TREATISE ON THE STEAM ENGINE, in its application to Mines, Mills, Steam Navigation, Railways, and Agriculture. With 37 Plates and 546 Woodcuts. 4to. 42s.

CATECHISM OF THE STEAM ENGINE, in its various Applications to Mines, Mills, Steam Navigation, and Agriculture. With 89 Woodcuts. Fcp. 8vo. 6s.

HANDBOOK OF THE STEAM ENGINE; a Key to the Author's Catechism of the Steam Engine. With 67 Woodcuts. Fcp. 8vo. 9s.

RECENT IMPROVEMENTS IN THE STEAM ENGINE. With 124 Woodcuts. Fcp. 8vo. 6s.

EXAMPLES OF STEAM AND GAS ENGINES of the most recent Approved Types. With 54 Plates and 356 Woodcuts. 4to. 70s.

BRAMSTON & LEROY. — *HISTORIC WINCHESTER;* England's First Capital. By A. R. BRAMSTON and A. C. LEROY. Cr. 8vo. 6s.

BRANDE'S *DICTIONARY OF SCIENCE, LITERATURE, AND ART.* Re-edited by the Rev. Sir G. W. Cox, Bart., M.A. 3 vols. medium 8vo. 63s.

BRASSEY. — *WORKS BY LADY BRASSEY.*

A VOYAGE IN THE 'SUNBEAM,' OUR HOME ON THE OCEAN FOR ELEVEN MONTHS. By Lady BRASSEY. With Map and 65 Wood Engravings. Library Edition, 8vo. 21s. Cabinet Edition, crown 8vo. 7s. 6d. School Edition, fcp. 2s. Popular Edition, 4to. 6d.

SUNSHINE AND STORM IN THE EAST; or, Cruises to Cyprus and Constantinople. With 2 Maps and 114 Illustrations engraved on Wood. Library Edition, 8vo. 21s. Cabinet Edition, cr. 8vo. 7s. 6d.

IN THE TRADES, THE TROPICS, AND THE 'ROARING FORTIES'; or, Fourteen Thousand Miles in the *Sunbeam* in 1883. By Lady BRASSEY. With nearly Two Hundred and Fifty Illustrations engraved on Wood from drawings by R. T. Pritchett, and Eight Maps and Charts. Library Edition, 8vo. 21s.

BROWNE.—*AN EXPOSITION OF THE* 39 *ARTICLES,* Historical and Doctrinal. By E. H. BROWNE, D.D., Bishop of Winchester. 8vo. 16s.

BUCKLE.—*HISTORY OF CIVILISATION IN ENGLAND AND FRANCE, SPAIN AND SCOTLAND.* By HENRY THOMAS BUCKLE. 3 vols. crown 8vo. 24s.

BUCKTON.— *WORKS BY MRS. C. M. BUCKTON.*

FOOD AND HOME COOKERY; a Course of Instruction in Practical Cookery and Cleaning. With 11 Woodcuts. Crown 8vo. 2s. 6d.

HEALTH IN THE HOUSE: Twenty-five Lectures on Elementary Physiology. With 41 Woodcuts and Diagrams. Crown 8vo. 2s.

BULL.— *WORKS BY THOMAS BULL, M.D.*

HINTS TO MOTHERS ON THE MANAGEMENT OF THEIR HEALTH during the Period of Pregnancy and in the Lying-in Room. Fcp. 8vo. 1s. 6d.

THE MATERNAL MANAGEMENT OF CHILDREN IN HEALTH AND DISEASE. Fcp. 8vo. 1s. 6d.

BURTON.—*MY HOME FARM.* By Mrs. JOHN HILL BURTON. Crown 8vo. 3s. 6d.

CABINET LAWYER, The; a Popular Digest of the Laws of England, Civil, Criminal, and Constitutional. Fcp. 8vo. 9s.

CALVERT.—*THE WIFE'S MANUAL;* or Prayers, Thoughts, and Songs on Several Occasions of a Matron's Life. By the late W. CALVERT, Minor Canon of St. Paul's. Printed and ornamented in the style of *Queen Elizabeth's Prayer Book.* Crown 8vo. 6s.

CARLYLE. — *THOMAS AND JANE WELSH CARLYLE.*

THOMAS CARLYLE, a History of the first Forty Years of his Life, 1795-1835. By J. A. FROUDE, M.A. With 2 Portraits and 4 Illustrations, 2 vols. 8vo. 32s.

CARLYLE'S LIFE IN LONDON: from 1834 to his death in 1881. By JAMES A. FROUDE, M.A. with Portrait engraved on steel. 2 vols. 8vo. 32s.

REMINISCENCES. By THOMAS CARLYLE. Edited by J. A. FROUDE, M.A. 2 vols. crown 8vo. 18s.

LETTERS AND MEMORIALS OF JANE WELSH CARLYLE. Prepared for publication by THOMAS CARLYLE, and edited by J. A. FROUDE, M.A. 3 vols. 8vo. 36s.

CATES. — *A DICTIONARY OF GENERAL BIOGRAPHY.* By W. L. R. CATES. 8vo. 28s.

CHESNEY.—*WATERLOO LECTURES;* a Study of the Campaign of 1815. By Col. C. C. CHESNEY, R.E. 8vo. 10s. 6d.

CHRIST OUR IDEAL, an Argument from Analogy. By the Author of 'The Gospel for the Nineteenth Century 8vo. 8s. 6d.

CICERO.—*THE CORRESPONDENCE OF CICERO:* a revised Text, with Notes and Prolegomena.—Vol. I., The Letters to the end of Cicero's Exile. By ROBERT Y. TYRRELL, M.A., Fellow of Trinity College, Dublin, 12s.

COATS.—*A MANUAL OF PATHOLOGY.* By JOSEPH COATS, M.D. Pathologist to the Western Infirmary and the Sick Children's Hospital, Glasgow ; formerly Pathologist to the Royal Infirmary, and President of the Pathological and Clinical Society of Glasgow. With 339 Illustrations engraved on Wood. 8vo. 31s. 6d.

COLENSO.—*THE PENTATEUCH AND BOOK OF JOSHUA CRITICALLY EXAMINED.* By J. W. COLENSO, D.D., late Bishop of Natal. Crown 8vo. 6s.

CONDER.—*A Handbook to the Bible*, or Guide to the Study of the Holy Scriptures derived from Ancient Monuments and Modern Exploration. By F. R. Conder, and Lieut. C. R. Conder, R.E. Post 8vo. 7s. 6d.

CONINGTON. — *Works by John Conington, M.A.*

The Æneid of Virgil. Translated into English Verse. Crown 8vo. 9s.

The Poems of Virgil. Translated into English Prose. Crown 8vo. 9s.

CONTANSEAU.—*Works by Professor Léon Contanseau.*

A Practical Dictionary of the French and English Languages. Post 8vo. 3s. 6d.

A Pocket Dictionary of the French and English Languages; being a careful Abridgment of the Author's 'Practical French and English Dictionary.' Square 18mo. 1s. 6d.

CONYBEARE & HOWSON.—*The Life and Epistles of St. Paul.* By the Rev. W. J. Conybeare, M.A., and the Very Rev. J. S. Howson, D.D. Dean of Chester.

Library Edition, with all the Original Illustrations, Maps, Landscapes on Steel, Woodcuts, &c. 2 vols. 4to. 42s.

Intermediate Edition, with a Selection of Maps, Plates, and Wood-cuts. 2 vols. square crown 8vo. 21s.

Student's Edition, revised and condensed, with 46 Illustrations and Maps. 1 vol. crown 8vo. 7s. 6d.

COOKE. — *Tablets of Anatomy and Physiology.* By Thomas Cooke, F.R.C.S. Being a Synopsis of Demonstrations given in the Westminster Hospital Medical School, A.D. 1871–1875. Anatomy, complete, Second Edition, 4to. 15s. Physiology, complete, Second Edition, 4to. 10s.

** These Tablets *may still be had in separate Fasciculi as originally published.*

COX. — *A General History of Greece:* from the Earliest Period to the Death of Alexander the Great; with a Sketch of the Subsequent History to the Present Time. By the Rev. Sir G. W. Cox, Bart. M.A. With 11 Maps and Plans. Crown 8vo. 7s. 6d.

CRAWFORD.—*Across the Pampas and the Andes.* By Robert Crawford, M.A. With Map and 7 Illustrations. Crown 8vo. 7s. 6d.

CREIGHTON. — *History of the Papacy During the Reformation.* By the Rev. M. Creighton, M.A. Vol. I. the Great Schism—the Council of Constance, 1378–1418. Vol. II. the Council of Basel—The Papal Restoration, 1418–1464. 2 vols. 8vo. 32s.

CRESY.—*Encyclopædia of Civil Engineering,* Historical, Theoretical, and Practical. By Edward Cresy. With above 3,000 Woodcuts, 8vo. 25s.

CULLEY.—*Handbook of Practical Telegraphy.* By R. S. Culley, M. Inst. C.E. Plates and Woodcuts. 8vo. 16s.

DAVIDSON.—*An Introduction to the Study of the New Testament,* Critical, Exegetical, and Theological. By the Rev. S. Davidson, D.D. LL.D. Revised Edition. 2 vols. 8vo. 30s.

DEAD SHOT, The, *or Sportsman's Complete Guide;* a Treatise on the Use of the Gun, with Lessons in the Art of Shooting Game of all kinds, and Wild-Fowl, also Pigeon-Shooting, and Dog-Breaking. By Marksman. With 13 Illustrations. Crown 8vo. 10s. 6d.

DECAISNE & LE MAOUT.— *A General System of Botany.* Translated from the French of E. Le Maout, M.D., and J. Decaisne, by Mrs. Hooker; with Additions by J. D. Hooker, C.B. F.R.S. Imp. 8vo. with 5,500 Woodcuts, 31s. 6d.

DE ·TOCQUEVILLE.—*Democracy in America.* By Alexis de Tocqueville. Translated by H. Reeve. 2 vols. crown 8vo. 16s.

DEVAS.—*Groundwork of Economics.* By C. S. Devas. 8vo. 16s.

DEWES.—*The Life and Letters of St. Paul.* By Alfred Dewes, M.A. LL.D. D.D. Vicar of St. Augustine's, Pendlebury. With 4 Maps. 8vo. 7s. 6d.

DIXON.—*Rural Bird Life;* Essays on Ornithology, with Instructions for Preserving Objects relating to that Science. By Charles Dixon. With 45 Woodcuts. Crown 8vo. 5s.

DOWNING.—*Elements of Practical Construction,* for the Use of Students in Engineering and Architecture. By Samuel Downing, LL.D. Part I. Structures in Direct Tension and Compression. With numerous Woodcuts and a Folio Atlas of 14 Plates, 8vo. 14s

DICKINSON. — *DISEASES OF THE KIDNEY AND URINARY DERANGEMENTS.* By W. HOWSHIP DICKINSON, M.D. Cantab. F.R.C.P. &c. Physician to, and Lecturer on Medicine at, St. George's Hospital. In Three Parts. PART I.— *Diabetes*, with 3 Plates of Figures and 17 Woodcuts. 8vo. price 10s. 6d. PART II.—*Albuminuria*, with 11 Plates and 31 Woodcuts, price 20s.

⁎ The Two Parts may be had separately, each an independent work : PART I.—*Diabetes*, price 12s. cloth. PART II.—Being the Second Edition Revised of Dr. DICKINSON'S 'Pathology and Treatment of Albuminuria,' price 21s. cloth. PART III., completing the work, is in the Press.

DOYLE.—*THE ENGLISH IN AMERICA;* Virginia, Maryland, and the Carolinas. By J. A. DOYLE, Fellow of All Souls' College, Oxford. 8vo. Map, 18s.

DRESSER.—*JAPAN ; ITS ARCHITEC-TURE, ART, AND ART MANUFACTURES.* By CHRISTOPHER DRESSER, Ph.D. F.L.S. &c. With 202 Graphic Illustrations engraved on Wood for the most part by Native Artists in Japan, the rest by G. Pearson, after Photographs and Drawings made on the spot. Square crown 8vo. 31s. 6d.

EASTLAKE.—*FIVE GREAT PAINTERS ;* Essays on Leonardo da Vinci, Michael Angelo, Titian, Raphael, Albert Dürer. By LADY EASTLAKE. 2 vols. Crown 8vo. 16s.

EASTLAKE.—*WORKS BY C. L. EASTLAKE, F.R.S. B.A.*

HINTS ON HOUSEHOLD TASTE IN FURNITURE, UPHOLSTERY, &c. With 100 Illustrations. Square crown 8vo. 14s.

NOTES ON FOREIGN PICTURE GALLERIES. Crown 8vo.

The Louvre Gallery, *Paris,* with 114 Illustrations, 7s. 6d.

The Brera Gallery, *Milan,* with 55 Illustrations, 5s.

The Old Pinaluthell, *Munich,* with 107 Illustrations, 7s. 6d.

EDERSHEIM. — *THE LIFE AND TIMES OF JESUS THE MESSIAH.* By the Rev. ALFRED EDERSHEIM, M.A. Oxon, D.D. Ph.D. Warburtonian Lecturer at Lincoln's Inn. 2 vols. 8vo. 42s.

EDWARDS.—*OUR SEAMARKS.* By E. PRICE EDWARDS. With numerous Illustrations of Lighthouses, Lightships, Lighting Appliances, &c. engraved on Wood by G. H. Ford. Crown 8vo. 8s. 6d.

ELLICOTT. — *WORKS BY C. J. ELLICOTT, D.D.,* Bishop of Gloucester and Bristol.

A CRITICAL AND GRAMMATICAL COMMENTARY ON ST. PAUL'S EPISTLES. 8vo. Galatians, 8s. 6d. Ephesians, 8s. 6d. Pastoral Epistles, 10s. 6d. Philippians, Colossians, and Philemon, 10s. 6d. Thessalonians, 7s. 6d.

HISTORICAL LECTURES ON THE LIFE OF OUR LORD JESUS CHRIST. 8vo. 12s.

EPOCHS OF ANCIENT HISTORY. Edited by the Rev. Sir G. W. Cox, Bart. M.A. and C. SANKEY, M.A.

Beesly's Gracchi, Marius and Sulla, 2s. 6d.
Capes's Age of the Antonines, 2s. 6d.
—— Early Roman Empire, 2s. 6d.
Cox's Athenian Empire, 2s. 6d.
—— Greeks and Persians, 2s. 6d.
Curteis's Macedonian Empire, 2s. 6d.
Ihne's Rome to its Capture by the Gauls, 2s. 6d.
Merivale's Roman Triumvirates, 2s. 6d.
Sankey's Spartan and Theban Supremacies, 2s. 6d.
Smith's Rome and Carthage, 2s. 6d.

EPOCHS OF MODERN HISTORY. Edited by C. COLBECK, M.A.

Church's Beginning of the Middle Ages, 2s. 6d.
Cox's Crusades, 2s. 6d.
Creighton's Age of Elizabeth, 2s. 6d.
Gairdner's Lancaster and York, 2s. 6d.
Gardiner's Puritan Revolution, 2s. 6d.
—— Thirty Years' War, 2s. 6d.
—— (Mrs.) French Revolution, 2s. 6d.
Hale's Fall of the Stuarts, 2s. 6d.
Johnson's Normans in Europe, 2s. 6d.
Longman's Frederick the Great, 2s. 6d.
Ludlow's War of American Independence, 2s. 6d.
M'Carthy's Epoch of Reform, 1830–1850, 2s. 6d.
Morris's Age of Anne, 2s. 6d.
Seebohm's Protestant Revolution, 2s. 6d.
Stubbs' Early Plantagenets, 2s. 6d.
Warburton's Edward III. 2s. 6d.

ERICHSEN.—*WORKS BY JOHN ERIC ERICHSEN, F.R.S.*

THE SCIENCE AND ART OF SURGERY: Being a Treatise on Surgical Injuries, Diseases, and Operations. Illustrated by Engravings on Wood. 2 vols 8vo. 42s. ; or bound in half-russia, 60s.

ON CONCUSSION OF THE SPINE, NERVOUS SHOCKS, and other Obscure Injuries of the Nervous System in their Clinical and Medico-Legal Aspects. Crown 8vo. 10s. 6d.

EVANS.—*THE BRONZE IMPLEMENTS, ARMS, AND ORNAMENTS OF GREAT BRITAIN AND IRELAND.* By JOHN EVANS, D.C.L. LL.D. F.R.S. With 540 Illustrations. 8vo. 25s.

EWALD.—*WORKS BY PROFESSOR HEINRICH EWALD,* of Göttingen.

THE ANTIQUITIES OF ISRAEL. Translated from the German by H. S. SOLLY, M.A. 8vo. 12s. 6d.

THE HISTORY OF ISRAEL. Translated from the German. Vols. I.–V. 8vo. 63s. Vol. VI. *Christ and his Times,* 8vo. 16s. Vols. VII. and VIII. *The Apostolic Age,* 8vo. 21s.

FAIRBAIRN.—*WORKS BY SIR W. FAIRBAIRN, BART, C.E.*

A TREATISE ON MILLS AND MILL-WORK, with 18 Plates and 333 Woodcuts. 1 vol. 8vo. 25s.

USEFUL INFORMATION FOR ENGINEERS. With many Plates and Woodcuts. 3 vols. crown 8vo. 31s. 6d.

FARRAR.—*LANGUAGE AND LANGUAGES.* A Revised Edition of *Chapters on Language and Families of Speech.* By F. W FARRAR, D.D. Crown 8vo. 6s.

FITZWYGRAM. — *HORSES AND STABLES.* By Major-General Sir F. FITZWYGRAM, Bart. With 39 pages of Illustrations. 8vo. 10s. 6d.

FOX.—*THE EARLY HISTORY OF CHARLES JAMES FOX.* By the Right Hon. G. O. TREVELYAN, M.P. Library Edition, 8vo. 18s. Cabinet Edition, cr. 8vo. 6s.

FRANCIS.—*A BOOK ON ANGLING;* or, Treatise on the Art of Fishing in every branch; including full Illustrated Lists of Salmon Flies. By FRANCIS FRANCIS. Post 8vo. Portrait and Plates, 15s.

FREEMAN.—*WORKS BY E. A. FREEMAN, D.C.L.*

THE HISTORICAL GEOGRAPHY OF EUROPE. With 65 Maps. 2 vols. 8vo. 31s. 6d.

SOME IMPRESSIONS OF THE UNITED STATES. Crown 8vo. 6s.

FRENCH. — *NINETEEN CENTURIES OF DRINK IN ENGLAND,* a History. By RICHARD VALPY FRENCH, D.C.L. LL.D. F.S.A. ; Author of ' The History of Toasting ' &c. Crown 8vo. 10s. 6d.

FROUDE.—*WORKS BY JAMES A FROUDE, M.A.*

THE HISTORY OF ENGLAND, from the Fall of Wolsey to the Defeat of the Spanish Armada. Cabinet Edition, 12 vols. cr. 8vo. £3. 12s. Popular Edition, 12 vols. cr. 8vo. £2. 2s.

SHORT STUDIES ON GREAT SUBJECTS. 4 vols. crown 8vo. 24s.

THE ENGLISH IN IRELAND IN THE EIGHTEENTH CENTURY. 3 vols. crown 8vo. 18s.

THOMAS CARLYLE, a History of the first Forty Years of his Life, 1795 to 1835. 2 vols. 8vo. 32s.

CARLYLE'S LIFE IN LONDON : from 1834 to his death in 1881. By JAMES A. FROUDE, M.A. with Portrait engraved on steel. 2 vols. 8vo. 32s.

GANOT.—*WORKS BY PROFESSOR GANOT.* Translated by E. ATKINSON, Ph.D. F.C.S.

ELEMENTARY TREATISE ON PHYSICS, for the use of Colleges and Schools. With 5 Coloured Plates and 898 Woodcuts. Large crown 8vo. 15s.

NATURAL PHILOSOPHY FOR GENERAL READERS AND YOUNG PERSONS. With 2 Plates and 471 Woodcuts. Crown 8vo. 7s. 6d.

GARDINER.—*WORKS BY SAMUEL RAWSON GARDINER, LL.D.*

HISTORY OF ENGLAND, from the Accession of James I. to the Outbreak of the Civil War, 1603-1642. Cabinet Edition, thoroughly revised. 10 vols. crown 8vo. price 6s. each.

OUTLINE OF ENGLISH HISTORY, B.C. 55-A.D. 1880. With 96 Woodcuts, fcp. 8vo. 2s. 6d.

** For Professor Gardiner's other Works, *see* ' Epochs of Modern History,' p. 9.

GARROD. — *WORKS BY ALFRED BARING GARROD, M.D. F.R.S.*

A TREATISE ON GOUT AND RHEUMATIC GOUT (RHEUMATOID ARTHRITIS). With 6 Plates, comprising 21 Figures (14 Coloured), and 27 Illustrations engraved on Wood. 8vo. 21s.

THE ESSENTIALS OF MATERIA MEDICA AND THERAPEUTICS. Revised and edited, under the supervision of the Author, by E. B. BAXTER, M.D. F.R.C.P. Professor of Materia Medica and Therapeutics in King's College, London. Crown 8vo. 12s. 6d.

GOETHE.—*Faust.* Translated by T. E. Webb, LL.D. Reg. Prof. of Laws and Public Orator in the Univ. of Dublin. 8vo. 12*s*. 6*d*.

Faust. A New Translation, chiefly in Blank Verse ; with a complete Introduction and Copious Notes. By James Adey Birds, B.A. F.G.S. Large crown 8vo. 12*s*. 6*d*.

Faust. The German Text, with an English Introduction and Notes for Students. By Albert M. Selss, M.A. Ph.D. Crown 8vo. 5*s*.

GOODEVE.—*Works by T. M. Goodeve, M.A.*

Principles of Mechanics. With 253 Woodcuts. Crown 8vo. 6*s*.

The Elements of Mechanism. With 342 Woodcuts. Crown 8vo. 6*s*.

GOSPEL FOR THE NINETEENTH CENTURY (The). 8vo. 10*s*. 6*d*.

GRANT.—*Works by Sir Alexander Grant, Bart. LL.D. D.C.L. &c.*

The Story of the University of Edinburgh during its First Three Hundred Years. With numerous Illustrations. 2 vols. 8vo. 36*s*.

The Ethics of Aristotle. The Greek Text illustrated by Essays and Notes. 2 vols. 8vo. 32*s*.

GRAY. — *Anatomy, Descriptive and Surgical.* By Henry Gray, F.R.S. late Lecturer on Anatomy at St. George's Hospital. With 557 large Woodcut Illustrations ; those in the First Edition after Original Drawings by Dr. Carter, from Dissections made by the Author and Dr. Carter ; the additional Drawings in the Second and subsequent Editions by Dr. Westmacott, and other Demonstrators of Anatomy. Re-edited by T. Pickering Pick, Surgeon to St. George's Hospital. Royal 8vo. 30*s*.

GREVILLE. — *Journal of the Reigns of King George IV. and King William IV.* By the late C. C. F. Greville. Edited by H. Reeve, C.B. 3 vols. 8vo. 36*s*.

GWILT.—*An Encyclopædia of Architecture,* Historical, Theoretical, and Practical. By Joseph Gwilt, F.S.A. Illustrated with more than 1,100 Engravings on Wood by R. Branston from Drawings by J. S. Gwilt. Revised, with Alterations and Considerable Additions, by Wyatt Papworth. Additionally illustrated with nearly 400 Wood Engravings by O. Jewitt, and nearly 200 other Woodcuts. 8vo. 52*s*. 6*d*.

GROVE.—*The Correlation of Physical Forces.* By the Hon. Sir W. R. Grove, F.R.S. &c. 8vo. 15*s*.

HALLIWELL-PHILLIPPS. — *Outlines of the Life of Shakespeare.* By J. O. Halliwell-Phillipps, F.R.S. 8vo. 7*s*. 6*d*.

HAMILTON.—*Life of Sir William R. Hamilton,* Kt. LL.D. D.C.L. M.R.I.A. &c. Including Selections from his Poems, Correspondence, and Miscellaneous Writings. By the Rev. R. P. Graves, M.A. Vol. I. 8vo. 15*s*.

HARTE.—*On the Frontier.* Three Stories. By Bret Harte. 16mo. 1*s*.

HARTWIG.—*Works by Dr. G Hartwig.*

The Sea and its Living Wonders 8vo. with many Illustrations, 10*s*. 6*d*.

The Tropical World. With abou 200 Illustrations. 8vo. 10*s*. 6*d*.

The Polar World ; a Description of Man and Nature in the Arctic and Antarctic Regions of the Globe. Maps, Plates, and Woodcuts. 8vo. 10*s*. 6*d*.

The Arctic Regions (extracted from the 'Polar World'). 4to. 6*d*. sewed.

The Subterranean World. With Maps and Woodcuts. 8vo. 10*s*. 6*d*.

The Aerial World ; a Popular Account of the Phenomena and Life of the Atmosphere. Map, Plates, Woodcuts. 8vo. 10*s*. 6*d*.

HASSALL. — *Works by Arthur Hill Hassall, M.D.*

Food ; its Adulterations and the Methods for their Detection. Illustrated. Crown 8vo. 24*s*.

San Remo, climatically and medically considered. With 30 Illustrations. Crown 8vo. 5*s*.

HAUGHTON. — *Six Lectures on Physical Geography,* delivered in 1876, with some Additions. By the Rev. Samuel Haughton, F.R.S. M.D. D.C.L. With 23 Diagrams. 8vo. 15*s*.

HAVELOCK. — *Memoirs of Sir Henry Havelock, K.C.B.* By John Clark Marshman. Crown 8vo. 3*s*. 6*d*.

HAWARD.—*A Treatise on Orthopædic Surgery.* By J. Warrington Haward, F.R.C.S. Surgeon to St. George's Hospital. With 30 Illustrations engraved on Wood. 8vo. 12*s*. 6*d*.

HELMHOLTZ.—*POPULAR LECTURES ON SCIENTIFIC SUBJECTS.* By Professor HELMHOLTZ. Translated and edited by EDMUND ATKINSON, Ph.D. F.C.S. With a Preface by Professor TYNDALL, F.R.S. and 68 Woodcuts. 2 vols. Crown 8vo. 15*s.* or separately, 7*s.* 6*d.* each.

HERSCHEL.—*OUTLINES OF ASTRONOMY.* By Sir J. F. W. HERSCHEL, Bart. M.A. With Plates and Diagrams. Square crown 8vo. 12*s.*

HEWITT. — *WORKS BY GRAILY HEWITT, M.D.*

THE DIAGNOSIS AND TREATMENT OF DISEASES OF WOMEN, INCLUDING THE DIAGNOSIS OF PREGNANCY. New Edition, in great part re-written and much enlarged, with 211 Engravings on Wood, of which 79 are new in this Edition. 8vo. 24*s.*

THE MECHANICAL SYSTEM OF UTERINE PATHOLOGY. With 31 Life-size Illustrations prepared expressly for this Work. Crown 4to. 7*s.* 6*d.*

HICKSON. — *IRELAND IN THE SEVENTEENTH CENTURY;* or, The Irish Massacres of 1641-2, their Causes and Results. Illustrated by Extracts from the unpublished State Papers, the unpublished MSS. in the Bodleian Library, Lambeth Library, &c. ; a Selection from the unpublished Depositions relating to the Massacres, and the Reports of the Trials in the High Court of Justice, 1652-4, from the unpublished MSS. By MARY HICKSON. With a Preface by J. A. Froude, M.A. 2 vols. 8vo. 28*s.*

HOBART.—*THE MEDICAL LANGUAGE OF ST. LUKE:* a Proof from Internal Evidence that St. Luke's Gospel and the Acts were written by the same person, and that the writer was a Medical Man. By the Rev. W. K. HOBART, LL.D. 8vo. 16*s.*

HOLMES.—*A SYSTEM OF SURGERY,* Theoretical and Practical, in Treatises by various Authors. Edited by TIMOTHY HOLMES, M.A. Surgeon to St. George's Hospital ; and J. W. HULKE, F.R.S. Surgeon to the Middlesex Hospital. In 3 Volumes, with Coloured Plates and Illustrations on Wood. 3 vols. royal 8vo. price Four Guineas.

HORACE.—*HORATII OPERA,* Library Edition ; the Text carefully corrected, with Notes, Marginal References, and Various Readings. Edited by the Rev. J. E. YONGE, M.A. Assistant Master, Eton. 8vo. 21*s.*

HOMER.—*THE ILIAD OF HOMER,* Homometrically translated by C. B. CAYLEY. 8vo. 12*s.* 6*d.*

THE ILIAD OF HOMER. The Greek Text, with a Verse Translation, by W. C. GREEN, M.A. Vol. I. Books I.-XII. Crown 8vo. 6*s.*

HOPKINS.—*CHRIST THE CONSOLER;* a Book of Comfort for the Sick. By ELLICE HOPKINS. Fcp. 8vo. 2*s.* 6*d.*

HORSES AND ROADS; or How to Keep a Horse Sound on His Legs. By FREE-LANCE. Crown 8vo. 6*s.*

HORT.—*THE NEW PANTHEON,* or an Introduction to the Mythology of the Ancients. By W. J. HORT. 18mo. 2*s.* 6*d.*

HOWITT.—*VISITS TO REMARKABLE PLACES,* Old Halls, Battle-Fields, Scenes illustrative of Striking Passages in English History and Poetry. By WILLIAM HOWITT. With 80 Illustrations engraved on Wood. Crown 8vo. 7*s.* 6*d.*

HULLAH.—*WORKS BY JOHN HULLAH, LL.D.*

COURSE OF LECTURES ON THE HISTORY OF MODERN MUSIC. 8vo. 8*s.* 6*d.*

COURSE OF LECTURES ON THE TRANSITION PERIOD OF MUSICAL HISTORY. 8vo. 10*s.* 6*d.*

HULME.—*ART-INSTRUCTION IN ENGLAND.* By F. E. HULME, F.L.S. F.S.A. Fcp. 8vo. 3*s.* 6*d.*

HUME.—*THE PHILOSOPHICAL WORKS OF DAVID HUME.* Edited by T. H. GREEN, M.A. and the Rev. T. H. GROSE, M.A. 4 vols. 8vo. 56*s.* Or separately, Essays, 2 vols. 28*s.* Treatise on Human Nature. 2 vols. 28*s.*

HUSBAND. — *EXAMINATION QUESTIONS IN ANATOMY, PHYSIOLOGY, BOTANY, MATERIA MEDICA, SURGERY, MEDICINE, MIDWIFERY, AND STATE-MEDICINE.* Arranged by H. A. HUSBAND, M.B. M.C. M.R.C.S. L.S.A. &c. 32mo. 4*s.* 6*d.*

INGELOW. —*POETICAL WORKS OF JEAN INGELOW.* New Edition, reprinted, with Additional Matter, from the 23rd and 6th Editions of the two volumes respectively. With 2 Vignettes. 2 vols. Fcp. 8vo. 12*s.*

IN THE OLDEN TIME.—A Novel. By the Author of 'Mademoiselle Mori.' Crown 8vo. 6s.

JAMESON.—*Works by Mrs. Jameson.*

Legends of the Saints and Martyrs. With 19 Etchings and 187 Woodcuts. 2 vols. 31s. 6d.

Legends of the Madonna, the Virgin Mary as represented in Sacred and Legendary Art. With 27 Etchings and 165 Woodcuts. 1 vol. 21s.

Legends of the Monastic Orders. With 11 Etchings and 88 Woodcuts. 1 vol. 21s.

History of the Saviour, His Types and Precursors. Completed by Lady Eastlake. With 13 Etchings and 281 Woodcuts. 2 vols. 42s.

JEFFERIES.—*Works by Richard Jefferies.*

The Story of My Heart: My Autobiography. Crown 8vo. 5s.

Red Deer. Crown 8vo. 4s. 6d.

JOHNSON.—*The Patentee's Manual;* a Treatise on the Law and Practice of Letters Patent, for the use of Patentees and Inventors. By J. Johnson and J. H. Johnson. 8vo. 10s. 6d.

JOHNSTON.—*A General Dictionary of Geography,* Descriptive, Physical, Statistical, and Historical; a complete Gazetteer of the World. By Keith Johnston. Medium 8vo. 42s.

JONES. — *The Health of the Senses: Sight, Hearing, Voice, Smell and Taste, Skin;* with Hints on Health, Diet, Education, Health Resorts of Europe, &c. By H. Macnaughton Jones, M.D. Crown 8vo. 3s. 6d.

JUKES.—*Works by the Rev. Andrew Jukes.*

The New Man and the Eternal Life. Crown 8vo. 6s.

The Types of Genesis. Crown 8vo. 7s. 6d.

The Second Death and the Restitution of all Things. Crown 8vo. 3s. 6d.

The Mystery of the Kingdom. Crown 8vo. 2s. 6d.

JUSTINIAN.—*The Institutes of Justinian;* Latin Text, chiefly that of Huschke, with English Introduction, Translation, Notes, and Summary. By Thomas C. Sandars, M.A. Barrister-at-Law. 8vo. 18s.

KALISCH. — *Works by M. M. Kalisch, M.A.*

Bible Studies. Part I. The Prophecies of Balaam. 8vo. 10s. 6d. Part II. The Book of Jonah. 8vo. 10s. 6d.

Commentary on the Old Testament; with a New Translation. Vol. I. Genesis, 8vo. 18s. or adapted for the General Reader, 12s. Vol. II. Exodus, 15s. or adapted for the General Reader, 12s. Vol. III. Leviticus, Part I. 15s. or adapted for the General Reader, 8s. Vol. IV. Leviticus, Part II. 15s. or adapted for the General Reader, 8s.

KANT. — *Critique of Practical Reason,* and other Works on the Theory of Ethics. By Emmanuel Kant. Translated by Thomas Kingsmill Abbott, B.D. With Memoir and Portrait. 8vo. 12s. 6d.

KEARY.—*Outlines of Primitive Belief among the Indo-European Races.* By Charles F. Keary, M.A. 8vo. 18s.

KELLER.—*The Lake Dwellings of Switzerland,* and other Parts of Europe. By Dr. F. Keller, President of the Antiquarian Association of Zürich. Translated and arranged by John E. Lee, F.S.A. F.G.S. 2 vols. royal 8vo. with 206 Illustrations, 42s.

KERL.—*A Practical Treatise on Metallurgy.* By Professor Kerl. Adapted from the last German Edition by W. Crookes, F.R.S. &c. and E. Röhrig, Ph.D. 3 vols. 8vo. with 625 Woodcuts, £4. 19s.

KILLICK.—*Handbook to Mill's System of Logic.* By the Rev. A. H. Killick, M.A. Crown 8vo. 3s. 6d.

KOLBE.—*A Short Text-book of Inorganic Chemistry.* By Dr. Hermann Kolbe. Translated from the German by T. S. Humpidge, Ph.D. With a Coloured Table of Spectra and 66 Illustrations. Crown 8vo. 7s. 6d.

LANG.—*Works by Andrew Lang,* late Fellow of Merton College.

Custom and Myth; Studies of Early Usage and Belief. With Illustrations. Crown 8vo. 7s. 6d.

The Princess Nobody: a Tale of Fairyland. After the Drawings by Richard Doyle, printed in colours by Edmund Evans. Post 4to. 5s. boards.

LATHAM.—*Works by Robert G. Latham, M.A. M.D.*

A *Dictionary of the English Language.* Founded on the Dictionary of Dr. JOHNSON. Four vols. 4to. £7.

A *Dictionary of the English Language.* Abridged from Dr. Latham's Edition of Johnson's Dictionary. One Volume. Medium 8vo. 14s.

Handbook of the English Language. Crown 8vo. 6s.

LECKY.—*Works by W. E. H. Lecky.*

History of England in the 18th Century. 4 vols. 8vo. 1700-1784, £3. 12s.

The History of European Morals from Augustus to Charlemagne. 2 vols. crown 8vo. 16s.

History of the Rise and Influence of the Spirit of Rationalism in Europe. 2 vols. crown 8vo. 16s.

Leaders of Public Opinion in Ireland. — Swift, Flood, Grattan, O'Connell. Crown 8vo. 7s. 6d.

LESLIE.—*Essays in Political and Moral Philosophy.* By T. E. CLIFFE LESLIE, Barrister-at-Law. 8vo. 10s. 6d.

LEWES.—*The History of Philosophy,* from Thales to Comte. By GEORGE HENRY LEWES. 2 vols. 8vo. 32s.

LEWIS. — *On the Influence of Authority in Matters of Opinion.* By Sir G. C. LEWIS, Bart. 8vo. 14s.

LINDLEY and MOORE. — *The Treasury of Botany,* or Popular Dictionary of the Vegetable Kingdom. Edited by J. LINDLEY, F.R.S. and T. MOORE, F.L.S. With 274 Woodcuts and 20 Steel Plates. Two Parts, fcp. 8vo. 12s.

LITTLE.—*On In-knee Distortion* (Genu Valgum) : Its Varieties and Treatment with and without Surgical Operation. By W. J. LITTLE, M.D. Assisted by MUIRHEAD LITTLE, M.R.C.S. With 40 Illustrations. 8vo. 7s. 6d.

LIVEING.—*Works by Robert Liveing, M.A. and M.D. Cantab.*

Handbook on Diseases of the Skin. With especial reference to Diagnosis and Treatment. Fcp. 8vo. 5s.

Notes on the Treatment of Skin Diseases. 18mo. 3s.

Elephantiasis Græcorum, or True Leprosy. Crown 8vo. 4s. 6d.

LLOYD.—*A Treatise on Magnetism,* General and Terrestrial. By H. LLOYD, D.D. D.C.L. 8vo. 10s. 6d.

LLOYD.—*The Science of Agriculture.* By F. J. LLOYD. 8vo. 12s.

LONGMAN.—*Works by William Longman, F.S.A.*

Lectures on the History of England from the Earliest Times to the Death of King Edward II. Maps and Illustrations. 8vo. 15s.

History of the Life and Times of Edward III. With 9 Maps, 8 Plates, and 16 Woodcuts. 2 vols. 8vo. 28s.

LONGMAN.—*Works by Frederick W. Longman, Balliol College, Oxon.*

Chess Openings. Fcp. 8vo. 2s. 6d.

Frederick the Great and the Seven Years' War. With 2 Coloured Maps. 8vo. 2s. 6d.

A *New Pocket Dictionary of the German and English Languages.* Square 18mo. 5s.

LONGMAN'S MAGAZINE. Published Monthly. Price Sixpence. Vols. 1-4, 8vo. price 5s. each.

LONGMORE.—*Gunshot Injuries;* Their History, Characteristic Features, Complications, and General Treatment. By Surgeon-General T. LONGMORE, C.B. F.R.C.S. With 58 Illustrations. 8vo. price 31s. 6d.

LOUDON.—*Works by J. C. Loudon, F.L.S.*

Encyclopædia of Gardening; the Theory and Practice of Horticulture, Floriculture, Arboriculture, and Landscape Gardening. With 1,000 Woodcuts. 8vo. 21s.

Encyclopædia of Agriculture; the Laying-out, Improvement, and Management of Landed Property; the Cultivation and Economy of the Productions of Agriculture. With 1,100 Woodcuts. 8vo. 21s.

Encyclopædia of Plants; the Specific Character, Description, Culture, History, &c. of all Plants found in Great Britain. With 12,000 Woodcuts. 8vo. 42s.

LUBBOCK.—*The Origin of Civilization and the Primitive Condition of Man.* By Sir J. LUBBOCK, Bart. M.P. F.R.S. 8vo. Woodcuts, 18s.

LYRA GERMANICA; Hymns Translated from the German by Miss C. WINKWORTH. Fcp. 8vo. 5s.

MACALISTER.—*An Introduction to the Systematic Zoology and Morphology of Vertebrate Animals.* By A. MACALISTER, M.D. With 28 Diagrams. 8vo. 10s. 6d.

MACAULAY. — *Works and Life of Lord Macaulay.*

HISTORY OF ENGLAND from the Accession of James the Second:
Student's Edition, 2 vols. crown 8vo. 12s.
People's Edition, 4 vols. crown 8vo. 16s.
Cabinet Edition, 8 vols. post 8vo. 48s.
Library Edition, 5 vols. 8vo. £4.

CRITICAL AND HISTORICAL ESSAYS:
Cheap Edition, 1 vol. crown 8vo. 2s. 6d.
Student's Edition, 1 vol. crown 8vo. 6s.
People's Edition, 2 vols. crown 8vo. 8s.
Cabinet Edition, 4 vols. post 8vo. 24s.
Library Edition, 3 vols. 8vo. 36s.

LAYS OF ANCIENT ROME, &c.
Illustrated by G. Scharf, fcp. 4to. 10s. 6d.
———————— Popular Edition, fcp. 4to. 6d. sewed, 1s. cloth.
Illustrated by J. R. Weguelin, crown 8vo. 3s. 6d. cloth extra, gilt edges.
Cabinet Edition, post 8vo. 3s. 6d.
Annotated Edition, fcp. 8vo. 1s. sewed, 1s. 6d. cloth, or 2s. 6d. cloth extra, gilt edges.

ESSAYS which may be had separately price 6d. each sewed, 1s. each cloth:
Addison and Walpole.
Frederick the Great.
Croker's Boswell's Johnson.
Hallam's Constitutional History.
Warren Hastings.
The Earl of Chatham (Two Essays).
Ranke and Gladstone.
Milton and Machiavelli.
Lord Bacon.
Lord Clive.
Lord Byron, and The Comic Dramatists of the Restoration.

The Essay on Warren Hastings annotated by S. HALES, 1s. 6d.
The Essay on Lord Clive annotated by H. COURTHOPE-BOWEN, M.A. 2s. 6d.

SPEECHES:
People's Edition, crown 8vo. 3s. 6d.

MISCELLANEOUS WRITINGS
Library Edition, 2 vols. 8vo. Portrait, 21s.
People's Edition, 1 vol. crown 8vo. 4s. 6d.

SELECTIONS FROM THE WRITINGS OF LORD MACAULAY. Edited, with Occasional Notes, by the Right Hon. G. O. TREVELYAN, M.P. Crown 8vo. 6s.

[*Continued above.*]

MACAULAY — *Works and Life of Lord Macaulay* —continued.

MISCELLANEOUS WRITINGS AND SPEECHES:
Student's Edition, in ONE VOLUME, crown 8vo. 6s.
Cabinet Edition, including Indian Penal Code, Lays of Ancient Rome, and Miscellaneous Poems, 4 vols. post 8vo. 24s.

THE COMPLETE WORKS OF LORD MACAULAY. Edited by his Sister, Lady TREVELYAN.
Library Edition, with Portrait, 8 vols. demy 8vo. £5. 5s.
Cabinet Edition, 16 vols. post 8vo. £4. 16s.

THE LIFE AND LETTERS OF LORD MACAULAY. By the Right Hon. G. O. TREVELYAN, M.P.
Popular Edition, 1 vol. crown 8vo. 6s.
Cabinet Edition, 2 vols. post 8vo. 12s.
Library Edition, 2 vols. 8vo. with Portrait, 36s.

MACFARREN.—*Lectures on Harmony,* delivered at the Royal Institution. By G. A. MACFARREN. 8vo. 12s.

MACKENZIE.—*On the Use of the Laryngoscope in Diseases of the Throat;* with an Appendix on Rhinoscopy. By MORELL MACKENZIE, M.D. Lond. With 47 Woodcut Illustrations. 8vo. 6s.

MACLEOD.—*Works by Henry D. Macleod, M.A.*

PRINCIPLES OF ECONOMICAL PHILOSOPHY. In 2 vols. Vol. I. 8vo. 15s. Vol. II. PART I. 12s.

THE ELEMENTS OF ECONOMICS. In 2 vols. Vol. I. crown 8vo. 7s. 6d.

THE ELEMENTS OF BANKING. Crown 8vo. 5s.

THE THEORY AND PRACTICE OF BANKING. Vol. I. 8vo. 12s. Vol. II. nearly ready.

ELEMENTS OF POLITICAL ECONOMY. 8vo. 16s.

ECONOMICS FOR BEGINNERS. 8vo. 2s. 6d.

LECTURES ON CREDIT AND BANKING. 8vo. 5s.

MACNAMARA. — *Himalayan and Sub-Himalayan Districts of British India,* their Climate, Medical Topography, and Disease Distribution. By F. N. MACNAMARA, M.D. With Map and Fever Chart. 8vo. 21s.

McCULLOCH. — *THE DICTIONARY OF COMMERCE AND COMMERCIAL NAVIGATION* of the late J. R. McCULLOCH, of H.M. Stationery Office. Latest Edition, containing the most recent Statistical Information by A. J. WILSON. 1 vol. medium 8vo. with 11 Maps and 30 Charts, price 63*s.* cloth, or 70*s.* strongly half-bound in russia.

MAHAFFY. — *A HISTORY OF CLASSICAL GREEK LITERATURE.* By the Rev. J. P. MAHAFFY, M.A. Crown 8vo. Vol. I. Poets, 7*s.* 6*d.* Vol. II. Prose Writers, 7*s.* 6*d.*

MALMESBURY. — *MEMOIRS OF AN EX-MINISTER:* an Autobiography. By the Earl of MALMESBURY, G.C.B. 2 vols. 8vo. 32*s.*

MANNING. — *THE TEMPORAL MISSION OF THE HOLY GHOST;* or, Reason and Revelation. By H. E. MANNING, D.D. Cardinal-Archbishop. Crown 8vo. 8*s.* 6*d.*

MARTINEAU. — *WORKS BY JAMES MARTINEAU, D.D.*

HOURS OF THOUGHT ON SACRED THINGS. Two Volumes of Sermons. 2 vols. crown 8vo. 7*s.* 6*d.* each.

ENDEAVOURS AFTER THE CHRISTIAN LIFE. Discourses. Crown 8vo. 7*s.* 6*d.*

MAUNDER'S TREASURIES.

BIOGRAPHICAL TREASURY. Reconstructed, revised, and brought down to the year 1882, by W. L. R. CATES. Fcp. 8vo. 6*s.*

TREASURY OF NATURAL HISTORY; or, Popular Dictionary of Zoology. Fcp. 8vo. with 900 Woodcuts, 6*s.*

TREASURY OF GEOGRAPHY, Physical, Historical, Descriptive, and Political. With 7 Maps and 16 Plates. Fcp. 8vo. 6*s.*

HISTORICAL TREASURY, Outlines of Universal History, Separate Histories of all Nations. Revised by the Rev. Sir G. W. Cox, Bart. M.A. Fcp. 8vo. 6*s.*

TREASURY OF KNOWLEDGE AND LIBRARY OF REFERENCE. Comprising an English Dictionary and Grammar, Universal Gazetteer, Classical Dictionary, Chronology, Law Dictionary, &c. Fcp. 8vo. 6*s.*

SCIENTIFIC AND LITERARY TREASURY: a Popular Encyclopædia of Science, Literature, and Art. Fcp. 8vo. 6*s.*

MAXWELL. — *DON JOHN OF AUSTRIA;* or, Passages from the History of the Sixteenth Century, 1547-1578. By the late Sir WILLIAM STIRLING MAXWELL, Bart. K.T. With numerous Illustrations engraved on Wood taken from Authentic Contemporary Sources. Library Edition. 2 vols. royal 8vo. 42*s.*

MAY. — *WORKS BY THE RIGHT HON. SIR THOMAS ERSKINE MAY, K.C.B.*

THE CONSTITUTIONAL HISTORY OF ENGLAND SINCE THE ACCESSION OF GEORGE III. 1760-1870. 3 vols. crown 8vo. 18*s.*

DEMOCRACY IN EUROPE; a History. 2 vols. 8vo. 32*s.*

MENDELSSOHN. — *THE LETTERS OF FELIX MENDELSSOHN.* Translated by Lady WALLACE. 2 vols. crown 8vo. 10*s.*

MERIVALE. — *WORKS BY THE VERY REV. CHARLES MERIVALE, D.D. Dean of Ely.*

HISTORY OF THE ROMANS UNDER THE EMPIRE. 8 vols. post 8vo. 48*s.*

THE FALL OF THE ROMAN REPUBLIC: a Short History of the Last Century of the Commonwealth. 12mo. 7*s.* 6*d.*

GENERAL HISTORY OF ROME FROM B.C. 753 TO A.D. 476. Crown 8vo. 7*s.* 6*d.*

THE ROMAN TRIUMVIRATES. With Maps. Fcp. 8vo. 2*s.* 6*d.*

MILES. — *WORKS BY WILLIAM MILES.*

THE HORSE'S FOOT, AND HOW TO KEEP IT SOUND. Imp. 8vo. 12*s.* 6*d.*

STABLES AND STABLE FITTINGS. Imp. 8vo. with 13 Plates, 15*s.*

REMARKS ON HORSES' TEETH, addressed to Purchasers. Post 8vo. 1*s.* 6*d.*

PLAIN TREATISE ON HORSE-SHOEING. Post 8vo. Woodcuts, 2*s.* 6*d.*

MILL. — *ANALYSIS OF THE PHENOMENA OF THE HUMAN MIND.* By JAMES MILL. With Notes, Illustrative and Critical. 2 vols. 8vo. 28*s.*

MILL. — *WORKS BY JOHN STUART MILL.*

PRINCIPLES OF POLITICAL ECONOMY. Library Edition, 2 vols. 8vo. 30*s.* People's Edition, 1 vol. crown 8vo. 5*s.*

[*Continued on next page.*

MILL.— *WORKS BY JOHN STUART MILL*—continued.

A SYSTEM OF LOGIC, Ratiocinative and Inductive.
Library Edition, 2 vols. 8vo. 25s.
People's Edition, crown 8vo. 5s.

ON LIBERTY. Crown 8vo. 1s. 4d.

ON REPRESENTATIVE GOVERNMENT. Crown 8vo. 2s.

AUTOBIOGRAPHY, 8vo. 7s. 6d.

ESSAYS ON SOME UNSETTLED QUESTIONS OF POLITICAL ECONOMY. 8vo. 6s. 6d.

UTILITARIANISM. 8vo. 5s.

THE SUBJECTION OF WOMEN. Crown 8vo. 6s.

EXAMINATION OF SIR WILLIAM HAMILTON'S PHILOSOPHY. 8vo. 16s.

DISSERTATIONS AND DISCUSSIONS. 4 vols. 8vo. £2. 6s. 6d.

NATURE, THE UTILITY OF RELIGION, AND THEISM. Three Essays. 8vo. 10s. 6d.

MILLER.— *WORKS BY W. ALLEN MILLER, M.D. LL.D.*

THE ELEMENTS OF CHEMISTRY, Theoretical and Practical Re-edited, with Additions, by H. MACLEOD, F.C.S. 3 vols. 8vo.
Part I. CHEMICAL PHYSICS, 16s.
Part II. INORGANIC CHEMISTY, 24s.
Part III. ORGANIC CHEMISTRY, 31s. 6d.

AN INTRODUCTION TO THE STUDY OF INORGANIC CHEMISTRY. With 71 Woodcuts. Fcp. 8vo. 3s. 6d.

MILLER. — *READINGS IN SOCIAL ECONOMY.* By Mrs. F. FENWICK MILLER, Member of the London School Board. Library Edition, crown 8vo. 5s. Cheap Edition for Schools and Beginners, crown 8vo. 2s.

MILLER.— *WINTERING IN THE RIVIERA;* with Notes of Travel in Italy and France, and Practical Hints to Travellers. By W. MILLER. With 12 Illustrations. Post 8vo. 7s. 6d.

MILNER. — *COUNTRY PLEASURES;* the Chronicle of a Year, chiefly in a Garden. By GEORGE MILNER. With Vignette. Crown 8vo. 6s.

MITCHELL.— *A MANUAL OF PRACTICAL ASSAYING.* By JOHN MITCHELL, F.C.S. Revised, with the Recent Discoveries incorporated. By W. CROOKES, F.R.S. 8vo. Woodcuts, 31s. 6d.

MODERN NOVELIST'S LIBRARY (THE). Price 2s. each boards, or 2s. 6d. each cloth :—

By the Earl of BEACONSFIELD, K.G.
Endymion.

Lothair.	Henrietta Temple.
Coningsby.	Contarini Fleming, &c.
Sybil.	Alroy, Ixion, &c.
Tancred.	The Young Duke, &c.
Venetia.	Vivian Grey, &c.

By Mrs. OLIPHANT.
In Trust.

By BRET HARTE.
In the Carquinez Woods.

By ANTHONY TROLLOPE.
Barchester Towers.
The Warden.

By Major WHYTE-MELVILLE.

Digby Grand	Good for Nothing.
General Bounce.	Holmby House.
Kate Coventry.	The Interpreter.
The Gladiators.	Queen's Maries.

By Various Writers.
The Atelier du Lys.
Atherstone Priory.
The Burgomaster's Family.
Elsa and her Vulture.
Mademoiselle Mori.
The Six Sisters of the Valleys.
Unawares.

MONCK. — *AN INTRODUCTION TO LOGIC.* By WILLIAM H. STANLEY MONCK, M.A. Prof. of Moral Philos. Univ. of Dublin. Crown 8vo. 5s.

MONSELL.— *SPIRITUAL SONGS FOR THE SUNDAYS AND HOLIDAYS THROUGHOUT THE YEAR.* By J. S. B. MONSELL, LL.D. Fcp. 8vo. 5s. 18mo. 2s.

MOORE.— *THE WORKS OF THOMAS MOORE.*

LALLA ROOKH, TENNIEL'S Edition, with 68 Woodcut Illustrations. Crown 8vo. 10s. 6d.

IRISH MELODIES, MACLISE'S Edition, with 161 Steel Plates. Super-royal 8vo. 21s.

MOREHEAD.—*CLINICAL RESEARCHES ON DISEASE IN INDIA.* By CHARLES MOREHEAD, M.D. Surgeon to the Jamsetjee Jeejeebhoy Hospital. 8vo. 21s.

MORELL. — *HANDBOOK OF LOGIC*, adapted especially for the Use of Schools and Teachers. By J. D. MORELL, LL.D. Fcp. 8vo. 2s.

MOZLEY.—*REMINISCENCES CHIEFLY OF ORIEL COLLEGE AND THE OXFORD MOVEMENT.* By the Rev. THOMAS MOZLEY, M.A. 2 vols. crown 8vo. 18s.

MÜLLER. — *WORKS BY F. MAX MÜLLER, M.A.*

BIOGRAPHICAL ESSAYS. Crown 8vo. 7*s.* 6*d.*

SELECTED ESSAYS ON LANGUAGE, MYTHOLOGY AND RELIGION. 2 vols. crown 8vo. 16*s.*

LECTURES ON THE SCIENCE OF LANGUAGE. 2 vols. crown 8vo. 16*s.*

INDIA, WHAT CAN IT TEACH US? A Course of Lectures delivered before the University of Cambridge. 8vo. 12*s.* 6*d.*

HIBBERT LECTURES ON THE ORIGIN AND GROWTH OF RELIGION, as illustrated by the Religions of India. Crown 8vo. 7*s.* 6*d.*

INTRODUCTION TO THE SCIENCE OF RELIGION: Four Lectures delivered at the Royal Institution ; with Notes and Illustrations on Vedic Literature, Polynesian Mythology, the Sacred Books of the East, &c. Crown 8vo. 7*s.* 6*d.*

A SANSKRIT GRAMMAR FOR BEGINNERS, in Devanagari and Roman Letters throughout. Royal 8vo. 7*s.* 6*d.*

MURCHISON. — *WORKS BY CHARLES MURCHISON, M.D. LL.D. F.R.C.S. &c.*

A TREATISE ON THE CONTINUED FEVERS OF GREAT BRITAIN. New Edition, revised by W. CAYLEY, M.D. Physician to the Middlesex Hospital. 8vo. with numerous Illustrations, 25*s.*

CLINICAL LECTURES ON DISEASES OF THE LIVER, JAUNDICE, AND ABDOMINAL DROPSY. New Edition, revised by T. LAUDER BRUNTON, M.D. 8vo. with numerous Illustrations.
[*In preparation.*

NEISON. — *THE MOON,* and the Condition and Configurations of its Surface. By E. NEISON, F.R.A.S. With 26 Maps and 5 Plates. Medium 8vo. 31*s.* 6*d.*

NEVILE. — *WORKS BY GEORGE NEVILE, M.A.*

HORSES AND RIDING. With 31 Illustrations. Crown 8vo. 6*s.*

FARMS AND FARMING. With 13 Illustrations. Crown 8vo. 6*s.*

NEWMAN. — *APOLOGIA PRO VITÂ SUÂ;* being a History of his Religious Opinions by Cardinal NEWMAN. Crown 8vo. 6*s.*

NEW TESTAMENT (THE) of our Lord and Saviour Jesus Christ. Illustrated with Engravings on Wood after Paintings by the Early Masters chiefly of the Italian School. New and Cheaper Edition. 4to. 21*s.* cloth extra, or 42*s.* morocco.

NORTHCOTT. — *LATHES AND TURNING,* Simple, Mechanical, and Ornamental. By W. H. NORTHCOTT. With 338 Illustrations. 8vo. 18*s.*

OWEN. — *WORKS BY SIR RICHARD OWEN, K.C.B. &c.*

THE COMPARATIVE ANATOMY AND PHYSIOLOGY OF THE VERTEBRATE ANIMALS. With 1,472 Woodcuts. 3 vols. 8vo. £3. 13*s.* 6*d.*

EXPERIMENTAL PHYSIOLOGY, ITS BENEFITS TO MANKIND; with an Address on Unveiling the Statue of William Harvey at Folkestone, August 1881. Crown 8vo. 5*s.*

PAGET. — *WORKS BY SIR JAMES PAGET, BART. F.R.S. D.C.L. &c.*

CLINICAL LECTURES AND ESSAYS. Edited by F. HOWARD MARSH, Assistant-Surgeon to St. Bartholomew's Hospital. 8vo. 15*s.*

LECTURES ON SURGICAL PATHOLOGY. Delivered at the Royal College of Surgeons of England. Re-edited by the AUTHOR and W. TURNER, M.B. 8vo. with 131 Woodcuts, 21*s.*

PALEY. — *VIEW OF THE EVIDENCES OF CHRISTIANITY AND HORAE PAULINAE.* By Archdeacon PALEY. With Notes and an Analysis, and a Selection of Questions. By ROBERT POTTS, M.A. 8vo. 10*s.* 6*d.*

PASTEUR. — *LOUIS PASTEUR,* his Life and Labours. By his SON-IN-LAW. Translated from the French by Lady CLAUD HAMILTON. Crown 8vo. 7*s.* 6*d.*

PAYEN. — *INDUSTRIAL CHEMISTRY;* a Manual for Manufacturers and for Colleges or Technical Schools ; a Translation of PAYEN'S 'Précis de Chimie Industrielle.' Edited by B. H. PAUL. With 698 Woodcuts. Medium 8vo. 42*s.*

PAYN. — *THICKER THAN WATER.* A Novel. By JAMES PAYN, Author of 'Lost Sir Massingberd' &c. Crown 8vo. 6*s.*

PENNELL. — *'FROM GRAVE TO GAY':* a Volume of Selections from the complete Poems of H. CHOLMONDELEY-PENNELL, Author of 'Puck on Pegasus' &c. Fcp. 8vo. 6*s.*

PEREIRA. — *MATERIA MEDICA AND THERAPEUTICS.* By Dr. PEREIRA. Abridged, and adapted for the use of Medical and Pharmaceutical Practitioners and Students. Edited by Professor R. BENTLEY, M.R.C.S. F.L.S. and by Professor T. REDWOOD, Ph.D. F.C.S. With 126 Woodcuts, 8vo. 25*s.*

PERRY. — *A Popular Introduction to the History of Greek and Roman Sculpture*, designed to Promote the Knowledge and Appreciation of the Remains of Ancient Art. By WALTER C. PERRY. With 268 Illustrations. Square crown 8vo. 31s. 6d.

PIESSE. — *The Art of Perfumery*, and the Methods of Obtaining the Odours of Plants; with Instructions for the Manufacture of Perfumes, &c. By G. W. S. PIESSE, Ph.D. F.C.S. With 96 Woodcuts, square crown 8vo. 21s.

PLATO. — *The Parmenides of Plato*; with Introduction, Analysis, and Notes. By THOMAS MAGUIRE, LL.D. D.Lit. Fellow and Tutor, Trinity College, Dublin. 8vo. 7s. 6d.

POLE. — *The Theory of the Modern Scientific Game of Whist.* By W. POLE, F.R.S. Fcp. 8vo. 2s. 6d.

PROCTOR. — *Works by R. A. Proctor.*

The Sun; Ruler, Light, Fire, and Life of the Planetary System. With Plates and Woodcuts. Crown 8vo. 14s.

The Orbs Around Us; a Series of Essays on the Moon and Planets, Meteors and Comets, the Sun and Coloured Pairs of Suns. With Chart and Diagrams, crown 8vo. 7s. 6d.

Other Worlds than Ours; The Plurality of Worlds Studied under the Light of Recent Scientific Researches. With 14 Illustrations, crown 8vo. 10s. 6d.

The Moon; her Motions, Aspects, Scenery, and Physical Condition. With Plates, Charts, Woodcuts, and Lunar Photographs, crown 8vo. 10s. 6d.

Universe of Stars; Presenting Researches into and New Views respecting the Constitution of the Heavens. With 22 Charts and 22 Diagrams, 8vo. 10s. 6d.

New Star Atlas for the Library, the School, and the Observatory, in 12 Circular Maps (with 2 Index Plates). Crown 8vo. 5s.

Larger Star Atlas for the Library, in 12 Circular Maps, with Introduction and 2 Index Pages. Folio, 15s. or Maps only, 12s. 6d.

Light Science for Leisure Hours; Familiar Essays on Scientific Subjects, Natural Phenomena, &c. 3 vols. crown 8vo. 7s. 6d. each.

[*Continued above.*]

PROCTOR — *Works by R. A. Proctor* continued.

Studies of Venus-Transits; an Investigation of the Circumstances of the Transits of Venus in 1874 and 1882. With 7 Diagrams and 10 Plates. 8vo. 5s.

Transits of Venus. A Popular Account of Past and Coming Transits from the First Observed by Horrocks in 1639 to the Transit of 2012. With 20 Lithographic Plates (12 Coloured) and 38 Illustrations engraved on Wood, 8vo. 8s. 6d.

Essays on Astronomy. A Series of Papers on Planets and Meteors, the Sun and Sun-surrounding Space, Stars and Star Cloudlets. With 10 Plates and 24 Woodcuts, 8vo. 12s.

A Treatise on the Cycloid and on all Forms of Cycloidal Curves, and on the use of Cycloidal Curves in dealing with the Motions of Planets, Comets, &c. and of Matter projected from the Sun. With 161 Diagrams. Crown 8vo. 10s. 6d.

Pleasant Ways in Science, with numerous Illustrations. Crown 8vo. 6s.

Myths and Marvels of Astronomy, with numerous Illustrations. Crown 8vo. 6s.

THE 'KNOWLEDGE' LIBRARY. Edited by RICHARD A. PROCTOR.

Science Byways. A Series of Familiar Dissertations on Life in Other Worlds. By RICHARD A. PROCTOR. Crown 8vo. 6s.

The Poetry of Astronomy. A Series of Familiar Essays on the Heavenly Bodies. By RICHARD A. PROCTOR. Crown 8vo. 6s.

Nature Studies. Reprinted from *Knowledge.* By GRANT ALLEN, ANDREW WILSON, THOMAS FOSTER, EDWARD CLODD, and RICHARD A. PROCTOR. Crown 8vo. 6s.

Leisure Readings. Reprinted from *Knowledge.* By EDWARD CLODD, ANDREW WILSON, THOMAS FOSTER, A. C. RUNYARD, and RICHARD A. PROCTOR. Crown 8vo. 6s.

The Stars in their Seasons. An Easy Guide to a Knowledge of the Star Groups, in Twelve Large Maps. By RICHARD A. PROCTOR. Imperial 8vo. 5s.

QUAIN'S ELEMENTS of ANATOMY. The Ninth Edition. Re-edited by ALLEN THOMSON, M.D. LL.D. F.R.S.S. L. & E. EDWARD ALBERT SCHÄFER, F.R.S. and GEORGE DANCER THANE. With upwards of 1,000 Illustrations engraved on Wood, of which many are Coloured. 2 vols. 8vo. 18s. each.

QUAIN.—*A DICTIONARY OF MEDICINE.* Including General Pathology, General Therapeutics, Hygiene, and the Diseases peculiar to Women and Children. By Various Writers. Edited by R. QUAIN, M.D. F.R.S. &c. With 138 Woodcuts. Medium 8vo. 31s. 6d. cloth, or 40s. half-russia ; to be had also in 2 vols. 34s. cloth.

RAWLINSON. — *THE SEVENTH GREAT ORIENTAL MONARCHY;* or, a History of the Sassanians. By G. RAWLINSON, M.A. With Map and 95 Illustrations. 8vo. 28s.

READER.—*VOICES FROM FLOWER-LAND,* in Original Couplets. By EMILY E. READER. A Birthday-Book and Language of Flowers. 16mo. 2s. 6d. limp cloth ; 3s. 6d. roan, gilt edges.

REEVE. — *COOKERY AND HOUSE-KEEPING;* a Manual of Domestic Economy for Large and Small Families. By Mrs. HENRY REEVE. With 8 Coloured Plates and 37 Woodcuts. Crown 8vo. 7s. 6d.

RICH.—*A DICTIONARY OF ROMAN AND GREEK ANTIQUITIES.* With 2,000 Woodcuts. By A. RICH, B.A. Crown 8vo. 7s. 6d.

RIVERS. — *WORKS BY THOMAS RIVERS.*

THE ORCHARD-HOUSE; or, the Cultivation of Fruit Trees under Glass. Crown 8vo. with 25 Woodcuts, 5s.

THE ROSE AMATEUR'S GUIDE. Fcp. 8vo. 4s. 6d.

ROGERS. — *WORKS BY HENRY ROGERS.*

THE ECLIPSE OF FAITH; or, a Visit to a Religious Sceptic. Fcp. 8vo. 5s.

DEFENCE OF THE ECLIPSE OF FAITH. Fcp. 8vo. 3s. 6d.

ROGET.—*THESAURUS OF ENGLISH WORDS AND PHRASES,* classified and arranged so as to facilitate the expression of Ideas, and assist in Literary Composition. By PETER M. ROGET, M.D. Crown 8vo. 10s. 6d.

RONALDS. — *THE FLY-FISHER'S ENTOMOLOGY.* By ALFRED RONALDS. With 20 Coloured Plates. 8vo. 14s.

SALTER.—*DENTAL PATHOLOGY AND SURGERY.* By S. J. A. SALTER, M.B. F.R.S. With 133 Illustrations. 8vo. 18s.

SCOTT.—*WORKS BY JOHN SCOTT.*

RENTS AND PURCHASES; or, the Valuation of Landed Property, Woods, Minerals, Buildings, &c. Crown 8vo. 6s.

THE FARM-VALUER. Crown 8vo. 5s.

SEEBOHM.—*WORKS BY FREDERICK SEEBOHM.*

THE OXFORD REFORMERS—JOHN COLET, ERASMUS, AND THOMAS MORE; a History of their Fellow-Work. 8vo. 14s.

THE ENGLISH VILLAGE COMMUNITY Examined in its Relations to the Manorial and Tribal Systems, and to the Common or Openfield System of Husbandry. 13 Maps and Plates. 8vo. 16s.

THE ERA OF THE PROTESTANT REVOLUTION. With Map. Fcp. 8vo. 2s. 6d.

SENNETT.—*THE MARINE STEAM ENGINE;* a Treatise for the use of Engineering Students and Officers of the Royal Navy. By RICHARD SENNETT, Chief Engineer, Royal Navy. With 244 Illustrations. 8vo. 21s.

SEWELL.—*WORKS BY ELIZABETH M. SEWELL.*

STORIES AND TALES. Cabinet Edition, in Eleven Volumes, crown 8vo. 3s. 6d. each, in cloth extra, with gilt edges :—

> Amy Herbert. Gertrude.
> The Earl's Daughter.
> The Experience of Life.
> A Glimpse of the World.
> Cleve Hall. Ivors.
> Katharine Ashton.
> Margaret Percival.
> Laneton Parsonage. Ursula.

PASSING THOUGHTS ON RELIGION. Fcp. 8vo. 3s. 6d.

PREPARATION FOR THE HOLY COMMUNION; the Devotions chiefly from the works of JEREMY TAYLOR. 32mo. 3s.

NIGHT LESSONS FROM SCRIPTURE. 32mo. 3s. 6d.

SEYMOUR.—*THE PSALMS OF DAVID;* a new Metrical English Translation of the Hebrew Psalter or Book of Praises. By WILLIAM DIGBY SEYMOUR, Q.C. LL.D. Crown 8vo. 2s. 6d.

SHORT.—*SKETCH OF THE HISTORY OF THE CHURCH OF ENGLAND TO THE REVOLUTION OF 1688.* By T. V. SHORT, D.D. Crown 8vo. 7s. 6d,

SHAKESPEARE.—*BOWDLER'S FA-MILY SHAKESPEARE*. Genuine Edition, in 1 vol. medium 8vo. large type, with 36 Woodcuts, 14*s*. or in 6 vols. fcp. 8vo. 21*s*.

OUTLINES OF THE LIFE OF SHAKE-SPEARE. By J. O. HALLIWELL-PHIL-LIPPS, F.R.S. 8vo. 7*s*. 6*d*.

SIMCOX.—*A HISTORY OF LATIN LITERATURE*. By G. A. SIMCOX, M.A. Fellow of Queen's College, Oxford. 2 vols. 8vo. 32*s*.

SKOBELEFF AND THE SLAVONIC CAUSE. By O. K. Honorary Member of the Benevolent Slavonic Society. 8vo. with Portrait, 14*s*.

SMITH, Rev. SYDNEY.—*THE WIT AND WISDOM OF THE REV. SYDNEY SMITH*. Crown 8vo. 3*s*. 6*d*.

SMITH, R. BOSWORTH. — *CAR-THAGE AND THE CARTHAGINIANS*. By R. BOSWORTH SMITH, M.A. Maps, Plans, &c. Crown 8vo. 10*s*. 6*d*.

SMITH, R. A.—*AIR AND RAIN;* the Beginnings of a Chemical Climatology. By R. A. SMITH, F.R.S. 8vo. 24*s*.

SMITH, JAMES.—*THE VOYAGE AND SHIPWRECK OF ST. PAUL*. By JAMES SMITH, of Jordanhill. With Dissertations on the Life and Writings of St. Luke, and the Ships and Navigation of the Ancients. With numerous Illustrations. Crown 8vo. 7*s*. 6*d*.

SMITH, T.—*A MANUAL OF OPERA-TIVE SURGERY ON THE DEAD BODY*. By THOMAS SMITH, Surgeon to St. Bartholomew's Hospital. A New Edition, re-edited by W. J. WALSHAM. With 46 Illustrations. 8vo. 12*s*.

SMITH, H. F.—*THE HANDBOOK FOR MIDWIVES*. By HENRY FLY SMITH, M.B. Oxon. M.R.C.S. late Assistant-Surgeon at the Hospital for Sick Women, Soho Square. With 41 Woodcuts. Crown 8vo. 5*s*.

SOPHOCLES.—*SOPHOCLIS TRAGŒ-DIÆ* superstites ; recensuit et brevi Anno-tatione instruxit GULIELMUS LINWOOD, M.A. Ædis Christi apud Oxonienses nuper Alumnus. Editio Quarta, auctior et emendatior. 8vo. 16*s*.

THE THEBAN TRILOGY OF SOPHO-CLES; Oedipus Rex, Oedipus Coloneus, Antigone: Greek Text, with copious Explanatory English Notes. By the Rev. W. LINWOOD, M.A. Crown 8vo. 7*s*. 6*d*.

SOUTHEY.—*THE POETICAL WORKS OF ROBERT SOUTHEY*, with the Author's last Corrections and Additions. Medium 8vo. with Portrait, 14*s*.

THE CORRESPONDENCE OF ROBERT SOUTHEY WITH CAROLINE BOWLES. Edited by EDWARD DOWDEN, LL.D. 8vo. Portrait, 14*s*.

STANLEY.—*A FAMILIAR HISTORY OF BIRDS*. By E. STANLEY, D.D Revised and enlarged, with 160 Wood-cuts. Crown 8vo. 6*s*.

STEEL.—*A TREATISE ON THE DIS-EASES OF THE OX;* being a Manual of Bovine Pathology specially adapted for the use of Veterinary Practitioners and Students. By J. H. STEEL, M.R.C.V.S. F.Z.S. With 2 Plates and 116 Wood-cuts. 8vo. 15*s*.

STEPHEN.—*ESSAYS IN ECCLESIAS-TICAL BIOGRAPHY*. By the Right Hon. Sir J. STEPHEN, LL.D. Crown 8vo. 7*s*. 6*d*.

'STONEHENGE.'—*THE DOG IN HEALTH AND DISEASE*. By 'STONE-HENGE.' With 78 Wood Engravings. Square crown 8vo. 7*s*. 6*d*.

THE GREYHOUND. By 'STONEHENGE.' With 25 Portraits of Greyhounds, &c. Square crown 8vo. 15*s*.

STURGIS.—*MY FRIENDS AND I.* By JULIAN STURGIS. With Frontispiece. Crown 8vo. 5*s*.

SULLIVAN.—*'STRAY SHOTS;'* Politi-cal, Military, Economical, and Social. By Sir EDWARD SULLIVAN, Bart. 8vo. 10*s*. 6*d*.

SULLY.—*OUTLINES OF PSYCHOLOGY*, with Special Reference to the Theory of Education. By JAMES SULLY, M.A. 8vo. 12*s*. 6*d*.

SUPERNATURAL RELIGION; an Inquiry into the Reality of Divine Reve-lation. Complete Edition, thoroughly revised. 3 vols. 8vo. 36*s*.

SWINBURNE.—*PICTURE LOGIC;* an Attempt to Popularise the Science of Reasoning. By A. J. SWINBURNE, B.A. Post 8vo. 5*s*.

SWINTON.—*THE PRINCIPLES AND PRACTICE OF ELECTRIC LIGHTING*. By ALAN A. CAMPBELL SWINTON. With 54 Illustrations engraved on Wood Crown 8vo. 5*s*.

TAYLOR.—*Student's Manual of the History of India*, from the Earliest Period to the Present Time. By Colonel MEADOWS TAYLOR, C.S.I. Crown 8vo. 7s. 6d.

TAYLOR.—*The Complete Works of Bishop Jeremy Taylor*. With Life by Bishop Heber. Revised and corrected by the Rev. C. P. EDEN. 10 vols. £5. 5s.

TEXT-BOOKS OF SCIENCE: a Series of Elementary Works on Science, Mechanical and Physical, forming a Series of Text-books of Science, adapted for the use of Students in Public and Science Schools. Fcp. 8vo. fully illustrated with Woodcuts.

Abney's Photography, 3s. 6d.
Anderson's Strength of Materials, 3s. 6d.
Armstrong's Organic Chemistry, 3s. 6d.
Ball's Elements of Astronomy, 6s.
Barry's Railway Appliances, 3s. 6d.
Bauerman's Systematic Mineralogy, 6s.
—————— Descriptive Mineralogy, 6s.
Bloxam and Huntington's Metals, 5s.
Glazebrook's Physical Optics, 6s.
Gore's Electro-Metallurgy, 6s.
Griffin's Algebra and Trigonometry, 3s. 6d.
Jenkin's Electricity and Magnetism, 3s. 6d.
Maxwell's Theory of Heat, 3s. 6d.
Merrifield's Technical Arithmetic, 3s. 6d.
Miller's Inorganic Chemistry, 3s. 6d.
Preece and Sivewright's Telegraphy, 5s.
Rutley's Petrology, or Study of Rocks, 4s. 6d.
Shelley's Workshop Appliances, 4s. 6d.
Thomé's Structural and Physiological Botany, 6s.
Thorpe's Quantitative Analysis, 4s. 6d.
Thorpe and Muir's Qualitative Analysis, 3s. 6d.
Tilden's Chemical Philosophy, 3s. 6d. With Answers to Problems, 4s. 6d.
Unwin's Machine Design, 6s.
Watson's Plane and Solid Geometry, 3s. 6d.

THOMSON.—*An Outline of the Necessary Laws of Thought*; a Treatise on Pure and Applied Logic. By W. THOMSON, D.D. Archbishop of York. Crown 8vo. 6s.

THOMSON'S CONSPECTUS *Adapted to the British Pharmacopœia*. By EDMUND LLOYD BIRKETT, M.D. &c. Latest Edition. 18mo. 6s.

THREE IN NORWAY. By Two of THEM. With a Map and 59 Illustrations on Wood from Sketches by the Authors. Crown 8vo. 6s.

TREVELYAN. — *Works by the Right Hon. G. O. Trevelyan, M.P.*

The Life and Letters of Lord Macaulay. By the Right Hon. G. O. TREVELYAN, M.P.
LIBRARY EDITION, 2 vols. 8vo. 36s.
CABINET EDITION, 2 vols. crown 8vo. 12s.
POPULAR EDITION, 1 vol. crown 8vo. 6s.

The Early History of Charles James Fox. Library Edition, 8vo. 18s. Cabinet Edition, crown 8vo. 6s.

TWISS.—*Works by Sir Travers Twiss.*

The Rights and Duties of Nations, considered as Independent Communities in Time of War. 8vo. 21s.

On the Rights and Duties of Nations in Time of Peace. 8vo. 15s.

TYNDALL.—*Works by John Tyndall, F.R.S. &c.*

Fragments of Science. 2 vols. crown 8vo. 16s.

Heat a Mode of Motion. Crown 8vo. 12s.

Sound. With 204 Woodcuts. Crown 8vo. 10s. 6d.

Essays on the Floating-Matter of the Air in relation to Putrefaction and Infection. With 24 Woodcuts. Crown 8vo. 7s. 6d.

Lectures on Light, delivered in America in 1872 and 1873. With Portrait, Plate, and Diagrams. Crown 8vo. 7s. 6d.

Lessons in Electricity at the Royal Institution, 1875-76. With 58 Woodcuts. Crown 8vo. 2s. 6d.

Notes of a Course of Seven Lectures on Electrical Phenomena and Theories, delivered at the Royal Institution. Crown 8vo. 1s. sewed 1s. 6d. cloth.

Notes of a Course of Nine Lectures on Light, delivered at the Royal Institution. Crown 8vo. 1s. sewed, 1s. 6d. cloth.

Faraday as a Discoverer. Fcp. 8vo. 3s. 6d.

URE.—*A Dictionary of Arts, Manufactures, and Mines.* By Dr. URE. Seventh Edition, re-written and enlarged by R. HUNT, F.R.S. With 2,064 Woodcuts. 4 vols. medium 8vo. £7. 7s.

VILLE.—*On Artificial Manures,* their Chemical Selection and Scientific Application to Agriculture. By GEORGES VILLE. Translated and edited by W. CROOKES, F.R.S. With 31 Plates. 8vo. 21s.

VIRGIL.—*Publi Vergili Maronis Bucolica, Georgica, Æneis;* the Works of VIRGIL, Latin Text, with English Commentary and Index. By B. H. KENNEDY, D.D. Crown 8vo. 10s. 6d.

The Æneid of Virgil. Translated into English Verse. By J. CONINGTON, M.A. Crown 8vo. 9s.

The Poems of Virgil. Translated into English Prose. By JOHN CONINGTON, M.A. Crown 8vo. 9s.

WALKER.—*The Correct Card;* or, How to Play at Whist; a Whist Catechism. By Major A. CAMPBELL-WALKER, F.R.G.S. Fcp. 8vo. 2s. 6d.

WALPOLE.—*History of England from the Conclusion of the Great War in 1815 to the Year 1841.* By SPENCER WALPOLE. 3 vols. 8vo. £2. 14s.

WATSON.—*Lectures on the Principles and Practice of Physic,* delivered at King's College, London, by Sir THOMAS WATSON, Bart. M.D. With Two Plates. 2 vols. 8vo. 36s.

WATTS.—*A Dictionary of Chemistry and the Allied Branches of other Sciences.* Edited by HENRY WATTS, F.R.S. 9 vols. medium 8vo. £15. 2s. 6d.

WEBB.—*Celestial Objects for Common Telescopes.* By the Rev. T. W. WEBB, M.A. Map, Plate, Woodcuts. Crown 8vo. 9s.

WELLINGTON.—*Life of the Duke of Wellington.* By the Rev. G. R. GLEIG, M.A. Crown 8vo. Portrait, 6s.

WEST.—*Lectures on the Diseases of Infancy and Childhood.* By CHARLES WEST, M.D. &c. Founder of, and formerly Physician to, the Hospital for Sick Children. 8vo. 18s.

WHATELY.—*English Synonyms.* By E. JANE WHATELY. Edited by her Father, R. WHATELY, D.D. Fcp. 8vo. 3s.

WHATELY.—*Works by R. Whately, D.D.*

Elements of Logic. 8vo. 10s. 6d. Crown 8vo. 4s. 6d.

Elements of Rhetoric. 8vo. 10s. 6d. Crown 8vo. 4s. 6d.

Lessons on Reasoning. Fcp. 8vo. 1s. 6d.

Bacon's Essays, with Annotations. 8vo. 10s. 6d.

WHITE.—*A Concise Latin-English Dictionary,* for the Use of Advanced Scholars and University Students. By the Rev. J. T. WHITE, D.D. Royal 8vo. 12s.

WHITE & RIDDLE.—*A Latin-English Dictionary.* By J. T. WHITE, D.D. Oxon. and J. E. RIDDLE, M.A. Oxon. Founded on the larger Dictionary of Freund. Royal 8vo. 21s.

WILCOCKS.—*The Sea Fisherman.* Comprising the Chief Methods of Hook and Line Fishing in the British and other Seas, and Remarks on Nets, Boats, and Boating. By J. C. WILCOCKS. Profusely Illustrated. New and Cheaper Edition, much enlarged, crown 8vo. 6s.

WILLICH.—*Popular Tables* for giving Information for ascertaining the value of Lifehold, Leasehold, and Church Property, the Public Funds, &c. By CHARLES M. WILLICH. Edited by MONTAGU MARRIOTT. Crown 8vo. 10s.

WITT.—*Works by Prof. Witt,* Head Master of the Alstadt Gymnasium, Königsberg. Translated from the German by FRANCES YOUNGHUSBAND.

The Trojan War. With a Preface by the Rev. W. G. RUTHERFORD, M.A. Head-Master of Westminster School. Crown 8vo. 2s.

Myths of Hellas; or, Greek Tales. Crown 8vo. 3s. 6d.

WOOD.—*WORKS BY REV. J. G. WOOD.*

HOMES WITHOUT HANDS; a Description of the Habitations of Animals, classed according to the Principle of Construction. With about 140 Vignettes on Wood. 8vo. 10s. 6d.

INSECTS AT HOME; a Popular Account of British Insects, their Structure, Habits, and Transformations. 8vo. Woodcuts, 10s. 6d.

INSECTS ABROAD; a Popular Account of Foreign Insects, their Structure, Habits, and Transformations. 8vo. Woodcuts, 10s. 6d.

BIBLE ANIMALS; a Description of every Living Creature mentioned in the Scriptures. With 112 Vignettes. 8vo. 10s. 6d.

STRANGE DWELLINGS; a Description of the Habitations of Animals, abridged from 'Homes without Hands.' With Frontispiece and 60 Woodcuts. Crown 8vo. 5s. Popular Edition, 4to. 6d.

OUT OF DOORS; a Selection of Original Articles on Practical Natural History. With 6 Illustrations. Crown 8vo. 5s.

COMMON BRITISH INSECTS: BEETLES, MOTHS, AND BUTTERFLIES. Crown 8vo. with 130 Woodcuts, 3s. 6d.

PETLAND REVISITED. With numerous Illustrations, drawn specially by Miss Margery May, engraved on Wood by G. Pearson. Crown 8vo. 7s. 6d.

WYLIE.—*HISTORY OF ENGLAND UNDER HENRY THE FOURTH.* By JAMES HAMILTON WYLIE, M.A. one of Her Majesty's Inspectors of Schools. Vol. 1, crown 8vo. 10s. 6d.

YONGE.—*THE NEW ENGLISH-GREEK LEXICON,* containing all the Greek words used by Writers of good authority. By CHARLES DUKE YONGE, M.A. 4to. 21s.

YOUATT. — *WORKS BY WILLIAM YOUATT.*

THE HORSE. Revised and enlarged by W. WATSON, M.R.C.V.S. 8vo. Woodcuts, 7s. 6d.

THE DOG. Revised and enlarged. 8vo. Woodcuts. 6s.

ZELLER. — *WORKS BY DR. E. ZELLER.*

HISTORY OF ECLECTICISM IN GREEK PHILOSOPHY. Translated by SARAH F. ALLEYNE. Crown 8vo. 10s. 6d.

THE STOICS, EPICUREANS, AND SCEPTICS. Translated by the Rev. O. J. REICHEL, M.A. Crown 8vo. 15s.

SOCRATES AND THE SOCRATIC SCHOOLS. Translated by the Rev. O. J. REICHEL, M.A. Crown 8vo. 10s. 6d.

PLATO AND THE OLDER ACADEMY. Translated by S. FRANCES ALLEYNE and ALFRED GOODWIN, B.A. Crown 8vo. 18s.

THE PRE-SOCRATIC SCHOOLS; a History of Greek Philosophy from the Earliest Period to the time of Socrates. Translated by SARAH F. ALLEYNE. 2 vols. crown 8vo. 30s.

Spottiswoode & Co. Printers, New-street Square, London.

www.ingramcontent.com/pod-product-compliance
Lightning Source LLC
Chambersburg PA
CBHW031400270326
41929CB00010BA/1258